Victor Auguste Dechamps

The Second Eve or the Mother of Life

Recollections and Prayers for Every Day in the Month of Mary and for the Other

Days Consecrated to the Mother of God

Victor Auguste Dechamps

The Second Eve or the Mother of Life
Recollections and Prayers for Every Day in the Month of Mary and for the Other Days Consecrated to the Mother of God

ISBN/EAN: 9783337274924

Printed in Europe, USA, Canada, Australia, Japan

Cover: Foto ©Lupo / pixelio.de

More available books at **www.hansebooks.com**

THE SECOND EVE;

OR,

THE MOTHER OF LIFE.

Recollections and Prayers

FOR EVERY DAY IN THE MONTH OF MARY, AND FOR THE OTHER DAYS CONSECRATED TO THE MOTHER OF GOD.

By V. DECHAMPS,

OF THE CONGREGATION OF THE MOST HOLY REDEEMER; BISHOP OF NAMUR.

Authorised Translation.

O Domine, quia ego servus tuus, et filius Ancillæ tuæ, dirupisti vincula mea ("O my God, I am Thy servant, and the son of Thy Handmaid, and Thou hast broken my bonds").—*Ps.* cxv.

LONDON:
BURNS, LAMBERT, & OATES, 17, 18 PORTMAN STREET,
AND 63 PATERNOSTER ROW.

Imprimatur.

✠ HENRY EDWARD,
Archbishop of Westminster.

LONDON:
LEVEY AND CO., PRINTERS, GREAT NEW STREET,
FETTER LANE, E.C.

CONTENTS.

	PAGE
PREFACE	ix
OFFERING TO MARY	xvi

CHAPTER I.
THE SECOND EVE—MATER VIVENTIUM . . 1

CHAPTER II.
MARY THE MEDIATRIX OF GRACE TO ALL GENERATIONS OF MANKIND 6

CHAPTER III.
MARY IN TYPE AND IN PROPHECY . . . 17

God thought of Mary from the beginning of all things, impressed her image upon the centuries which preceded her, and announced her by the mouth of the prophets.

CHAPTER IV.
THE DIGNITY OF MARY 22

A mere creature cannot be raised to a higher dignity than was conferred on Mary by her Divine Maternity in the Incarnation of the Word.

CHAPTER V.
THE GRACE OF MARY, OR MARY FULL OF GRACE . 28

The grace bestowed on Mary is immeasurably superior to all the graces which have ever been granted to Angels or to men.

CHAPTER VI.
THE IMMACULATE CONCEPTION, OR MARY EVER SPOTLESS 34

Definition of the Dogma.

CHAPTER VII.
THE IMMACULATE CONCEPTION, OR MARY EVER SPOTLESS 43

Definition of the Dogma (*continued*).

CHAPTER VIII.
MARY, VIRGIN AND MOTHER 50

CHAPTER IX.
MARY EVER VIRGIN 57

Heresy has ever been offended at the brightness of her purity—Heresy deceives by the perversion of Holy Scripture—The compassion which those deserve who are thus deceived.

CHAPTER X.
THE MERIT OF MARY 65

CHAPTER XI.
THE GLORY OF MARY 70

Mary glorified in body and soul.

CHAPTER XII.
MARY THE UNIVERSAL MEDIATRIX . . . 78

CHAPTER XIII.
MARY THE UNIVERSAL MEDIATRIX (*continued*) . 88

CHAPTER XIV.

THE CULTUS OF MARY 104

The cultus of hyperdulia—Tokens of this cultus in the sanctuaries, offices, and festivals of the Church.

CHAPTER XV.

THE FESTIVALS OF MARY 112

The life of Mary the light of ours—Feast of the Immaculate Conception—Fidelity to grace.

CHAPTER XVI.

THE NATIVITY 115

A sign foreshadowing the revival of grace.

CHAPTER XVII.

THE PRESENTATION 117

The great law of grace, which obliges all men to give themselves wholly to God.

CHAPTER XVIII.

THE ANNUNCIATION 122

Humility.

CHAPTER XIX.

THE VISITATION 127

The mystery of faith, charity, humility, grace, and consolation.

CHAPTER XX.

THE PURIFICATION OF MARY AND THE PRESENTATION OF JESUS IN THE TEMPLE 133

The Mosaic law—The primitive law—The fulfilment of prophecy.

CHAPTER XXI.

THE PURIFICATION OF MARY (*continued*) . . 141

Humble obedience.

CHAPTER XXII.

THE PRESENTATION OF JESUS IN THE TEMPLE (*continued*) 146

Jesus a sign to be spoken against—The sword of Mary—Faith and incredulity.

CHAPTER XXIII.

THE FEAST OF THE COMPASSION, OR THE SORROWS OF MARY 156

Faith, hope, love, sorrow, patience, conformity to the will of God.

CHAPTER XXIV.

PREPARATION FOR THE FESTIVALS OF MARY . . 163

CHAPTER XXV.

SATURDAY: MARY'S DAY 173

CHAPTER XXVI.

THE MONTH OF MARY 182

CHAPTER XXVII.

CHARACTERISTICS OF TRUE DEVOTION TOWARDS THE BLESSED VIRGIN 189

Veneration, love, confidence.

CHAPTER XXVIII.

CHARACTERISTICS OF TRUE DEVOTION TOWARDS THE BLESSED VIRGIN (*continued*) . . . 193

The love of Mary.

CHAPTER XXIX.

CHARACTERISTICS OF TRUE DEVOTION TOWARDS THE BLESSED VIRGIN (*continued*) . . . 203

Confidence in her intercession.

CHAPTER XXX.

OF VARIOUS PIOUS PRACTICES IN HONOUR OF THE BLESSED VIRGIN FOR EVERY DAY, WEEK, MONTH, OR YEAR 206

The Hail Mary—The Rosary—The daily visit—The consecration of the Saturday—The Feasts—The Month of Mary—The frequent invocation of the name of Mary.

CHAPTER XXXI.

THE ROSARY 213

CHAPTER XXXII.

THE SCAPULAR 222

CHAPTER XXXIII.

THE IMITATION OF MARY 229

CHAPTER XXXIV.

THE ARK OF THE COVENANT, MARY, AND THE CHURCH 233

APPROVALS.

Auctoritate a Reverendissimo Patre Nuncio Mauron, Superiore Generali Congregationis SS. Redemptoris, nobis commissa, licentiam dedimus R. Patri Dechamps in lucem edendi opus, cui titulus, *La Nouvelle Eve, ou la Mère de la Vie,* a duobus ordinis nostri Theologis ad id deputatis perlectum et adprobatum.

J. KOCKEROLS, C.S.S.,
De Red. Sup. Prov. Belg.

Brusellis, die 7 Martii 1862.

Nous avons lu, conformément aux intentions de Mgr. l'Evêque, un livre intitulé, *La Nouvelle Eve, ou la Mère de la Vie; Souvenirs et Prières,* &c., par le R. P. Dechamps. Nous avons remarqué dans cet ouvrage, approuvé par les Supérieurs de la Congrégation du très Saint Rédempteur, un heureux ensemble de considerations sur les grandeurs, les grâces, les vertus de la Sainte Vierge, sur le culte qui lui est dû, et les pratiques de piété qui s'y attachent. Cet ouvrage, qui respire la foi la plus vive, et la confiance la plus entière dans la puissante protection de la Mère de Dieu, nous a paru propre à démontrer tout ce que la dévotion envers la Sainte Vierge renferme de solide, de suave, et d'efficace, et combien des âmes desireuses de leur perfection doivent y être fidèles.

Nous en autorisons l'impression, et nous en recommandons tout particulièrement la lecture pendant le mois de Marie.

A. P. V. DESCAMPS,
Vic. Gen.

Tournai, Fête de N. D. des Sept Douleurs,
11 Avril 1862.

PREFACE.

WE have given the title of *Recollections* to this work, that our readers may not be tempted to seek or even to suppose they can find any thing new in it. The thoughts and the prayers of which it is composed are, in fact, recollections of what the faith, the wisdom, and the piety of our fathers have handed down to us from age to age, from the very first centuries of the Church. If they appear here and there in a new light, it is because truth has never been grasped on all sides, nor has ever been embraced entirely by the mind of man, and that no one can gaze attentively on that truth which is always old without discovering there beauties which are always new.

But what are these Recollections? Are they meditations? Doubtless they contain matter for meditation, but they are not meditations. They are religious reflections, the greater part of which require only a little modification to become instructions on the knowledge and the cultus or worship of the Blessed Virgin.

We had at first, indeed, intended to give them this general title, which we afterwards changed for that of *The Second Eve; or, the Mother of Life,* as corresponding more entirely to their fundamental idea, and as better suited for a work intended chiefly for persons in the world.

We hope, however, that this little book may not prove wholly without use to our colleagues in the Sacred Ministry, many of whom have, doubtless, experienced what befell ourselves at the conclusion of our theological studies. From the impossibility of fathoming, in the course of a few years, all the depths of the science of sciences, our notions were far more imperfect than they are now of many truths relating to the Mother of God, and her intimate union with the mysteries of the Incarnation and Redemption,—such as the order of her dignity, her grace, her merit, her unrivalled place in the Divine economy of man's salvation, her quality or function of universal Mediatrix of prayer and intercession. On these different points, and on many others, we might, then, and in perfect good faith, have treated the most sublime and certain truths as pious exaggerations, because the great theological works which treat these subjects with the fulness which they deserve were then unknown to us. If any one had then given us an analysis of at least their most important contents, he would have rendered us a most essential service. The first part of this work contains such an analysis, but in a form which may suit all readers, because, as we have said, it is intended principally for persons in the world.

We are persuaded that all the pages of this book, not only those of the second part, which is the longest and most practical, but also those of the first, are perfectly within the reach of the faithful. The chapter which requires the greatest attention to be fully understood is unquestionably the second, which, nevertheless, is entirely founded on a long passage from an *ascetical* work of S. Francis of Sales, his *Treatise on the Love of God*, in which the Saint has brought together the subjects of sermons preached by himself *to the people*.

Those who wish to use this little book during the Month of Mary, will do well to take the 26th chapter first. It would have been placed at the beginning of the book, had it not been our intention to offer to the faithful a work which might be equally useful to them at every period of the year. They will find here a series of lectures, religious, dogmatic, moral, and ascetic, on the privileges of Mary, and on the graces which correspond to those privileges; on the life of the Mother of God according to the Gospels, and on the lessons which it contains; on the cultus or the worship which is due to her, and on the practices of piety flowing from it. All these lectures, like the chapters of S. Liguori's *Glories of Mary*, are followed by prayers.

It may, perhaps, be matter of surprise that one of his disciples and children should have thought of writing another book in honour of Mary, when S. Alphonsus himself has written a work on the glories of his Mother, so full of life and unction, that truly pious souls cannot read a single page of it without being deeply moved and enlightened thereby. We can enter into this feeling; but we believe, nevertheless, that S. Alphonsus loves to see us follow his steps, and that he desires to hear us speak of Mary after our poor fashion to the Christians of our own day, in their own language; so as to draw to their Mother souls which, in order to love her better, need chiefly to know her better, and who require to be led to the *Glories of Mary*.

But the motive which induced us to write will be

better understood by the relation of a fact which suggested it.

One day, when we were visiting a learned and pious friend, we found the *Glories of Mary* among the books which covered his table. He saw that we had observed it, and took it up, saying: "This is my spiritual thermometer; when I am in some degree faithful to grace, a few words from this book enlighten and encourage me; when I am careless and lukewarm, it no longer suits me; it becomes, as it were, too strong for me. When I feel this, I look into myself, and I soon find that it is not the light which has grown dim, but the interior eye which is no longer able to bear its brightness. I then labour to restore this eye of the soul to its strength and purity; and the thermometer soon rises, or rather the soul rises, and soon finds itself in union with this precious book."

We have been careful not to draw from this isolated fact a general conclusion which would be incorrect, for experience proves daily that the *Glories of Mary* touches sinners and brings them back to God, as it consoles the just and encourages them to perseverance; but it is no less true that there is a certain spiritual state unhappily too often experienced, a state of languor and darkness, in which we find the necessity of varying our reading, and of being brought back gently to books which seem at those times to be beyond us.

We therefore offer this book to the world in the hope that it will be of service to those who have yet to learn to enjoy the *Glories of Mary*.

For this reason we determined to give to it the character of which we have spoken above, and which distinguishes several pious books by S. Alphonsus, especially his great *Treatise on Prayer*, which is at the same time ascetic and dogmatic, and in which he refutes the Jansenistic errors then popular, as we refute here and there, and especially in the 9th chapter, the errors which men are making strenuous efforts to render popular in our day, and which we have heard maintained by poor artisans in our streets, perfectly *au fait* at the arguments of Protestantism, by which they are constituted doctors of free examination at a very cheap rate. The work of S. Alphonsus is even more dogmatic than ours, in which we have abstained from purely theological terms in order to be useful to a greater number of souls, after the example of our holy founder, who afterwards simplified his admirable *Treatise on Prayer*. The same desire for general utility has induced us to translate the Latin quotations which are to be met with in this work, or at least to give their meaning in the passage of the text which precedes or follows them.

We have only now to express to our readers the consolation which we feel in offering to them these Recollections and Prayers, or rather in offering them, through their hands, to our common Mother, under the pontificate of a Pope whom she has so visibly marked as her own. Pius IX. has been her favoured son from his baptism, when he received the name of John Mary, and has been predestined by Divine Providence, among all the successors of Peter, to the high privilege of solemnly defining the belief of Christendom in all ages in the second Eve's plenitude of grace.

Do we wonder after this that Mary has chosen Pius IX. to stand nearest to her at the foot of the Cross?

Did she not choose S. John to be with her there, the beloved Apostle whom Jesus gave her to be her son, and to be the first who should treasure up those blessed words: "Behold thy Mother"?

But if the beloved disciple shared most closely and most deeply the sufferings of his Master and of his Divine Mother, if he was the nearest to them in sorrow, he was the nearest to them also in joy, and the first of the disciples to confess his faith in the Resurrection. We see, then, why the great heart of Pius IX., which is so full of sadness, is so full of hope—or rather, of the certain expectation—of the triumph of the Church; and we can find no words to express that sadness and that hope but those of the inspired Psalmist, who was himself so admirable a figure of Christ suffering and triumphant. He expressed beforehand what has been always experienced in a certain measure by all the living members of Christ, all the true children of His grace, but which is experienced in its fulness in our day by the visible head of the mystical body of the New Man, the Vicar of the Man-God Himself.

Credidi, propter quod locutus sum: I have spoken to the world the words of faith, not only on the greatness of Mary ever Immaculate, but on the greatness of the stain which pollutes itself, and on the depths of the evil whence all its iniquities proceed. Nations and kings have heard those words, but have not followed them: *Ego autem humiliatus sum nimis.* In my desolation I sought whether no man loves the truth among those who have power to defend it, and I found none among the mighty, not even among those who call themselves my sons. I have found nothing but the love of falsehood: *Ego dixi in excessu meo: Omnis homo mendax.* But what I found not among the mighty, I have found among the weak, and I have heard the voice of a great multitude of nations calling me father! *Quid retribuam Domino, pro omnibus quæ retribuit mihi?* What shall I do for these children whom God makes so faithful to me? *Calicem salutaris accipiam: et nomen Domini invocabo.* O my God, I am ready to suffer for the whole Catholic world; I am ready to die for it, if such be Thy will, as Thou didst die for it Thyself: *Vota mea Domino reddam coram omni populo ejus: pretiosa in conspectu Domini mors sanctorum ejus.* But whether it be my life or my death which is to be to it the source of grace, I know, O Lord, that that grace shall be full. *O Domine, quia ego servus tuus: ego servus tuus, et filius ancillæ tuæ.* Yes, I know that grace shall be full, for I am thy servant, and the son of thy handmaid, him whom she has deigned to choose among Thy Vicars upon earth to make known the full sense of that salutation: "Hail, full of grace!" Yes, I shall obtain the grace of the liberty of the Church, the liberty of the Holy See. *Dirupisti vincula mea: tibi sacrificabo hostiam laudis.* And for that liberty I shall bless Thee, O Lord, either from the bosom of the Church militant or in the bosom of the Church triumphant. *Vota mea Domino reddam in conspectu omnis populi ejus: in atriis domus Domini, in medio tui Jerusalem.*[1]

[1] Psalm cxv.

OFFERING TO MARY.

O Thou of whom Jesus was born, Woman blessed among all women, living Ark of the eternal alliance between the human and Divine natures; City of God, wherein the light of the Lamb reveals to us such wonderful things; peerless Virgin foretold by the prophets, and whom all generations call blessed; holy Mother of God made man,—I come to lay at thy feet the humble homage of one of the poorest of thy children; the memorial of what he has seen, of what he has learnt, of what he has heard, of thee,—of what he believes of thy greatness, on the word of God Himself; of what he knows of thy love by the experience which all men may easily verify by their own.

To speak of thee, Blessed Mary, is to awaken a spring of gratitude in many a heart; it is also to lead those who know thee not as thou shouldst be known to attest by their own experience all that can be said of thy goodness and thy power. Cast, then, thy merciful eyes upon this offering, unworthy, indeed, of thee, but which comes from a heart which loves thee. Let thy maternal indulgence accept and bless it, and may that benediction cause these recollections and these prayers to live in a multitude of other hearts. Prostrate together at thy feet, we hail thee "full of grace," and we beseech thee with perfect confidence to obtain for us some measure of that fulness, now and at the hour of our death. Amen.

THE SECOND EVE;

OR,

THE MOTHER OF LIFE

CHAPTER I.

THE SECOND EVE—MATER VIVENTIUM.

HAVE you never experienced a deep feeling of compassion on meeting with some unhappy Christian who has been born and brought up in a country in which the faith has been mutilated by error, and where the true sense of the Gospel has been so miserably lost that Mary is spoken of simply as one among other holy women to be revered for their virtues alone? Have such poor Christians never opened the Gospels, that they know not her who is blessed among women,[1] her whom all the nations call blessed,[2] because the Almighty has done great things in her?[3] Have they never been struck by those great and ineffable words: *De qua natus est Jesus, qui vocatur Christus* ("Mary, of whom was born Jesus, who is called Christ")?[4] Let us look upon Mary in the light of these words, and we shall behold in her the Mother of life, *Mater viventium*,[5] the true

[1] Luke i. 28. [2] Luke i. 48. [3] Luke i. 49.
[4] Matt. i. 16. [5] Gen. iii. 20.

Mother of the human race; in very truth the second Eve, more truly our Mother than the first, because the life which we receive from her is immeasurably higher than that derived from Eve.

That we may fully understand this, let us remember that the Creator and Principle of all life has shed abroad various kinds of life in His creation: *In ipso vita erat* ("In Him was life");[1] *et omnia per ipsum facta sunt* ("and all things were made by Him").[2] He has been pleased to combine in us these various lives, which form a kind of hierarchy, of which human nature is the centre and the bond. We share *vegetable* life with the plants, *sensitive* life with the animals, *intellectual* life with the Angels. We participate with pure spirits in the divine life of grace, that life of which the Gospel speaks in these words: *Non ex voluntate carnis, sed ex Deo nati sunt* ("Who are born, not of the will of the flesh, but of God").[3] But how do we partake of this life? Our Lord Himself has told us: "I am the Vine," He says, "you the branches;[4] as the branch cannot bear fruit of itself, unless it abide in the vine, so neither can you unless you abide in Me;[5] he that abideth in Me and I in him, the same beareth much fruit; for without Me you can do nothing." The Incarnate Word is the one source of the divine life of which He here speaks. The Vine and its branches must be of the same nature; and as the Word is God, and we have not the nature of God, He became man in order that human nature, being united to the Divinity, might become in Him that Vine of which we might be the branches,[6] and that the divine life of grace might be thereby communicated to us. The Incarnation, therefore, is to us the source of the life of grace; a life so incomparably higher than the life of nature, that every faithful Christian ought to be ready to sacrifice the one to preserve the other.

But how did the Word become Incarnate? how did

[1] John i. 4. [2] John i. 3. [3] John i. 13.
[4] John xv. 5. [5] Ibid. [6] St. Aug., Tract 80, *in Joan.*

He unite Himself to our nature, that He might make us partakers of that divine life: *divinæ consortes naturæ* ("partakers of the Divine nature")?[1]

The answer to this great question is in the Catholic Creed, and we have heard it a hundred times upon our knees: *Et incarnatus est de Spiritu Sancto ex Maria Virgine, et homo factus est.* It was, therefore, in Mary and by Mary that He gave Himself to the world; it is in and by her that He has communicated to men that new life which renders them sons of God. *Dedit eis potestatem filios Dei fieri, his qui credunt in nomine ejus. Qui non ex sanguinibus, neque ex voluntate carnis, neque ex voluntate viri, sed ex Deo nati sunt*[2] ("But as many as received Him, He gave them power to be made the sons of God; to them that believe in His name. Who are born, not of blood, nor of the will of the flesh, nor of the will of man, but of God"). And with perfect truth does the Church call Mary the Mother of that divine life: *Mater divinæ gratiæ*. It is not, doubtless, by her own power that Mary is our Mother in the order of grace; neither was it by their own power, according to the words of the mother of the Machabees to her sons, that our mothers bestowed on us our bodily life. To each of them belong justly the words of the first woman: *Possedi hominem per Deum*[3] ("I have gotten a man through God"); and with like fulness of truth might the second Eve, when she conceived the new Adam, have said: I have conceived Him by the power of the Most High, that I might regenerate the whole race of mankind to a new life. Even so, for God has as truly given us the divine life of grace by the fruitful Virginity of Mary, as He gave us our human life by our natural parents. When we say that Mary gave us life, that she regenerated us to a new life by the power of God, we are using no figurative language, but plain and literal terms, such as express the full and perfect truth. For is not Jesus our Life? Has He

---

[1] 2 Pet. i. 4.   [2] John i. 12, 13.   [3] Gen. iv. 1.

not affirmed Himself so to be?—*Ego sum Vita*[1] ("I am the Resurrection and the Life; I am the Way, and the Truth, and the Life"). And how did He give Himself to men? By Mary. By her, therefore, He gave us life. She is, therefore, our Mother. To whom do men owe the name of mother? To her who, by her own consent, positively and freely contributed to give them life, and who afterwards brought them forth in sorrow. Thus God was pleased that Mary should contribute positively and freely to give us life by consenting to the Incarnation of the Word, and that she should bring us forth in sorrow; not in pain of body, but in anguish of soul, because she was to give us the life of the soul. Did she not say freely to the Angel of God: *Fiat mihi secundum verbum tuum* ("Be it done to me according to thy word")? Did not the Divine Word, the Only Eternal and Consubstantial Son of God, await the consent of Mary to take upon Him our nature in time, to become man in the womb of the second Eve, the woman destined from the beginning to become the sanctuary of the eternal alliance between God and man? He willed, therefore, that she should coöperate positively in giving supernatural life to mankind. And was not this coöperation full of anguish? It was so; not only when, standing at the foot of the cross, in submission to the will of the Father, who gave His Son to death for us, Mary united her heart to the Heart of Jesus in that flame of love which redeemed the world; but it was so also in the Incarnation, when the *Fiat mihi* of the Virgin of virgins made her from that moment the Mother of Sorrows, because from that moment she beheld in the Blessed Fruit of her womb the Lamb laden with the sins of men, and felt the sharpness of the sword which was to transfix her whole life, and pierce to the very bottom of her soul: *Et tuam ipsius animam pertransibit gladius*[2] ("And thy own soul a sword shall pierce").

---

[1] John xi. 25; xiv. 6.   [2] Luke ii. 35.

Prayer.

O Lord, I can now more fully understand those divine words which flowed from the Cross, and were treasured up on Calvary by the best beloved of Thy disciples: "Behold thy Mother!" I see that they were spoken to the children of grace throughout all ages; that they extend even to me, and relate to me. I see that I am truly the child of Thy humble Handmaid, and that Thy Mother is also mine, because my life was given me by her, because it has pleased Thee to give it to me through her. O Divine Wisdom! Thou dost nothing imperfectly; when Thou gavest us a Mother, Thou didst give to her a mother's heart; when Thou gavest us a Divine Mother, Thou didst enkindle her heart with the fire of Divine love. Blessed be Thou, O my God, for this ineffable gift! I would fain prove my gratitude by awakening the like in the hearts of others, and by seizing every opportunity of saying to the ungrateful and the blind of heart: *If you did but know the gift of God!* If you did but know what a Mother's heart is loving you in heaven! Only put that heart to the proof, and you will soon attest by your own experience the truth which you now receive on faith. Mary, my own true Mother, I will not rest content with loving thee myself; I desire to make thee known, to make thee to be loved! *Dignare me laudare te Virgo sacrata.* It will be no hard task. It is not difficult to make thee loved. It is enough to tell men what thou art. God Himself draws all men to thy love; for when He made thee their Mother, He made them thy children; and when He filled thy heart with love for them, He infused also into their hearts a child-like instinct, which awakens at thy presence. There is something supernatural in the heart of man which speaks to him of thee; and whoever resists that divine attraction revolts against the order of God, and falls from the supernatural love which he rejects into the supernatural hatred to which he becomes subject. Yes, love and hatred are the distinctive characteristics here below of the children of God and the children of Satan,—that father of pride, who has ever detested in thee the humility which vanquished him. I will labour, then, to win hearts for thee. I will tell them of thy greatness, thy beauty, thy motherly love. I will teach them to trust to thy prayers; and as my reward, most sweet and holy Mother, thou wilt pray for me with all the tender compassion of which I stand in need. Amen.

CHAPTER II.

MARY THE MEDIATRIX OF GRACE TO ALL GENERATIONS OF MANKIND.

GOD has impressed the character of unity on all His works; but He has been especially jealous of the unity of the human race, which is, as it were, His own family, created to His own image and likeness: *Ipsius genus sumus*[1] ("for we are also His offspring"). Thus, not only did He ordain that the whole human race should issue from one primitive family, and that family the offspring of the first marriage between one man and one woman, the father and the mother of all generations of mankind,—but He formed the first woman herself from the first man, the first Eve from the first Adam; thus constituting the perfect unity of the natural life. The gift of supernatural life has not broken that unity; for it was of a daughter of Eve, according to nature, that the second Adam, the Principle of the life of grace, vouchsafed to be born; the Creator Word becoming thus incarnate to redeem and to restore His work without dividing it.

[1] Acts xvii. 28.

The unity of the supernatural life is not less perfect in the human race than the unity of the natural life; for if all generations have received the one from the first Adam by the first Eve, all likewise, without excepting the first man and the first woman, have received the other from the second Adam by the second Eve.

Mary, in fact, did not first become the Mother of grace at the moment of the Incarnation, but from the very origin of mankind; as Jesus is the Source of grace, the Principle of the superior life of mankind, not only from the moment of the Incarnation, but from the beginning of the world—*ab origine mundi*.[1] It is of faith that grace was restored to the first man by virtue of his foreseen redemption by the "Lamb slain from the beginning."[2] Jesus Christ, therefore, was the true Principle of life to the first man and to all his descendants.

But by whom did God *will* from the beginning to give us Jesus Christ? By Mary. It was, therefore, by her that from the beginning He *willed* to restore us to life; and Mary is thus the Mother of grace *ab initio* ("from the beginning of all things"), by the will of God.

But to place this truth in its full light, it ought to be viewed in relation to another, explained very clearly by S. Francis of Sales in his *Treatise on the Love of God*, in which he shows that not only was grace *restored* to the first man with a view to redemption, but that it was originally *given* to him with a view to the Incarnation; because the Incarnation of the Word, and therewith the Divine Maternity which was the condition freely chosen for it by Providence (freely chosen as was the Incarnation itself), belonged to the original purpose of the Creator; a divine purpose which would have been realised without the fall of man (to which the order of redemption corresponds), by some other free effect of the infinite mercy of God.

[1] Apoc. xiii. 8.   [2] Ibid.

But we will cite the very words of St. Francis of Sales, both because they are so full of light, and because they show us how the Saints treat ascetical subjects, carefully basing piety on the sweet and interior knowledge of divine truth; and lastly, because they will lead us to our conclusion by a process of reasoning so forcible and so sublime as might be accounted over-bold in our mouth had we not borrowed it from the spiritual science of the saintly Bishop of Geneva.

"Every thing which God has done," says he, "was destined for the salvation of men and angels; but this is the order of His Providence with regard to them, as we have been able to discover it by diligent attention to Holy Scripture and to the teaching of antiquity; and we are now about to speak of it so far as our weakness will permit.

"God knew from all eternity that He had power to create an innumerable host of creatures to whom He might communicate Himself; and considering that, among all the different modes of such communication, the most excellent was so to unite Himself to some created being, that the creature should be, as it were, ingrafted into the Divinity, so as to form but one person with It, His infinite goodness, which was led of itself and by itself to that communication, resolved to make it after this manner, in order that, as from eternity there is an *essential communication in God*, by which the Father, in begetting the Son, communicates to Him all His infinite and indivisible Divinity; and the Father and the Son together, producing the Holy Spirit, communicate also to Him their proper Divinity,—so this Sovereign Goodness was in the Incarnation so perfectly communicated out of itself to a created nature, that that nature and the Divinity, each preserving its own properties, were nevertheless so perfectly united together as to form but One Person.

"Now, among all the created beings which it was in the power of Almighty God to produce, He thought fit to choose the humanity which was afterwards actually united to the Person of God the Son, to raise it to the incomparable dignity of a personal union with His Divine Majesty, that through all eternity it might preeminently enjoy the treasures of His infinite glory. Next, having thus chosen for this supreme felicity the Sacred Humanity of our Saviour, the Eternal Father determined not to restrict His bounty to the Person of His well-beloved Son alone, but *for His sake* to bestow it upon a great multitude of His creatures; and among all the innumerable variety of possible creatures, He chose to create *men and Angels* to bear His Son company, to share His graces and His glory, and to adore and praise Him eternally.

"And because Almighty God saw that His Son might become truly incarnate in many different ways,—His body, for example, as well as His soul, might have been created out of nothing, or (as in the creation of Adam and Eve) His Body might have been formed out of previously existing matter, or by the way of ordinary generation, or by extraordinary generation of a Virgin,[1] —He willed that the Incarnation should be brought to pass in this latter way; and among all the women whom He might have chosen for that end, He made choice of the most Blessed Virgin Mary, that by her means the Saviour of our souls might become, not only Man, but *the Child of the human race.*[2]

"Moreover, Divine Providence 'determined to pro-

---

[1] Of the Virgin promised from the beginning, of her whom Isaias calls *the* Virgin, whose image appears in all the traditions of mankind, and even in the fables of paganism, combined with the idea of the Incarnation, as we have shown elsewhere, from the sacred books of the nations of antiquity. Our fathers, in the forests of the North, thus raised altars to the Virgin who was to bring forth a child, *Virgini pariturœ*. See the second part of *Le Christ et les Antichrists*, tom. i., "Jesus Christ dans l'Histoire."

[2] See what we have just said in the beginning of this second chapter on the *unity* of the work of God.

duce all other things, whether natural or supernatural, for the sake of the Redeemer,' in order that 'Angels' and 'men,' by serving Him, might 'become partakers of His glory.'[1] Now when I say that God has seen and willed first one thing, and then another,—thus marking an order in His wills,—I am to be understood, as I before said, to affirm that although all this passed in one absolutely single and simple act, yet by that act the order, distinction, and dependence of things was no less strictly observed than if there had been several distinct acts in the intelligence and will of God. And as every rightly disposed will chooses and loves best and before all other objects, equally present to it, that which is most worthy of love, it follows that the Supreme Providence of God, in His eternal purpose and design for all that He was minded to produce, willed and loved in the first place, with a special and surpassing preference, the object most worthy of His love, even our Redeemer, and next, in their order, His creatures, according to the measure in which they were to serve Him and to promote His honour and glory.

"Thus all things were created for that Man-God who is therefore called the 'First-born of every creature,'[2] 'possessed by the Divine Majesty before He made any thing from the beginning;'[3] 'for in Him were all things created, and He is before all, and by Him all things consist, and He is the Head of the body the Church, that in all things He may hold the primacy.'[4] The vine is planted chiefly for the sake of the fruit, and consequently the fruit is the first thing desired and looked for, though the leaves and the flowers are produced before it. Thus our Divine Saviour was the first in the intention of God; and in His eternal purpose for His creation, and with a view to that blessed fruit, the

[1] *Traité de l'Amour de Dieu*, l. ii. ch. iv.
[2] Coloss. i. 15. Observe well this magnificent exposition of the texts of St. Paul and of the Book of Proverbs.
[3] Prov. viii. 22.   [4] Coloss. i. 16-18.

vine of the universe was planted, and the succession of many generations was ordained; which, like leaves and flowers, were to precede Him as a fit preparation for the production of that celestial fruit which the heavenly Spouse extols in the Canticle, the juice whereof rejoices God and men.[1]

"Who then will doubt the abundance of our means of salvation, since we have so mighty a Saviour, 'for Whose sake we were created, and by Whose merits we have been redeemed'?"[2]

You see that S. Francis of Sales not only says that we were redeemed by the merits of Jesus Christ, Who became the voluntary Victim for our sins, but he affirms that it was for the sake of Jesus Christ that we were made; that all things were created for the Man-God; that this Man-God was first in the Divine intention, and for this reason that all other things, whether natural or supernatural, were produced for Him; and that Angels and men were created to share His graces and His glory. According to this doctrine, which the holy and learned Bishop of Geneva, in company with many other illustrious theologians, has drawn (as he says himself) from the fountains of Holy Scripture and antiquity, the fall of man occasioned the order of redemption, because it induced the Incarnate Word to offer Himself freely, *ab origine*, for the salvation of mankind; but it did not occasion the order of the Incarnation, which would have been accomplished (though under other conditions) even if mankind had remained faithful to original grace, and so had stood in no need of redemption.

Let us now endeavour to grasp the whole extent of this great truth, that we may enjoy the full glory of its light.

The Incarnation of the Word is the end, freely but positively determined, of the works of God. For what is, in fact, the declared end of creation? Is it not the glory of the Creator? is it not the felicity of creatures,

[1] Ps. ciii. 15.   [2] *Traité de l'Amour de Dieu*, l. ii. ch. v.

the salvation of Angels and of men; which is again the glory of God, because the love which renders the creature happy by uniting it to the Creator is also that which glorifies Him? God is glorified by His justice only in the creature which freely refuses His love, and that justice again is in God nothing but the love of good, a love unchangeable in itself, and which only becomes justice in us and by us when it meets with evil. *De suo bonus, de nostro justus.* Thus the flame whose brightness is reflected by a placid lake is the same which burns up inflammable substances. But if the love which glorifies the Creator, and makes His creatures happy by their union with Him,—if this love or this union is the end of creation, God has been pleased that the supreme degree of this union should be its supreme end; and that supreme union which, with liberty equal to His wisdom, He has willed, is the personal or hypostatic union of the created with the uncreated nature.

Reason, then, under the teaching of revealed truth, learns that the union of intelligent creatures with God is the end of creation, and that its supreme end is the most perfect or personal union.

By the same attention to Scripture and tradition we learn again why this personal union of the Creator and the creature was accomplished immediately in the "Person of the Word" (*sub relatione filiationis*). It was because the Word is the infinite uncreated Image (*Figura substantiæ ejus*)[1] of Him of whom all creatures produced in time are in their different degrees finite images. God's eternal idea of Himself, His living and necessary Likeness, His only Son by nature, the uncreated Archetype of all possible beings, by Whom and after Whose image all things were made—*per ipsum omnia facta sunt, et sine ipso factum est nihil*[2]—has, then, united Himself to His mortal brethren, the created children of God.

[1] Heb. i. 3.   [2] John i. 3.

But to which of all created natures shall that Creator-Word thus personally unite Himself?

Human nature manifestly comprises all creation, because it combines within itself all the different kingdoms of nature, both in the spiritual and corporal creation. It is, therefore, the link between the two worlds of bodies and of spirits. When the Divine Word assumed that nature, He therefore united Himself in it and by it to all His works—*omni creaturæ* ("to every creature")—according to the interpretation given to these words by St. Gregory the Great; and it is thus that the Word, who from all eternity is the "splendour and the glory of the Father,"[1] transforms all creation in time into a hymn of infinite love to the glory of God: *Per ipsum, et cum ipso, et in ipso, est tibi Deo Patri, in unitate Spiritus Sancti, omnis honor et gloria.*[2]

Once more, then, the first Adam is subordinate to the second, and the Man-God is the first in the divine intention, the true end of God in all His works.

Now, the designs of God are without repentance; and if His mercy has raised man from His fall, if the dawn of redemption has gilded from the beginning the mighty ruin of our nature, it is because the Word, Who willed to become incarnate, willed also from the very beginning of all things to redeem us and to take upon Him our death, that He might restore us to life. *Occisus ab origine mundi*[3] ("slain from the beginning of the world"), the Incarnate Word, the Man-God, Jesus Christ, "the First-born of every creature,"—that is to say, He Who in His human nature was willed by the Creator before all other creatures,—has also been from the beginning of time to all mankind the cause of the life of grace, of that divine life, surpassing the life of nature, which was granted to the father of the human race as the seed and principle of the life of glory. And when the first man had lost that divine life, it was for the sake of the sacrifice of the Lamb slain, in the purpose of God, from

---

[1] Heb. i. 3.   [2] Canon of the Mass.   [3] Apoc. xiii. 8.

the beginning of the world, that it was offered once more to him and to all his descendants.[1]

But if the Incarnation of the Word belongs to the primeval design of God in creation, and if it is evident that it cannot have been conceived independently of the mode chosen by Divine Providence to bring it to pass,—that is to say, of the Divine Maternity of her who is blessed among women, and whom Isaias thus foretold: "Behold a Virgin shall conceive and bear a Son, and His name shall be called Emmanuel"[2]—"God with us,"[3] —the second Adam cannot be separated from the second Eve, human nature in Jesus Christ from her in whose womb He assumed it for the love of us: *Spiritus Sanctus superveniet in te, et virtus Altissimi obumbrabit tibi. Ideoque et quod nascetur ex te Sanctum, vocabitur Filius Dei*[4] (" The Holy Ghost shall come upon thee, and the power of the Most High shall overshadow thee. And therefore also the Holy which shall be born of thee, shall be called the Son of God").

We now perfectly understand how it is that the Church ventures to apply to the Mother those words which directly relate to the Son, the Word made Flesh, the Incarnate Wisdom—" I came out of the mouth of the Most High, the First-born before all creatures. From the beginning and before the world was I created."[5] " The Lord possessed me in the beginning of His ways, before He made any thing from the beginning. I was set up from eternity, and of old before the world was made. The depths were not as yet, and I was already conceived."[6] Yes, we understand it; for *if the Redeemer was first in the Divine intention in God's eternal purpose for the production of creatures*, His Mother was also first conceived with Him, because in the Divine decree the Incarnation of the Word was one with the Divine Maternity. The first Eve, according to the words of S. Francis of Sales, in her *production*, was, therefore, subordinate in the

---

[1] See *La Question religieuse*, ch. xii. [2] Ibid. [3] Ibid.
[4] Luke i. 35. [5] Eccl. xxiv. 5, 14. [6] Prov. viii. 22-24.

Divine plan to the second, who holds the first place, not only because she is the highest in dignity, but because she was the first conceived, the first in the Divine intention, the first in the eternal idea, or in the providential design of the work of creation. Let us bear in mind, however, with S. Francis of Sales, when we use these expressions of *first* and *second*, that we are speaking of Divine things in human language, since the hierarchy of creatures, the unity in the diversity of beings, the work of God as a whole, the order of creation, in short, was conceived by a single act of the Divine intelligence, an infinitely simple act, which is no other than the Divinity itself.[1] But although infinitely simple in the eternal idea,—*i.e.* in the Word,—that order does not the less constitute in itself a true order, in which all things are established in *number, weight,* and *measure.*[2]

Lastly, if we would still further dispel the clouds which shroud from our eyes the full light of this doctrine, as in this life they always obscure the vision of the most luminous truths, let us remember that time, like space, is a fact full of mystery, and that the order of time, though most real in itself, does not, and evidently cannot, prevent the possibility of *all points* of time being at an *equal* distance[3] from eternity, or rather of their being at *no distance* from eternity, because they all touch it immediately at once.[4] Therefore it is that the Lamb slain in the midst of time was slain, in the sight of God, at its beginning. And therefore also it is that the second Eve, the Mother of the Lamb and the Mother of grace, was such in the sight of God from the beginning. *Dominus possedit me in initio viarum suarum,*

---

[1] God Himself acting.   [2] Wis. xi. 21.
[3] The circle in which all the points of the circumference are at an equal distance from the centre is the image of this truth. Days, years, and centuries are points of time; but their motion does not prevent their being attached to the centre by one and *the same* radius.
[4] Because the Eternal is He whose centre is every where, and His circumference nowhere.

antequam quidquam faceret a principio. Ab æterno ordinata sum, nondum erant abyssi, et ego jam concepta eram.[1]

Prayer.

Since thou, my Mother, wast the first of all creatures in the mind of the Word Who created them, thou shalt be, next to Him, the first also in my mind and in my heart. How sweet a thought it is that His Incarnation, the most divine of his works, is inseparable from thine ineffable Maternity! And how blessed am I to see and understand that, in order to pronounce the name of Jesus with full understanding, it must not be separated from the name of Mary, the true Mother of the Word made flesh to raise mankind to the love of God Himself! These names of Jesus and Mary, thus indissolubly united in the mind of God, shall be thus united also in mine. Blessed names! I will keep for you the worship of the heart, which ever repeats over and over again the names which it loves; and I pray of you, the one by the other, the Son by the Mother, to grant me grace to invoke you faithfully in all my needs, in all my weakness, in all my infirmities, in all my labours, in all my troubles, in all my sorrows, and, above all, in the last,—*in tribulatione magna,*—that I may live and die with those sacred names on my lips, and, above all, with those saving names engraven on my heart by that holy faith which reveals them to us as the sources of hope, of love, of penance, and of perseverance. Amen, Amen.

[1] Prov. viii. 22-24.

CHAPTER III.

MARY IN TYPE AND IN PROPHECY.

God thought of Mary from the beginning of all things, impressed her image upon the centuries which preceded her, and announced her by the mouth of the prophets.

WE have already seen that the second Eve was the first in the idea of God; and we will now follow the working out of the Divine idea throughout the course of time. But it would require many volumes to exhaust this subject, and the human intellect would still be unequal to the task; we must therefore content ourselves here with tracing that impress which God left of His great design on the works and acts which were to serve as a preparation for it at the principal epochs of the history of the world.

The works or acts of Providence which characterise these epochs are—(1) the creation of man and the promise of the redemption after the fall; (2) the restoration of the human race through a second parent family; (3) after the deluge the choice of a third family, from which was to proceed a central people, a people placed at the confluence of the great nations now become infidel, and which would serve as an everlasting protest against their infidelity, and as a living memorial of the creation, the original revelation, and the expected redemption; (4) the constitution of that people (in its threefold office, commemorative, figurative, and prophetical), whose mighty voice was to bear to the Gentiles with greater or less distinctness the echo of primitive tradition, even to the dawn of redemption, the first Advent of Jesus Christ.

Now, in the creation of man, in the restoration of the human race, in the choice of the family from which was to proceed the people of God, in the formation of this family, God was pleased throughout to join the image of Mary with that of her Son.

In creation, the first Eve is the image of the second.

A sad image, indeed, perhaps we may exclaim; but it was not thus sad when it came forth from the hand of God. And then, even in her fall, while drawing down a curse on herself, the first woman reminds us at every point, though in an opposite sense, of her who brought down on us a blessing. It was while conversing with the false Angel that Eve believed these words: "You shall be as gods;" it was while conversing with the faithful Angel that Mary believed these other words: "The Holy Ghost shall come upon thee, and the power of the Most High shall overshadow thee. And therefore also the Holy which shall be born of thee shall be called the Son of God."[1] Eve therefore believed the lying words which promised to make man God, and Mary believed the words of truth which announced that God willed to make Himself man. For having listened to the first, Eve heard the terrible sentence of condemnation, "In sorrow thou shalt bring forth children;"[2] and for having listened to the second, Mary heard the sentence full of grace and benediction, "Blessed art thou among women,"[3] and from henceforth all generations have called her blessed.[4] Again, because she doubted the word of God and rebelled against it, Eve, being overcome by the old serpent, became his slave; and because she believed the word of God and submitted to it, Mary, "the handmaid" of the Lord, crushed the head of the enemy of mankind by giving us the Saviour, according to the original promise, "I will put enmities between thee and the woman, and thy seed and her seed; she shall crush thy head."[5]

You see how, from the beginning, the mercy of God cast the shadow of the blessing of the second Eve even over the sad history of the malediction of the first.

And when the justice of God buried the old world in the waters of the deluge, this signal punishment was still surrounded by the same types of the mercy yet to come. Of what was that ark of salvation a figure which

[1] Luke i. 35. [2] Gen. xiv. 16. [3] Luke i. 42.
[4] Luke i. 48. [5] Gen. iii. 15.

sank not in the deep waters, but floated on them, giving shelter to the germ of future generations, to the vital principle of a new race? Was it not the type of the living Ark, which alone escaped the deep waters of sin, and rose superior to all their danger? Was it not manifestly the type of the sanctuary chosen to be the guardian of that Germ of the life of grace, of that Principle of divine life, which was to animate the new world —*orbem terræ futurum*—" the world to come"?[1]

We see these types become more exact and perfect in proportion as the work of God advances and draws near to its accomplishment. Abraham, the man whom God destines to be the father of believers, the father of a faithful people in the midst of idolatrous nations, has no descendants, and Sara cannot hope to give him any. Nevertheless a voice from heaven promises her a son, and Sara believes what is humanly impossible, and receives the child of promise, who himself obtains the blessing which makes him the father of a great people, because he obeyed even unto death, and himself carried the wood for his sacrifice up the Mountain of Vision. Is not Sara a touching image of Mary, who could not, humanly speaking, become a mother, because she had made a vow to God to remain a virgin; who believed the voice from heaven promising her the Divine Maternity, who brought forth Him of Whom Isaac was only the type, who gave us the Son of the eternal promise, the Father of the regenerate human race, Jesus Christ sacrificed on Calvary, whither He Himself carried the cross of His sacrifice—Jesus Christ, Who on that cross voluntarily took upon Himself the curse which we had deserved, and purchased for us blessings which we deserved not?

But a government is formed for the people of God; and its central point is the ark of the covenant. What is prefigured by this holy ark, which enclosed the tables of the law, the Word of God, and the manna of the

[1] Heb. ii. 5.

desert? It is evidently a figure of the Ark of the new covenant, which contains not the word of God graven on stone, and the manna which fed the people in the desert as they journeyed towards the promised land, but the living word of God, the Word of God Himself, and the living Bread which came down from heaven to be our nourishment in this dark pilgrimage, until the veil of time shall be rent asunder and our eyes behold the sanctuary of which the Lamb is the eternal Light!

In the remainder of the history of the chosen people, other types of Mary also appear in succession, grouped round the ark of the covenant, which have all been noticed by the holy Fathers: as the fleece of Gedeon and the cloud of Elias; they recognised her in the persons of Noemi, Judith, and Esther, and in others where the resemblance is equally striking and touching. Round the ark of the covenant also we hear the voices of the prophets announcing her of whom this ark was only a type, in words of wondrous clearness, of which we shall only give the most remarkable: those of the prophet Isaias, which are thus quoted in the Gospel narrative of the Incarnation: *Hoc autem totum factum est, ut adimpleretur quod dictum est a Domino per prophetam dicentem: Ecce Virgo in utero habebit, et pariet Filium: et vocabunt nomen ejus Emmanuel: quod est interpretatum, nobiscum Deus* ("Now all this was done that it might be fulfilled which the Lord spoke by the prophet, saying: Behold, a Virgin shall be with child, and bring forth a Son, and they shall call His name Emmanuel,[1] which, being interpreted, is God with us").[2]

Prayer.

Yes, Mary, my Mother, thou art the Virgin spoken of by Isaias! Thou art the promised Woman who should crush the head of the serpent, humble the pride of Satan, and deliver mankind from his power, by giving to the world the true Emmanuel, the Incarnate Word. Thou

---

[1] Isaias vii. 14.   [2] Matt. i. 22, 23.

art the Ark of everlasting salvation, where the life of man, forfeited, took shelter, that it might be mercifully restored to all generations. Thou thyself hast said: *Fecit mihi magna qui potens est, et sanctum nomen ejus. Et misericordia ejus a progenie in progenies timentibus eum* ("He that is mighty hath done great things unto me: and holy is His Name. And His mercy is from generation to generation unto them that fear Him").[1] Thou art the true Sara, the true Mother of the true Isaac. Thou art the Tabernacle of the New Testament, the living Ark of the eternal covenant, wherein are contained all the treasures of God; the Word which is our light, the Blood which is our reconciliation, the Bread which is our life. Thou, with thy Divine Son, art the realisation of the ancient types, the fulfilment of the prophecies, the love and the hope of all ages. Oh, how worthy of all compassion are the wilfully blind, who open the Gospel, and find not therein the source of this love for thee, this confidence in the prayers which rise for us to Jesus from the depths of thy maternal heart! We may, indeed, and we ought to go straight to Him our only Saviour; but is not our most direct way to His Heart through thine, through that heart which is so infinitely more humble, more pure, more loving, and more beloved than our own? Yes, my Saviour and my God, I will go straight to Thee; and that I may do so, I will take the way by which Thou Thyself didst come to us, that sweet way through Thy Blessed Mother.

[1] Luke i. 50.

CHAPTER IV.

THE DIGNITY OF MARY.

A mere creature cannot be raised to a higher dignity than was conferred on Mary by her Divine Maternity in the Incarnation of the Word.

OF a truth, the highest dignity to which a mere creature can be raised is that of the Divine Maternity; according to these words of S. Bernardin of Sienna: *Status maternitatis Dei erat summus status qui puræ creaturæ dari posset*[1] ("The state of the Divine Maternity is the highest which can be conferred upon a mere creature"); or, according to the equally expressive words of S. Albert the Great: *Deus Virgini summum donum donavit cujus pura creatura capax fuit*[2] ("God conferred upon the Virgin the highest gift of which a mere creature was capable").

In order thoroughly to appreciate this truth, we must first dispel a cloud which might obscure its glory.

The nature of creatures, however perfect and exalted they may be, is essentially finite; and so infinitely inferior to the absolute perfection of the Divine Nature. There is nothing, therefore, to hinder God, who is omnipotent, from creating at any time something more perfect than He has hitherto created; and we can never say, Here is a nature which has attained the highest perfection possible to created beings.

This is undeniable; and, therefore, the question here is not as to the nature of created beings, but as to the dignity to which God is pleased to raise them, a dignity which increases in proportion as God unites them more intimately to Himself—*i. e.* in proportion to the closeness of their union with Him.

Angelic nature is higher and more perfect in itself than human nature; nevertheless, human nature was

---

[1] *Pro Fest. V.M.*, Serm. 8, a. 3, c. 1.
[2] *Sup. Missus est*, q. 138.

raised to a dignity infinitely superior to that of the Angels, when the Word united it to His Divine Person in the Incarnation. Human nature, always essentially finite, has been actually raised to an infinite dignity by the Hypostatic Union. It is by reason of this personal union of the Divine nature and the human nature in the Incarnate Word, that Jesus Christ, Who is true man by His humanity, is nevertheless not a pure creature, but both true God and true man.

Hence it follows, that next to the personal or Hypostatic Union, there can be no closer union with God, no union consequently of a higher order, than that to which Mary was raised by the Divine Maternity; as S. Thomas of Aquin observes: *Est suprema quædam conjunctio cum persona infinita*[1] ("It is a supreme union with an Infinite Person"). Indeed, it belongs in a certain way to the order of the Hypostatic Union, since its relations with it are intrinsic and necessary; for the Word assumed in the womb of Mary that humanity to which He personally united Himself. Such is the opinion of Suarez, who does not hesitate to add that the dignity of Mother of God is *suo genere infinita*,[2] meaning by this that it touches immediately upon that which is infinite, and that the bond which unites it therewith is of the highest order possible for any creature. In a word, there is nothing above it but the Hypostatic Union itself: *Pertinet quodam modo ad ordinem unionis hypostaticæ: illam enim intrinsece respicit, et cum illa necessariam conjunctionem habet;*[3] *ita ut Beata Virgo magis Deo conjungi nisi fieret Deus, non potuerit.*[4]

It is on this account that the "Angel of the Schools" has said that the Blessed Virgin, as Mother of God, has been invested with a dignity in some sort infinite, by the union which she has contracted with an Infinite Person,

---

[1] *Apud* Suarez, *De Inc.*, q. 27, a. 1, d. 1, s. 2.
[2] *Loc. cit.*   [3] Suarez, *De Inc.*, q. 27, a. 1, d. 1, s. 2.
[4] Albert the Great. See Crasset *On True Devotion*, 1, 2; Treatise 1, a. 2.

with the Sovereign Good, which is God; and that because of this union with God, nothing can be greater or more perfect than the Divine Maternity: *Beata Virgo ex hoc quod est Mater Dei habet quamdam dignitatem infinitatem, ex bono infinito quod est Deus, et ex hac parte non potest aliquid fieri melius.*[1]

It was not, therefore, a mere impulse of the heart, but a firm conviction of the soul, which caused the Seraphic Doctor to say: "God could have created a greater world, and greater heavens, but He could not have created a greater Mother of God" (*Ipsa est qua majorem facere Deus non potest. Majorem mundum posset facere Deus, majus cœlum, majorem matrem quam Matrem Dei non posset facere*).[2]

Thus, when the tongue which can most worthily speak of this dignity breaks forth in thanksgiving to God in the canticle which has been chanted in every age and in every language, it exclaims: "He that is mighty hath done great things unto me" (*Fecit mihi magna qui potens est*)—great things even for Omnipotence.

But why does not Mary endeavour to explain this greatness to the world? Because it cannot be explained by human language, because it is ineffable (*Non explicat quænam hæc magna fuerint, quia inexplicabilia*).

But if we cannot succeed in forming a just conception of this greatness, such as it is in itself, and consequently cannot express it by human language, which is always inadequate to define exactly what touches on the infinite, let us at least endeavour to comprehend the greatness of Mary in her relations with finite beings, with all the chain of creatures of which she is the last and principal link,[3] the link which binds the Creator to the whole creation. What is the first link of this chain which is perceptible as it issues from nothingness,—not from

---

[1] S. Thomas of Aquin, *Summa*, p. 1, q. 25, a. 6.
[2] *Spec. B.V.*, Lect. 10.
[3] The last link of *mere* creatures.

nothingness as from its principle, but from its own nothingness, that is to say, from its nonexistence, that it may begin to exist by the omnipotence of Him Who has given not only the form but the substance to all created beings? What do we see at the bottom of the scale of creatures, at the lowest extremity of this hierarchy which ascends towards God?

Inert matter, matter without any kind of life.

In this inert matter God deposited the germ of life in its most imperfect form—vegetable life. But if a plant has not its root in the ground, it will not vegetate; though superior to the earth, it yet stands in need of it.

Now let us look at a creature, superior to the plants and to the earth. Here we discern inert matter and vegetable life also: but here God has deposited the germ of a life which does not depend so passively or so continually on what is exterior,—as the sap of a plant depends upon the earth into which it strikes its roots. Sensible and animal life finds its nourishment where it chooses to seek it; it moves itself by an interior principle, by instinct, and it goes whither its instinct leads it. Nevertheless, this animal life, though superior to vegetable life, cannot subsist without it.

Let us now behold creation ascending still higher in the scale. God stoops to His work to attach it more closely to Himself by the bond of resemblance. To the animal life, the principle of which is indeliberate instinct, He adds a life immeasurably superior, though dependent, at least in a certain degree, upon the first,—intellectual and moral life,—the principle of which is reason and liberty, and man becomes the living and immortal link which unites the material to the spiritual world, sensible creatures to pure spirits, and which completes the hierarchy we have just surveyed.

Is this all? No; God wills to unite created with uncreated life; he wills that a free and intelligent creature should live by His own Divine life: *Ut efficiamini divinæ consortes naturæ* ("That you may be made partakers of the Divine Nature").[1]

By what means will God unite the moral to the Divine life,—the natural life to the supernatural life of grace? "And the Word was made flesh, and dwelt among us."[2] The Word,—that is to say, the substantial, living, eternal Idea of God, the infinitely perfect knowledge which He has of Himself and of all things, the uncreated Wisdom, without which nothing was created, the ineffable prototype of all which is and of all which can be,—united Himself immediately with the work of His hands, and chose for this personal union the creature which contains in itself all creation, both bodily and spiritual: man, His image and His child; and it was in anticipation of the Incarnation of the Word that the divine life of grace was communicated to the pure spirits themselves, for Jesus Christ is the head of Angels as of men. Thus all created life, in all its forms, returns to its source—to Him who is the Fountain of life: *In ipso vita erat* ("In Him was life").

We have already seen that the Incarnation of the Word, ordained by the Creator from the beginning of time, has been to all generations of men the principle of that life of which the Incarnate Word, God made man, the Head of a supernatural humanity, Himself has said: "I am the Vine, you are the branches. If you abide not in Me, you have no life." It is by taking upon Himself our nature and our life that He has rendered us capable of partaking His life: *Unius quippe naturæ sunt vitis et palmites. Propter quod cum esset Deus, cujus natura non sumus, factus est homo, ut in illo esset vitis humana natura, cujus et nos homines palmites esse possemus*[3] ("For the vine and the branches are of the same nature; therefore, being God, of Whose nature we are not, He became man, that so He might be the Vine of which we men might be the branches"). He willed thus to make the communication of the Divine life to us de-

[1] 2 Peter i. 4. [2] John i. 14. [3] S. Aug. *in Joan*, Tr. 80.

pendent on the Incarnation, or personal union with human nature, with an inferior life which He had raised to an infinite life.

Is the humanity of Jesus Christ, then, the last link of the chain of creatures which immediately unites the whole creation to God?

In Jesus Christ the Humanity is not the Divinity, nor the Divinity the Humanity,—the two Natures, Divine and Human, being distinct; but these are inseparably united in One single Person, the Person of the "Only Son, eternally begotten in the bosom of the Father," so that in *Him* Man is truly God, and God truly Man. We must not say, then, of the Humanity of Jesus Christ, that it is the last link of the chain of *mere creatures* by which God unites the whole creation to Himself, since in Jesus Christ the Human Nature, without being confounded with the Divine, yet subsists only in the Person of the Word, and is, therefore, in this sense deified: *Non confusione substantiæ, sed unitate personæ* ("Not by confusion of substance, but by unity of person").[1]

The last link, then, of this chain is that creature, blessed above all others, in whose womb the Word became Incarnate, and to whom He has vouchsafed to owe that sacred Humanity which He took upon Himself for us: *Et incarnatus est de Spiritu Sancto, ex Maria Virgine* ("And was Incarnate by the Holy Ghost of the Virgin Mary").

Prayer.

Lord, I thank Thee that Thou hast given a place apart to Mary in creation, and hast raised her to such dignity that all other creatures are below her, and none above her but Thyself alone. In presence of this Thy greatest work, how blind do those appear who fear to say too much of Thy Mother! And how truly, Lord, hast Thou enlightened those who know and confess their inability to speak worthily of her, for the "great things"

[1] Symb. S. Athan.

which Thou hast done in her are truly beyond expression. But I thank Thee, not only for having made Mary so great, by choosing her for Thy Mother, and uniting her to Thyself by the closest bonds,—I thank Thee also, my God, for having made her so good, by making her our Mother also, and uniting her so closely to us by laying upon her the motherly care of our souls. Ah, yes, this I understand and see, and I shall never forget it, that Thy Mother is also mine; and if a Mother's heart cannot refuse to compassionate my miseries, and to hear me when I call upon her, neither can the Heart of her Son refuse to hearken to her and to grant her requests when she prays for me. Almighty God, only and eternal Son of the Father, Thou hast willed to become our Brother by becoming the Son of Mary! Grant, then, what she asks from Thee for us; grant what she asks from Thee for me; and I will live in penitence, and die in hope: *In pace in idipsum, dormiam et requiescam, quoniam tu, Domine, singulariter in spe constituisti me* ("In peace in the self-same, I will sleep and take my rest; for Thou only, O Lord, hast established me in hope").

CHAPTER V.

THE GRACE OF MARY, OR MARY FULL OF GRACE.

The grace bestowed on Mary is immeasurably superior to all the graces which have ever been granted to Angels or to men.

WE have now surveyed the scale of various lives, or rather of life in its different degrees,[1] and we have seen it coming forth from God and returning again to Him; becoming more perfect in proportion as He draws it closer to Himself, that He may unite it finally to His own life, to the Uncreated Life, by virtue of His union with our human nature, in which He had already combined the three degrees of created life.

[1] *Vide* pp. 24-27, *supra*.

But what shall we call that divine life in which it has pleased God to give His creatures a participation? It is called grace in time, and glory in eternity. Grace is the seed of glory, which God implants in us in this world, in order that with our coöperation it may bud and unfold here below to flourish eternally with Him in heaven.

What difference is there between the intellectual and moral life of human nature, and that divine life in which this nature participates by grace here on earth, and by glory in the bosom of God? There is this difference, that the intellectual and moral life is *like* that of God, whereas by the life of grace and glory we participate, in different degrees, in the Divine Life itself. By the first we are the image of God in intelligence and love; but we know and love Him only with a natural knowledge and love; we know Him by His works, and we love Him as the Author of nature and of all blessings; we know Him by the light of reason, and we love Him with the affections of the will, which follow from the intellectual light; or rather, we should thus naturally know and love Him, if the light of our understanding were not obscured by the darkness of ignorance and the force of our will weakened by concupiscence, because our nature, though still itself, is now but a ruin of what it was. But by the second life, *i.e.* the life of faith and of grace which leads us to glory, we begin to know God by a light superior to that of reason,—a light which dispels the darkness of our ignorance, elevates our understanding, takes possession of our soul, and fills it with unction: *Diligendo itaque nos Deus, ad imaginem suam nos reparat: et ut in nobis formam suæ bonitatis inveniat; dat unde ipsi quoque quod operatur, operemur, accendens scilicet mentium nostrorum lucernos, et igne nos suæ charitatis inflamens, ut non solum ipsum, sed etiam quidquid diligit, diligamus.*[1]

Give me a true Christian, and he will understand

[1] S. Leon., Serm. i., *De Jejunio.*

what S. Leo says here, because he will have had a taste of that light from on high which at once kindles and illuminates and makes us to know God in a way which human language cannot reach, because it is not human, but divine. Yes, the light of faith and grace gives us an insight, as it were, even in this world into the interior life of the living God, and helps us to know and love Him by the very light of His Word, and by His own spirit of love: *Dat unde ipsi quoque quod operatur, operemur;* though this greatest of gifts which He makes us of Himself be still hidden under the veil of time. But when death shall have torn asunder this veil, *in lumine suo videbimus lumen, et similes ei erimus quia videbimus eum sicuti est* ("In His light we shall see light, and we shall be like Him, for we shall see Him as He is"). We shall see the hidden treasure which we bear in the frail vessel of mortality; we shall see God face to face, and we shall be like living mirrors, resplendent with His eternal light, and burning with His eternal love.

The divine life of grace and glory does not, then, consist solely in knowing and loving God with the reason and the will, but in knowing and loving Him as He knows and loves Himself by His own light and with His own love, and thus penetrating into the sanctuary of the Divinity, and being united to the Father and the Son, by the Holy Ghost; the Eternal Bond between them who makes us children of adoption, by making us to live the very life of the Indivisible Trinity.

It is this life of grace in which Angels and men are called to participate, according to the measure determined by Divine Providence, that is to say, according to the capacity given to them, the degree of grace proportioned to that capacity, and the fidelity with which they have corresponded to it *during the time allotted for its increase.*

Now, it is a certain truth of theology, says S. Thomas, that every one receives grace according to the measure of his vocation, or in proportion to the greatness of his destiny, and the duties which it lays upon him: *Unicuique a Deo datur gratia secundum hoc ad quod eligitur*[1] ("God gives grace to every man according to that end whereto He calls him"). S. Bernardin of Sienna has expressed the same truth almost in the same words: *Regula firma est in sacra theologia, quod quandocumque Deus aliquem eligit ad aliquem statum, omnia dona illi dispenset quæ illi statui necessaria sunt, et illum copiose decorant*[2] ("It is a certain rule in theology, that when God calls a man to any state in life, He dispenses to him all the gifts which are needful to that state, and liberally endows him therewith").

What, then, was the grace which was given to Mary? Heaven proclaimed it to earth: "Hail, full of grace, the Lord is with thee!" But can earth understand this message from Heaven, and form a correct idea of the measure of grace proportioned to the dignity of Mother of God? Can it understand and form a correct idea of the grace which was necessary to fill the soul of that Mother of God, of the love which was necessary to fill the heart of that Mother of souls? No; for if, as we have seen, human reason is incapable of comprehending in all its greatness the dignity to which Mary was raised by the Divine Maternity, that dignity which borders on the infinite (*fines divinitatis attingit*), by its immediate, intimate, intrinsic relation to the Hypostatic Union, it is not the less incapable of comprehending in its fulness the grace proportioned to a dignity *suo genere infinita*, according to the expression of Suarez. But it is capable of comprehending that this grace must be immeasurably superior to all the graces bestowed upon Angels or men, because the vocation of Mary was immeasurably higher than that of Angels and men. The grace of Mary, then, is, like her dignity, of an order apart from any other, and nothing created approaches either to the one or the other: *Entra in un ordine superiore a tutto il creato*

---

[1] *Summa*, p. 3, q. 27, a. 5.
[2] *Pro. Fest. V.M.*, Serm. x., a. 2, c. 1.

("It belongs to an order superior to that of all other creatures").[1]

So much reason can and ought to infer from what revelation teaches it respecting Mary, and from what it knows of the harmony which pervades all the works of God.

But, besides these thoughts from Holy Scripture and the Fathers, which we have just given in the words of S. Thomas, we will not omit to add another, which the tender devotion of S. Alphonsus Liguori has likewise drawn from tradition, and which is itself full of grace and truth.

It is this: that the grace of the Mother of God not only became superior to that of all the Angels and Saints by reason of the admirable fidelity of Mary, which made it continually and marvellously to increase in her, but that it was so from the first moment of her life.[2]

And wherefore? Because at the moment when, in the Divine counsels, the Word resolved to become Incarnate, it was necessary that the human Mother of whom He willed to be born should be predestinated to the Divine Maternity. It is, therefore, certain that when, in the order of time, the eye of God fell upon Mary, He beheld in her the blessed creature whom He had chosen from all eternity to be His Mother. If, then, at that hour when the morning star appeared—the bright and heavenly harbinger of the rising of the sun of justice—Mary had not been endowed with a grace superior to that of all creatures, God would have loved her less at that moment than He loved some other creatures, since His love for them is necessarily proportioned to the measure of grace which He bestows on them. And how is it possible to believe, or even to imagine, that there ever was a time when the Word Incarnate in the counsels of God *ab origine mundi* ("from the beginning of the world") should, as He contemplated His Mother, have preferred any other of His works to her?

[1] F. Durazzo, S.J.   [2] Sermon on the Nativity.

What we have said here, is not certainly an article of faith, but it is a truth which faith instils into the soul which it illuminates, and which has always been equally approved by men of learning and of piety.

Prayer.

O Almighty God! infinitely wise, infinitely just, infinitely good! Thou owest nothing to that which is nothing, and, consequently, Thou owest us nothing, since we had no claim to the being which we have received from Thyself alone. And yet in Thy love Thou bestowest Thy gifts upon us all, and dispensest them in number, weight, and measure according to the order of Thy Providence. Blessed be Thou, O Lord, for having lavished them upon our Mother. She has suffered so much for us, and has manifested such constant love for us, that the love we bear her makes us happy in her happiness. Yes, my God, I am not afraid to say, in the name of all her children, that if, in order to be freed from my misery and my sorrows, I must see Thy Mother deprived of a single degree of that grace which makes her so dear to Thee, I would not hesitate to forego that deliverance. But to enrich me with Thy graces, it is not necessary that Thou shouldst impoverish my Mother. Thou hast already proved this; for how many graces have I received from Thee? Yes, I remember them all, and I wish always to remember them; but I remember my infidelities also, and I beseech Thee not to treat me as I deserve. How much more closely should I have been united to Thee, my God, if I had corresponded better to that chain of graces which Thou bringest before me in succession; how mightily should I have been enlightened, invigorated, and strengthened! I will, at least, suffer the obscurity, the void, the solitude, the desolation, which I experience in my soul, in expiation of my continued infidelities; and I offer them to Thee in union with the dereliction of Jesus on the cross. Thou wast there, my Mother, when He suffered it for Me. Obtain, then, in virtue of that dereliction, that I may not be left to myself; and obtain for me also, by thy loving heart, all the graces I have lost, with the grace henceforth to be more faithful to them. *Virgo fidelis* (" Virgin most faithful"), pray for me; pray for us all, now and at the hour of our death. Amen.

CHAPTER VI.

THE IMMACULATE CONCEPTION, OR MARY EVER SPOTLESS.

(Definition of the Dogma.)

IN the greatest of human societies, or rather in the superhuman society of the Church, there has ever prevailed a sweet and strong belief regarding the second Eve, the Mother of the true Life, the Virgin in whom the Word became Incarnate. Christendom has ever believed that the fall of man, which wounded us all, had no effect on her; that this second Mother of men, from the very beginning of her existence, was pure and stainless in a sense far higher than the first. But was this belief a simple conclusion of human wisdom, or a reflection of the light of God? Was it a truth of feeling, of reason, or of faith, that the Mother of Christ, who was saved like the rest of the human race by Him alone, was nevertheless saved after an exceptional manner, as beseemed the peerless creature chosen to give to the world the very Source of salvation? Is it of faith, in short, that the grace which raises us from the fall had preserved her from it?

The instinct of Christendom anticipated the answer, but it awaited it nevertheless with filial impatience. It was to obtain that answer that the Supreme Pontiff set the whole Church to pray. It was to obtain that answer that He questioned all the Bishops of the world as to the traditions of their Churches, and as to their own belief. And it was after having received that universal testimony, after having heard the voice of Catholicity like to that voice of mighty waters of which Scripture speaks, that the Vicar of Him Who commanded the sea and the storms spoke, in the midst of the universal silence, the words which thrilled through Christendom. No, the belief of ages as to the Immaculate Conception of Mary was not a human opinion, but a divine truth. That feeling of the universal Church originated, not in the heart of man, but in the Heart and in the revealed Will of the Son of God ; and it is of faith that the most holy Virgin Mary, " from the first moment of her Conception, by a special privilege of God, and by virtue of the merits of her Son Jesus Christ, the Saviour of mankind, was preserved from all stain of original sin."[1]

[1] Let us listen to the voice of Peter in his successor: " Being full of confidence in God, and persuaded that the fitting moment was come for defining the Immaculate Conception of the most holy Virgin Mother of God, which is attested and wonderfully illustrated by the Divine Oracles, venerable tradition, the permanent feeling of the Church, the admirable agreement of Catholic pastors and their flocks, and the solemn acts of our predecessors ; after having examined every thing with the greatest care, and offered assiduous and fervent prayers to God, it has seemed to us that we ought no longer to delay to sanction and define by our supreme judgment the Immaculate Conception of the Virgin, and thus to satisfy the pious desires of the Catholic world and our own devotion towards the most holy Virgin, in order to honour more and more, in her, her only Son our Lord Jesus Christ, since all the praise and honour which we give to the Mother redounds to the glory of the Son. Therefore, having offered unceasingly, with humility and fasting, our private prayers and the public prayers of the Church to God the Father, by His Son, that He would vouchsafe to strengthen and direct our soul by the power of the Holy Ghost; after having also implored the assistance of all the heavenly court and the aid of the Holy Spirit the Paraclete,—we, acting to-day under His inspiration, for the honour of the Most Holy and Undivided Trinity, for the glorification of the Virgin Mother of God, for the exaltation of the Catholic faith, and the increase of the Christian religion, by the authority of our

The Immaculate Conception of Mary, defined as a dogma of faith, thus expands like a flower of dazzling whiteness upon the immortal tree of revealed truth. We use the expression designedly, when we say that the definition of this dogma is the expansion of a truth. For it is not a new dogma, as ignorance supposes it to be, or as incredulity, in its jealousy of the progress of the faith, affects to believe it. No! it is not a new dogma, but the dogmatic declaration of a truth which has always been known and loved in the Church, and has always been contained in the deposit of revelation. It is an immutable truth, defined by the authority which Jesus Christ has instituted to be the guardian and interpreter of revelation : " Teach ; I am with you always, even unto the end of time." The Church never invents, she discerns ; and when she is asked if such or such a belief is a part of the dogma, she replies. Her answer to the heresy which denies, is an anathema ; to the good faith which hesitates, a consolation. It is thus that at different periods heresy, or even the weakness of the human mind (weak even in great men), has given occasion to the dogmatic declarations of the Church of Jesus Christ, and that the shock of errors and of opinions has struck out from the rock on which it is founded, not new truths, but new lights. It would take us too long a time to follow here the chain of these dogmatic definitions, but we shall not depart from our subject by re-

Lord Jesus Christ, of the blessed Apostles Peter and Paul, and by our own, we declare, pronounce, and define that the doctrine according to which the Blessed Virgin Mary was, from the first moment of her Conception, by a singular grace and special privilege of Almighty God, for the sake of the merits of Jesus Christ, the Saviour of mankind, preserved and exempted from all stain of original sin, is revealed by God, and consequently should be firmly and constantly believed by all the faithful. If, then, any one, which God forbid, has the presumption to think in his heart otherwise than we have defined, let him learn and know that being condemned by his own judgment, he has made shipwreck of the faith and forsaken the Church."

calling some of them, which will lead us back to it of themselves:

The Church anathematised the errors of the Manichees, and among these errors, that which denied the truth of the Flesh, and consequently of the Human Nature, of Jesus Christ She anathematised the error of the Arians, who denied His Divine Nature, and defined against them the consubstantiality of the Word of God. She condemned Nestorius, who, dividing these two natures instead of distinguishing them, made of them two persons, denied their union in the Person of the Word, and consequently the Divine Maternity of Mary, which was defined with so much fervour and solemnity at the celebrated Council of Ephesus. She condemned Eutyches, who, by confounding these two natures, destroyed them both. Lastly, she condemned the Monothelites, who, reviving in other terms the error of Eutyches, arrived as he did, whether intentionally or not, by the confusion of the human and Divine wills in Jesus Christ, to the same conclusion as Manes, Arius, and Nestorius, *i.e.* to the denial of the redemption of the human race by Him Who could not have expiated our sins if He had not been truly Man, and could not have given to His expiation the value required by His justice if He had not been truly God. He redeemed us because He was true God and true Man; Man to suffer, God to save.

Mary is the Mother of the Man-God. Her Divine Maternity is manifestly revealed: "Mary," says the Gospel, "of whom was born Jesus,"[1] and in whom "the Word was made flesh."[2] The declaration of the Council of Ephesus did not, then, establish a new dogma, but defined the faith of the Church against the heresies that strove to corrupt it.

The virginity of the Mother of God is also divinely affirmed in the Gospel: " The Holy Ghost shall come upon thee, and the power of the Most High shall over-

[1] Matt. i. 16.   [2] John i. 14.

shadow thee; therefore the Holy Child Who shall be born of thee shall be called the Son of God."[1] And again: "Joseph, thou son of David, fear not to take unto thee Mary thy wife, for that which is conceived in her is of the Holy Ghost."[2] And once more: "Jesus was about thirty years old, being (as was supposed) the Son of Joseph."[3] But here sectaries have attempted to obscure the glory of the Mother of God by denying the fact of her perpetual virginity. The Church has condemned them in several councils by the authority of the Apostolic tradition, which she simply defines.[4]

To this glory of virginity, this perfect integrity of purity, the Gospel adds another: the integrity and plenitude of grace,—"Hail, full of grace:"[5] words which we never find addressed to any other in Holy Scripture except to the Mother of God. They teach us that if the Living Temple of the Son of God was exempt from every stain, far more must the lamp of that temple, the flame which burns in that sanctuary, the soul of Mary, have been perfectly pure. Thus Catholic instinct has applied to Mary those words of the Holy Ghost: "Thou art all fair, my beloved, and there is no stain in thee."[6]

But now, according to heretics, questions arise. Are we to understand by this plenitude of grace and this exemption from all stain, the exemption only from such faults as destroy sanctifying grace, and not also from lesser faults and lighter stains? Is not this to ask if the Mother of God had ever offended God?

The Church answers by an abhorrent denial; and declares what the holy Fathers, and especially S. Augustine, had so clearly expressed, that there can be no question even of venial sin when we speak of the Mother

---

[1] Luke i. 35. [2] Matt. i. 20. [3] Luke iii. 23.

[4] Modern sectaries have renewed this old error, so learnedly demolished by St. Jerome. All heresies are marked by this lamentable characteristic, that they harbour something of the venomous enmity of the old serpent against her who has crushed his head. See chap. ix.

[5] Luke i. 28. [6] Cant. iv. 7.

of the Lord. But if it would have been unworthy of the Son of God to have been born of a Mother stained by venial sin, would it not have been still more unworthy of Him to have suffered her to be polluted, though only at the first moment of her life, by the guilt of the great original transgression? Would it not have been far more unworthy of the Divine Wisdom to have abandoned Mary, though but for a single moment, to the degrading dominion of him whose head she was destined to crush?[1] Hence the constant belief of Christendom in all ages that in her there was no kind of stain, either mortal, venial, or original, and that she was conceived without sin. In the Middle Ages, however, there were certain great and pious minds which, notwithstanding their attraction towards this truth, experienced a hesitation on the subject, which they submitted to the judgment of the Church. This hesitation arose from two causes: from a want of precision in the very idea of the Immaculate Conception; and from a fear which, though unfounded, is worthy of all respect, of admitting an exception to the general law of the contagion of original sin. The confusion of ideas arose from their not distinguishing in the Conception the action of second causes in the formation of the human body from the direct action of God in the creation of man. There is always, in fact, a direct action of God in the gift of life which He bestows on us. We have all learnt this in an admirable book which we read in our childhood, when we hardly understood it; and which we perhaps left off reading when we became capable of understanding it.

The Catechism asks: "Is God also your Father?" "Yes," we answer, "and far more so than our parents; because by them He formed our bodies, whilst He Himself created our souls out of nothing." Is God, then, always creating? Doubtless He is; and it is the creation of the soul and its union with the body which constitutes human nature. The Immaculate Conception, there-

[1] Gen. iii. 15.

fore, is a divine act,—the act by which God, in creating the soul of Mary and uniting it to the body which He destined for it, preserved it from the general contagion,[1] and exempted it from that common law which weighs upon all mankind, and of which an ancient writer has said: "It seems that our souls, on becoming united to the body, glide into a tomb." They feel, in fact, the effect of the original corruption of that human nature which is one in its two substances, and is infected in its source, being guilty and depraved in its origin (Adam), *in quo omnes peccaverunt*.[2]

Those, then, who feared to admit in the case of Mary an exception to that general law (of which we, alas, are a continual proof to ourselves), and who had not sufficiently observed that the exception here was a directly divine act, failed also to see that if the Conception of Mary was exceptional with regard to that of other men, it was, on the contrary, in perfect harmony with the whole design of God regarding her whom it is unreasonable to confound with the rest of mankind. "Give me another Mother of God," cries Bossuet, "and then fear to make an exception."[3]

Give me, I will add, another creature full of grace, blessed among women, in whom such great things have been wrought by the Most High, and whom all generations shall call blessed; and then dare to confound with the other children of Eve, in any thing whatsoever, a creature thus divinely exceptional in all things.

[1] Alexander VII., in his Constitutions, *Sollicitudo omnium Ecclesiarum*, of the 8th December 1661, thus declared the sense attached by the Church to the *cultus* of the Conception of Mary: "It is the ancient and pious belief of faithful Christians, that the soul of the Blessed Virgin Mary, from the first moment of its conception and of its union with the body, was, by a special privilege and grace of God, and for the sake of the merits of Jesus Christ her Son, the Redeemer of mankind, preserved and exempted from original sin: and it is in this sense that they honour and solemnly celebrate the Feast of her Conception."

[2] Romans xii.

[3] First Sermon on the Immaculate Conception.

Yes, in all things; for is not that a common law which was laid down by the Apostle: "In many things we all offend God" (*In multis offendimus omnes*)?[1] Yet here is a Virgin ever faithful, and a life without spot. Is it not by virtue of a common law that the glory of virginity is separated from the joys of maternity? Yet here is a Virgin Mother. Is it not by virtue of a common law that these joys are purchased by unspeakable sufferings—*in dolore paries*[2] ("in sorrow shalt thou bring forth")? Yet here is a childbirth without suffering. Is it not a common law which attaches agony to death? Yet here is a death without struggle and without agony. Is it not by a common law that man awaits his resurrection in the darkness of the tomb until the judgment of the last day? Yet here is an assumption without delay. You who hitherto have known little of Mary, learn at last to know your Mother, and acknowledge that if, for your sake, she was the Mother of sorrows and the most afflicted of all creatures, yet that her life was without sin, her death without suffering, her resurrection without delay. Tell me, then, is it fitting that in that living temple which the Divine Wisdom had made for Himself,[3] wherein all is peerless, incomparable, and exceptional, the corner-stone alone should be unworthy of the rest? Should it alone be excepted from the exception, and be out of harmony with the whole? Tell me in that soul, in that life, shall the principle of life itself—the Conception—be alone unworthy of them, the apparition of the soul itself as it issues from the hands of God be alone devoid of glory?

Think it not, believe it not; the Church has never believed it; and if for a time she tolerated fears to the contrary, because of the good faith of those who feared, she endured them with a maternal pity, soon to silence[4] them, to celebrate in her canticles the truth

---

[1] S. James iii. 2.   [2] Gen. v. 16.   [3] Prov. ix. 1.
[4] Paul V., Bull 97, an. 1616; Gregory XV., Bull 29, an. 1622.

which dispels[1] them, and at last to unveil it in this our day[2] in all the glory of her dogmatic decision, by which she shows it to have been contained in the divine tradition which Jesus Christ has impressed upon her mind and committed to her keeping even unto the end.

Prayer.

O Eternal Word, Incarnate for us in time, only Son of God and only Son of Mary, I thank Thee for having willed that Thy Mother should also be ours; and I bless Thee for having given her a heart so full of pity for our miseries, that it belongs to us by its compassion, as it belongs to Thee by its ever-spotless sanctity. But since thou art spotless, O my true Mother, cast thy merciful eyes upon my poor soul, which is stained by so many sins. Yes, look upon me, Immaculate Virgin, and pray for me to Him Who with one word can heal my soul of the sin which pollutes, of the leprosy which covers it. Wait not for the awful hour when I must appear before my Judge, but obtain for me even now an intense sorrow for my sins, the humble and sincere confession which obtains that sorrow, the fear and love of God, a true change of life, and fidelity to grace even unto death. Death approaches, my holy Mother; it draws nearer day by day—or rather, I am passing on quickly to meet it; but thou wilt be there, my Mother, at that hour of meeting, and thou wilt obtain for me the grace to die in faith, hope, love, and penitence, with an ardent desire to see God, and with a childlike confidence in being presented to Jesus by the same hands which bore Him, and by which He has shed all His graces upon me, and by the Mother's heart which always receives our prayers, and whose own are ever received by Him. Yes, I have a firm confidence that thou wilt then put into my mouth the aspiration which I offer to thee every evening of my

---

[1] Alexander VII. confirms and explains in 1661 the Constitution of Sixtus IV., of 1483, on the Feast of the Conception.
[2] Pius IX., 8th December 1854.

life: "Jesus, Mary, and Joseph, I give you my heart, my soul, my life;" above all, I hope that thou wilt put it into my heart, and that, after having said to thee so many thousand times, "Pray for us, now and at the hour of our death," I may obtain then what I have so often asked—thy prayer, to which God refuses nothing —that prevailing prayer, which will assuredly obtain for me perfect resignation, entire conformity to the Divine Will, the true life in Jesus by death, the *Adveniat regnum tuum*, by the *Fiat voluntas tua*. This is my hope, and it will not deceive me. *Memorare, O piissima Maria.*

CHAPTER VII.

THE IMMACULATE CONCEPTION, OR MARY EVER SPOTLESS.

(Definition of the Dogma—continued.)

THE faith in the Immaculate Conception of Mary, which, as we have seen, is confirmed by the general feeling of the faithful, has been consecrated also by the most sublime inspirations of Christian genius. We quoted just now a passage from Bossuet; but we know not if any thing more forcible or more sublime has ever been written on the Immaculate Conception of Mary than the whole discourse of that great man,[1] from which that passage is taken. We do not pretend here to make use of his words: they cannot be fairly called his own when detached from their context; but let us at least avail ourselves of his thoughts. The past, the present, and the future relate only to man: they are all present

---

[1] This great mind had its errors, that light its shadows. The Count de Maistre, who has brought them so prominently forward, did not the less admire the genius of Bossuet. He would fain have seen him finish his career with his admirable discourse on the Unity of the Church and the Primacy of Peter and his Successors, pronounced at the opening of the Assembly in 1682.

to the eternity of God. What He has resolved to do is before Him as if already accomplished. Hence the language of His prophets: they do not so much foretell the future as point it out, because it is before them. Thus also was Jesus Christ called "the Lamb slain from the foundation of the world,"[1] because He was thus slain in the decrees of God. But in those same decrees the Woman promised from the beginning was inseparable from her Son, the Mother of the Man-God from the Incarnation of the Word. Thus the Church, with that divine instinct which is her promised gift, applies to Mary those wonderful words which, in fact, relate to her in her maternal union with the Uncreated and Incarnate Wisdom: "The Lord possessed me from the beginning of His ways. I was in His thoughts, I was with Him before He created the world. I was established from the beginning, before the earth was made. The abyss was not as yet, and I was already conceived."[2]

From all eternity, then, the Word, who willed to be Incarnate in her, regarded her as His Mother. Was it ever possible that He could see her without loving her? And yet, if she had been conceived in sin, would it have been possible for Him to love her in a state infinitely opposed to His sanctity? The most perfect of Sons, then, must have been devoid of love for His Mother. What do I say? He must have regarded her with abhorrence. "No, no," cries Bossuet; "the honour of the Son compels me to affirm with all my power the Immaculate Conception of Mary, and to vindicate for her the singular prerogative of possessing in her God a Son who was before her." What a sublime cry is thus called forth by the eagle's glance upon the woman clothed with the Sun of Justice. This great man visibly suffered at having to await the definition of the dogma; and it would seem that, seeing now the Church militant glorifying on earth what he beholds in heaven, the joy of his soul has thrilled even through his tomb, and that

[1] Apoc. xiii. 8.   [2] Prov. viii.

he has obtained of God that his body, which has been lost for more than a century, should be found in our day and appear in his cathedral, as if to take part in the universal festivity.

But what, after all, is the voice of Bossuet compared with that concert of Fathers, Doctors, and great men of all ages, responding to the mighty voice of Peter, ever living in the Church to confirm his brethren? How majestic is that great stream of tradition which the Apostolic See causes to pass before us, bearing in its whole course the name of Mary ever stainless; above the earth, polluted in its whole extent,—above the human race, infected in all its generations! Mary alone corruption could not reach; Mary alone contagion could not touch; Mary alone is the one reserved spot which the deluge of sin has failed to reach, and where the Spirit of God rested, like the dove from the ark, to receive and to give to the human race the olive-branch of peace— salvation in Jesus Christ.

But if in this concert of great voices of all ages we have distinguished the cry of the eagle of our modern days, do we not also discern the sweeter accents of the dove of Geneva? It is S. Francis of Sales who, in accordance with the doctrine of Holy Scripture and the ancient Fathers, has shown us[1] the Incarnation of the Word in the primitive design of the Creator. He it is who has taught us how the second Adam, according to His production in the order of time, is truly the first in the Divine intention, in the eternal plan of Divine Providence for the production of creatures. But if the Incarnation of the Word could not have been decreed independently of the means chosen for its realisation—*i. e.* of the Divine Maternity of Mary—and if the Saviour was the first conceived in the plan of the Creator, as the end and aim of all His works, His Mother also was evidently first conceived together with Him. We therefore understand perfectly how the Eve first produced was really

[1] Page 8, *supra.*

subordinate to the second, who was truly the first in the Divine intention. We understand why Mary, the second Eve, was created in grace in a far higher sense than the first; why the grace of redemption preserved her from contagion, instead of healing her of its effects; why the flood of sin, which has never ceased from the beginning of time to roll its troubled waves from generation to generation, stopped before the living Ark of salvation, and let it pass; why He who was pleased to abide in that Ark, in order to raise the world from its fall, refused to suffer it to be touched by the common pollution.

And here we touch the other side of the dogma of the Immaculate Conception; for it reminds the proud world of the reality of its fall, and of its need of the hand of God for its restoration.

The great errors of modern times spring from the denial or the forgetfulness of the fall. Man, who fell by pride, would fain ignore his ruin. He will not acknowledge in the darkness wherein he is groping his way his need of that original light, but a feeble ray of which remains to him; of that sacred fire, of which he has preserved but a few sparks under the ashes; of that primeval strength, which made him master of himself and of the world, and of which he has preserved but a sorrowful remembrance. He will not confess the humiliating fact, to which his conscience bears witness, that he seeks truth, and faints in the pursuit of it; that his eyes are weary in the search, and never attain to its full possession; that his heart, which pines for liberty, finds itself in continual bondage; and that, notwithstanding its unconquerable desire of life, he finds at the end of all his ways the presence and sovereignty of death. He resists that divine voice within him[1] which protests against this vanity, and asks not, like the Apostle, "Who shall deliver me from the body of this death?"[2] because in his pride he will not consent to be saved

[1] Romans viii. 20.   [2] Romans vii. 24.

by grace.[1] No; from the depth of his misery he aims to be self-sufficient, as if he were his own principle and end. *Similis ero Altissimo*[2] (" I shall be like the Most High"), the principle of all errors, lurks in this apotheosis of man by himself. Idolatry was its popular, as Pantheism is its falsely scientific, form. In both alike the human mind is overcome by the spirit of falsehood, and yields once more to the original temptation, " You shall be as gods."[3] In both the creature would usurp the divine life, instead of receiving it; and aiming to possess as its own that which belongs to the Creator alone, is deprived by that very attempt of the grace and truth which make us to live the life of God.[4] But the Vicar of Christ, the divinely constituted organ of Him who said to man, " Thou must be born again" (*Oportet nasci denuo*),[5] recalls to the minds which have been deluded by the old lie the full extent and reality of our fall, by proclaiming that one creature alone has been exempted from it—the second Eve—the Mother of the new life, because she was to be the Mother of the Head of the regenerate human family.

Now, is it not plain that the world, which has been so long deaf to that voice, begins to lend it an attentive ear? It is at last compelled to acknowledge that every other regeneration but this would be fruitless, and that all other victories without the victory of Christ are powerless to save it even here below. The world seemed to have forgotten this truth so entirely as to be unconscious that its toilsome victories over matter were a proof of the fall and a carrying out of the sentence which condemned man to fertilise the earth by the sweat of his brow, and to reconquer some remains of his lost dominion over nature by dint of conflict, danger, and toil. It has been reminded of it at last, because it has pleased God to humble the pride of man in his physical conquests by moral defeats, and to make him feel that it

[1] Romans vii. 25.   [2] Isaias xiv. 14.   [3] Genesis iii. 5.
[4] Ephesians iv. 18.   [5] John iii. 7.

avails him little that nature obeys him if he knows not how to rule himself, and if at the moment when the elements acknowledge his sway all the souls of men are in revolt, and all the powers and kingdoms of the earth are tottering to their fall. A little while ago, intoxicated with success, proud of his riches, and dreaming of nothing but earthly enjoyment, he said to his soul, like the rich fool in the Gospel, "We have laboured and struggled, gathered up and conquered; it is time to enjoy ourselves in peace, and to live in security and glory, relieved by science from all the vain terrors of faith." But instead of enjoyment, behold sorrow; instead of repose, agitation and anguish; instead of peace, behold war; instead of life, behold death; and the world by these mighty warnings has been brought to the remembrance of itself, of its weakness and of its misery, and when it has been told of the help of God, and of that great bond which reunites to God and which is called religion, it has at last stretched out its hands to grasp it in the universal wreck.

This return of souls towards God and the irritation of those minds which do not take part in this returning movement, this progress towards the faith,[1] accounts for the excitement produced in the world by a dogmatic definition. It was not, in fact, piety alone which was moved by that decision; we believe its effects upon incredulity to be still more striking. There was a fact which touched all minds, a doctrinal, moral, and social event, which made every chord of love and hatred to vibrate. It was an event in doctrine; a flower, as we have seen, had expanded on the eternal tree of truth, and the eyes which are not attracted are dazzled by its

[1] The allocution, pronounced in the Consistory of the 9th of December 1854, says, that with the exception of secret societies, the perversity of unbelievers excites general abhorrence; that there is a certain disposition in the minds of men to return to faith and religion—a feeling of admiration for the Catholic religion; and that this is a great benefit, and a step towards truth.

brightness. It was an event in morals. The general impression which it has produced bears witness to the death-struggle of indifferentism in the nations of Christendom, and the presence of a spirit of religion which men had too hastily believed to be extinct. Those whom that spirit does not console are disturbed at its presence. It was a social event, and, as it were, an unexpected apparition of the supreme authority upon earth, of that spiritual and teaching authority which alone has children among all nations. Those to whom that authority brings not security, it strikes with consternation. And therefore it is that the impression produced by the definition of faith is universal. The one class are delighted to see, as they emerge from an age of doubt, that there is still a voice upon earth which has an echo full of love in every language. The others are more deeply wounded by such a prodigy, as they had believed it to be impossible. After having vainly endeavoured to disparage it, they have stooped to hypocrisy, and affected an anxious solicitude for the integrity of the faith. But believe not for a moment that they feel the slightest anxiety on the subject. No, they trouble themselves neither about the dogma of the Immaculate Conception, nor the doctrine of original sin; the one subject of their fears is the power of S. Peter, and the fresh proof which has just been given of its imperishable strength.

Prayer.

O my God, how happy am I in being a child of the Church, and in knowing by her teaching that Mary is the true Mother of my soul, and a Mother ever without spot! This truth fills me with hope; for, notwithstanding the depth of the evil which I bear within me, I believe, O Lord, that Thou wilt heal me and make me one day less unworthy of such a Mother. I know what is the stain of sin, alas, but too well; like oil penetrating a splendid garment, it has saturated my soul, and refuses to yield entirely to any of the means which I employ to efface it. *Amplius lava me ab iniquitate mea et a peccato meo munda me.* Purify me, then, Thyself, O Lord, and that more and more; for my sin is ever there, and Thou alone canst consume it in the fire of Thy love. I know, also, O my God, that to preserve us from the deepest of stains, the dark stain of pride, Thou wilt leave within us, even to the end of this poor life of ours, that which makes us to fear, to pray, to implore; that weakness which feels ever in danger of falling, that inclination to evil over which all the just have mourned; but grant, at least, O Lord, that I may mourn with them, that the presence of Thy grace may make me feel my misery, and that I may combat manfully the evil which I bear within me, that each victory of my life may be to me a consolation in death and a joy in eternity.

And thou, my Mother, in whom God has prepared a sanctuary worthy of His Son, by thine Immaculate Conception, obtain for thy poor child strength and courage in the conflict, patience in suffering, resignation to the will of God in death, and, above all, that perseverance in prayer which obtains all other graces; that, living and dying, pure in body and in heart, I may one day be admitted to kiss those motherly hands which have lavished so many graces upon me, and which I have a full confidence will open to me the gates of heaven. *Janua cœli, memorare.*

CHAPTER VIII.

MARY, VIRGIN AND MOTHER.

EVER since the fall of man, when he broke by his disobedience the bonds which united him with God, and thus lost the divine life of grace, he has been degraded in all his powers, but above all in the power of reproduction by the union which propagates natural life. In this power especially the original rebellion of his spirit has been punished, and punished by the degrading rebellion of the flesh; which, like an insolent slave, no longer obeys the command of the spirit, and whose blind instinct tends to enslave the intellectual nature of man, and to level it with that of the brutes. Thus the conscience of man has always and every where acknowledged the pollution attached to generation. It is not only the inspired Psalmist who mourns over it: *In peccatis concepit me mater mea;* it is not only the virgin Evangelist who extols virgins because they are without spot: *Hi sunt qui cum mulieribus non sunt coinquinati*[1] ("These are they who have not defiled themselves with women"); it is not only the Apostle who proclaims the superiority of virginity to the holiest marriage ("*Qui matrimonio jungit virginem suam, bene facit; qui non jungit, melius facit*[2] ("He that giveth his virgin in marriage, doth well; and he that giveth her not, doth better"). All ages, all nations, have felt the same, even at periods when reason was most degraded and morals most depraved. The Romans honoured vestals, even when they had ceased to exist among them; and never has the lily of purity budded upon this miserable earth without attracting the love of man, without touching his heart, or at least troubling his conscience.

This great fact remains, and must remain, inexplicable to all who do not acknowledge the fall of our nature, and the consequences which result from it. We Christians, who are conscious of both, know also why shame is ever attached to the communication of natural life, and why virginity always appears to the eyes of men as an aureola of the victory of the spirit over the flesh. It is not surprising, then, that the great victory of humanity, its great revenge upon its former conqueror, was begun by a virgin. That victory was promised to man immediately after the fall, and at the same time his defeat by redemption was foretold to Satan: *Inimicitias*

[1] 1 Cor. vii. 38.   [2] Apoc. xiv. 4.

ponam inter te et mulierem, inter semen tuum et semen illius : ipsa conteret caput tuum[1] ("I will put enmities between thee and the woman, between thy seed and her seed ; she shall crush thy head"). The woman who was to crush the serpent's head is called by Isaias, not only *a* virgin, but *the* virgin—*i. e.* the Virgin of virgins, whom the Gospel calls " the woman blest among all women."

Let us see, then, how the victory which was consummated on the cross began with virginity. "And in the sixth month, the Angel Gabriel was sent from God into a city of Galilee called Nazareth, to a virgin espoused to a man whose name was Joseph, of the house of David; and the name of the virgin was Mary. And the Angel being come in, said to her: Hail, full of grace, the Lord is with thee : blessed art thou among women. And when she had heard, she was troubled at his saying, and thought with herself what manner of salutation this should be. And the Angel said to her: Fear not, Mary, for thou hast found grace with God. Behold, thou shalt conceive in thy womb, and shalt bring forth a Son ; and thou shalt call His name Jesus. He shall be great, and shall be called the Son of the Most High ; and the Lord God shall give unto Him the throne of David His father ; and He shall reign in the house of Jacob for ever. And of His kingdom there shall be no end. And Mary said to the Angel : How shall this be done, because I know not man ? And the Angel answering, said to her : The Holy Ghost shall come upon thee, and the power of the Most High shall overshadow thee : and therefore also the Holy which shall be born of thee shall be called the Son of God. And behold thy cousin Elizabeth ; she hath also conceived a son in her old age; and this is the sixth month with her that is called barren : because no word is impossible with God. And Mary said : Behold the handmaid of the Lord ; be it done to me according to thy word"

[1] Gen iii. 15.

(*Ecce ancilla Domini; fiat mihi secundum verbum tuum*).[1]

All is divine in this dialogue; but the two sentences uttered by Mary show that virginity was the very condition of the Incarnation, both on the part of God and on the part of man; or rather, of human nature represented by the second Eve. It is manifest, in fact, that Mary refuses the glory offered her by God, if it is to be purchased at the cost of her virginity: *Quomodo fiat istud, quoniam virum non cognosco?* ("How can this be, because I know not man?") Unless these words express her irrevocable determination to remain a virgin, they have no meaning at all. Is it not clear, that if a young woman, to whom a child was promised, should simply reply: "How can this be, because I have hitherto observed continence in the marriage state?" the reply would be: "You will observe it no longer." The words of Mary, therefore, can bear no other sense than that of her unchangeable resolution to remain a virgin. And therefore it is that the saints have brought them forward as a proof of the vow of perpetual virginity by which she consecrated herself to the supreme object of her love. Yes, the *virum non cognosco* ("I know not man") has manifestly the same sense as the *lumen cœli non video*; and signifies not only "I know not," but "I cannot know;" as "I see not," in the mouth of the holy Tobias, signifies "I cannot see;" and as "I do not such a thing," in the mouth of one who is determined to abstain from it, signifies "I will not do it."

But for this resolution to remain a virgin, Mary would never have been the Mother of the New Man—of the second Adam—Who was to be like the first, though after a different manner—the immediate work of the Omnipotence of God, for the regeneration of the human race, wholly polluted in its source. The Word made Flesh would not receive that Flesh by the stream of generation, because that stream carried with it pollution

[1] Luke i. 38.

throughout its course. No, He first preserved from pollution the womb which was to bear Him, and then formed there Himself, by the operation of the Holy Ghost, the Sacred Body which was to be the Lamb without spot, the Victim for the whole world : *Spiritus Sanctus obumbrabit tibi, et quod nascetur ex te* SANCTUM *vocabitur Filius Dei.* The Eternal Word, the Uncreated Son of God, became thus the true Son of Man, because He was the true Son of Mary, who was herself, like all other human beings, the child of Adam ; but He became the Son of Man by a direct operation of the Almighty, as the first man was the work and the child of God by another direct operation of the power of Him who created him to His own Image. The virginity of Mary, therefore, was the condition of the Incarnation on the part of the Incarnate Word and on the part of His Mother. Mary did not consent to become a mother until assured that she should remain a virgin ; and the Word became Incarnate in her womb because He saw that this humble Virgin's love of purity was greater than her desire for the ineffable glory of the Divine Maternity.

The assurance given to Mary was followed by her consent ; and humility finished the work of virginity, by those words which the Spirit of God awaited, to perform the greatest of His works : *Ecce ancilla Domini ; fiat mihi secundum verbum tuum* ("Behold the handmaid of the Lord ; be it done unto me according to thy word").

The first who, after Mary herself, the holy Baptist, and his mother, received the revelation of that great work, was he who knew her resolution to remain, like himself, a virgin ; and who, unable to understand how she was about to become a mother, thought, in his anguish, of separating from her. "Joseph, thou son of David, said the Angel of God to him, fear not to take unto thee Mary thy wife; for that which is conceived in her is of the Holy Ghost."[1]

[1] Matt. i. 20.

And here the Gospel shows us the union of God's wisdom with His power, in the work of the Incarnation. That wisdom decreed that the mystery of salvation should not be made publicly known before its consummation on Calvary, and its glorification by the victory obtained over death by the risen Saviour.

By what means, then, was the miracle of the fruitfulness of the Virgin-Mother (the fulfilment of the prophecy of Isaias—" The Virgin shall conceive and bring forth"[1]) to be concealed from the eyes of men? By the veil of a marriage contracted between two persons both resolved, and both aware of each other's resolution, to preserve virginity unstained. He was chosen from all mankind who, being, like Mary, of royal descent, had, nevertheless, like her, embraced voluntary poverty; who was thus worthy to be the father of the poor, and to be in reality the confidant of the great counsel[2] of God, the work accomplished in Mary for the salvation of the world. And it was because Joseph was to receive the assurance of it from Heaven, that Mary waited in silence for that heavenly communication before she spoke herself to her husband of her ineffable election. From that moment the last and greatest of the Patriarchs knew what the Gospel afterwards revealed to the whole world, but which was to remain concealed upon earth until the beginning of the apostolical mission of Jesus : *Et ipse Jesus erat incipiens quasi annorum triginta, ut putabatur, filius Joseph* (" And Jesus Himself was beginning about the age of thirty years ; being—as it was supposed—the son of Joseph").[3] " What could be more worthy of God," exclaims St. Bernard, " than thus to veil the fruitful virginity of Mary under the appearance of the holiest of marriages? By this one counsel of His wisdom, this one design of His providence, He chose as the sharer of His heavenly secret and of the great work of the Incarnation the undeniable witness of the virginity

---

[1] Isaias vii. 14. [2] S. Bernard, *De Laud. V.M.*, Hom. 2.
[3] Luke iii. 23.

of Mary. He preserved the Holy of holies from the slanders of falsehood, and the sting of evil tongues; and sheltered, by His protection, both the virginal modesty and the fair fame of the Virgin Mother" (*Necessario igitur desponsata est Maria Joseph, quando per hoc et a canibus sanctum absconditur et a sponso virginitas comprobatur, et virginis tam verecundiæ parcitur quam famæ. Quid dignius divinâ providentiâ ? Uno tali consilio secretis cœlestibus et admittitur testis et excluditur hostis et integra servatur fama virginis matris*).[1]

Prayer.

My God, I thank Thee for the light which Thou hast given me, by which I read in the Gospel Thy Mother's ineffable purity. I see there that she would have sacrificed the glory of the Divine Maternity to the preservation of her virginity, and that it was because she would not consent to lose it that she was accounted worthy to be the Mother of Thy Word Incarnate in her chaste womb. I thank Thee also, O Lord, for having revealed to me the beauty of that other soul, elected from amongst all men to bear witness to Mary's perpetual virginity, and to be the Foster-Father of the Lamb of God in His voluntary humiliation for the salvation of the world. Yes, incomparably great, humble, noble, and pure must have been that patriarchal soul, to be so intimately united to the Holy of holies and the Virgin of virgins; and I believe, adorable Trinity of my God, that, after Jesus and Mary, nothing on earth has ever been dearer to Thee. May those names, then, of Jesus, Mary, and Joseph be inseparable in my heart, as they are in Thine ! May they ever remind me of the sublimity of the life hidden in God with Jesus Christ; of the vanity of the pomp and riches of the world; of the reality of that interior treasure which no rust can corrupt; of the glory which comes from on high, of which nothing can deprive

[1] S. Bernard, *De Laud. V.M.*, Hom. 2.

me; of the blessedness of suffering and being despised with Him Who makes all suffering and shame which is united with His, a seed of joy and glory and eternal life! May these three Sacred Names, Jesus, Mary, and Joseph, be ever on my lips : of Jesus, the Source of all grace ; of Mary, full of grace, and whose prayers obtain all grace for us ; of Joseph, whose name touches the heart of Mary, and moves it to that merciful and effectual prayer which brings grace into our own heart. Yes, Sacred Names of Jesus, Mary, and Joseph, you shall ever be to me an act of faith, of confidence, of love ; you shall be upon my lips and in my heart in every trial of my life ; and especially in the temptations which still remain for me to overcome. Above all, I hope that you will be the last words which my lips shall utter, and the aspiration which shall bear my soul into the bosom of the Father, the Son, and the Holy Ghost. Amen.

CHAPTER IX.

MARY EVER VIRGIN.

Heresy has ever been offended at the brightness of her purity—Heresy deceives by the perversion of Holy Scripture—The compassion which those deserve who are thus deceived.

WE have seen that the Gospel affirms not only the virginity of the Mother of Jesus, Who was born of the Holy Ghost (*Quod in ea natum est, de Spiritu Sancto est*),[1] but clearly reveals that Mary would have refused to become the Mother of Christ, if in order to obtain that privilege she must have ceased to be a virgin : *Quomodo fiet istud quoniam virum non cognosco.*[2]

Now, there are persons blind enough to raise the question whether this Virgin, who, as the Gospel shows us, refused to sacrifice her virginity even to become the

---

[1] Matt. i. 20. [2] Luke i. 34.

Mother of God, afterwards sacrificed it to become the Mother of men. There are souls so devoid of all spiritual sense, and even of simple common sense, as to set the Gospel in array against itself, by attempting to prove from its pages that, after having consented to become the sanctuary of the Divinity or the living Ark of the new covenant, only on the condition of preserving her virginity, Mary afterwards renounced that condition, and so delivered the holy Ark into the hands of the profane.

Alas, this blindness, this want of spiritual sense, and even of simple Christian common sense, is one of the distinctive characteristics of heresy. Heresy has always borne this token of its father, who is described in Holy Scripture as the father of lies;[1] it has always borne on its forehead this mark of the declared enemy of her who from the beginning he knew was destined to overcome him: *Inimicitias ponam inter te et mulierem.*[2]

Heresy, the offspring of Mary's enemy, has faithfully followed its father's method in its conflict with the truth. We find this method laid down in S. Matthew iv. There we see the fallen Angel, still ignorant of the Divinity of Christ, or only suspecting that which he wished to ascertain, endeavouring to deceive the second Adam as he had deceived the first. He came to tempt Him in the desert. But by what means did he endeavour to overcome Him? By basing his falsehoods on skilful perversions of Scripture, knowing well that error will not pass current in the world except under the disguise of some shreds of the truth. *Scriptum est* ("It is written"), says Satan to the Son of Man.

Heresy has always done the same. It has concealed the completeness and the divine harmony of revealed truth; it has turned a deaf ear to the unanimous tradition of the Church, which gives us its sense and shows us its unity; it has garbled Scripture by separating from each other the texts which mutually explain and

[1] John viii. 44. [2] Gen. iii. 15.

complete each other; and has forced that sacred Word, thus torn piecemeal, to contradict itself.

Thus it has seized upon texts which, taken by themselves and cunningly managed, seem to lend a colour to its infamous attacks against the perpetual virginity of the Mother of God, but which, when combined, triumphantly defend it.

Thus in S. Matthew xii. 46, we read not only of the Mother of Jesus, but of His brethren: *Ecce Mater ejus et fratres stabant foris quærentes loqui ei* ("Behold His Mother and His brethren stood without desiring to speak with Him"); and in ch. xiii. 55, the brethren of Jesus are mentioned by name: "His brethren James, and Joseph, and Simon, and Jude." Thus, again, S. Mark (vi. 2, 3) relates, that the Jews, having been struck with the wonderful wisdom of our Lord, and the superhuman power which He manifested by His miracles, said one to another: "How came this Man by all these things? and what wisdom is this that is given to Him, and such mighty works as are wrought by His hands? Is not this the carpenter, the Son of Mary, the brother of James, and Joseph, and Jude, and Simon?" You see, cry the Protestants, Jesus had brethren, and consequently Mary did not remain a virgin!

But were James the Less and Joseph, who, with Jude and Simon, are here called the brothers of the Lord, the sons of Mary the Mother of Jesus, or of another Mary, the kinswoman of the Blessed Virgin?

Let us open the Gospels: S. John[1] thus describes the awful scene on Calvary: *Stabant autem juxta crucem, Jesu Mater ejus, et soror Matris ejus Maria Cleophæ, et Maria Magdalene* ("Now there stood by the cross of Jesus, His Mother, and His Mother's sister, Mary of Cleophas, and Mary Magdalen"). Now, was this Mary Cleophas (the sister or kinswoman of the Mother of Jesus) the mother of James the Less and of Joseph, who, together with Simon and Jude, are called

[1] xix. 25.

the brethren of the Lord? Yes, replies the Evangelist S. Mark, as he describes in his 15th chapter and 40th verse the circumstances of the crucifixion: *Erant autem et mulieres de longe adspicientes: inter quas erat Maria Magdalene, et Maria Jacobi minoris et Joseph mater* ("And there were also women looking on afar off, among whom was Mary Magdalen, and Mary, the mother of James the Less and of Joseph"). Here again we see Mary Magdalen and another Mary, the mother of James the Less and of Joseph, gazing from afar off upon the cross before they draw near to it, to receive, together with the Virgin Mother, the last sigh and the last words of the Man-God. S. Matthew says the same thing in his 27th chapter and 56th verse: *Inter quas erat Maria Magdalene, et Maria Jacobi et Joseph mater* ("Among whom was Mary Magdalen, and Mary the mother of James and Joseph").

Why, then, are they called the brethren of the Lord?

Because, as S. John has told us, they were the sons of Mary, the sister and kinswoman of the Blessed Virgin, and because it was the known custom of the Hebrews to give the name of brother or sister to all the members of a family. Thus, to quote only two examples among many of this Hebrew custom, Holy Scripture calls Lot the nephew of Abraham his brother (Gen. xiii. 8; xii. 5), and gives the name of brother of Jacob to Laban his uncle (Gen. xxix. 15; xxviii. 2). James the Less and Joseph, together with Simon and Jude, are therefore called the brethren of the Lord, because they were the sons of Mary, the daughter of Cleophas and the wife of Alphæus, as we learn from St. Matthew in his 10th chapter and 3d verse, where he calls St. James the Less the son of Alphæus.[1]

---

[1] Some have supposed that Cleophas and Alphæus are two different translations of the same name in the original text, or two different ways of writing it. We have elsewhere followed this opinion; but, after mature examination, we are convinced,

Heresy has therefore ignored the customs of the Hebrews and the express words of Holy Scripture in order to rob Mary of the glory of her virginity, and thus to profane the living Ark of the new covenant.

No less vainly has it endeavoured to support its sacrilegious attempt by another text of S. Matthew: "And he knew her not till she brought forth her first-born Son, and he called His name Jesus" (Matt. i. 25). Heretics have attempted to draw from these words a twofold proof that, after the birth of the Man-God, Mary ceased to live in a state of virginity.

They adduce as their first proof the former part of the text, " He knew her not until she had brought forth ;" therefore, they conclude, he knew her after she had brought forth—as if these words "until" always indicated a change; whereas they are often employed

with Maldonatus, that Mary Cleophas was the daughter of Cleophas, and the wife of Alphæus. According to the wonderful revelations of Sœur Catharine Emmerich, by which the illustrious Görres was so deeply impressed, Mary Cleophas, the wife of Alphæus, and the mother of S. James the Less, called, like Joseph, Simon, and Jude, the brother of the Lord, was the daughter of Cleophas and of Mary of Heli, the sister of the Blessed Virgin. But it is unnecessary here to discuss this point, which has nothing to do with the principal question. This is clearly determined by the Gospel, in which we see that the brethren and sisters of the Lord were not the children of His Mother, but of another Mary, her kinswoman, and that they were called His brothers and sisters according to the Hebrew custom of giving those names to all the members of the family.

As we had already established the same thing in one of the dissertations of the Appendix to *Le Christ et les Antechrists*, a Protestant literary review at Geneva has thought fit to observe, that we have proved nothing, because we have not quoted the Greek text of the Gospels! The editors of this review would oblige us if they could show in the Greek text any expressions stronger than those of brothers and sisters, literally translated in the Vulgate, and consequently explain what they mean to say. We are certain that they know nothing of the matter. Being overcome by the evidence which results from the combination of the texts, they have had recourse to an evasion of equal pedantry and absurdity.

when no change is implied. As, for example, it is said of Michol, the daughter of Saul, that "she had no child till the day of her death" (2 Kings vi. 23). Are we to conclude from this that she had a child after her death? Again, the royal Prophet says in the 109th Psalm, " The Lord said unto my Lord, Sit thou on My right hand until I make Thy enemies Thy footstool." Are we to conclude from these words that after this victory Christ no longer reigns at the right hand of His Father?

In the same sense it is said of the raven which Noah sent out from the ark, that it did not return till the waters were dried up upon the earth (Gen. viii. 7). Does this mean that it did return after the drying up of the waters of the deluge?

By these words—" He knew her not till she had brought forth"—the Gospel affirms nothing to the contrary of what it had already told us of Mary's irrevocable purpose to remain always a virgin; but it confirms what it had said by revealing the birth of Jesus Christ of a Virgin Mother, and by repeating only what it had said before, that Mary had conceived the Saviour by the power of the Holy Ghost alone: *Antequam convenirent inventa est in utero habens de Spiritu Sancto* (Matt. i. 18). *Quod autem dicitur: Antequam convenirent* (says S. Jerome), *non sequitur ut postea convenirint; sed Scriptura quod factum non sit ostendit* (cap. Matt. i.) ("From what is here said, before they came together she was found with child of the Holy Ghost, it follows not that they afterwards came together, for Scripture shows that it was not so").

Equally vain is the attempt of heresy to seek its second proof in the latter words of the text, where Jesus Christ is called the First-born; for Holy Scripture often gives the name of first-born to an only son. Thus, for example, Machir, the only son of Manasses, is called his first-born (Jos. xvii. 1). God commands the offering of the first-born, though he were the only child, and Himself gives the name of His first-born to the nation which He so often calls His one chosen and peculiar people.

Jesus Christ, nevertheless, is the First-born of many brethren; but what manner of brethren are they? S. Paul teaches us, when he says of all the elect: *Ut sit ipse primogenitus in multis fratribus* (Rom. viii. 29). Mary is therefore the Mother of a multitude of children —that is, of all the children of God—who are born, not of blood, nor of the will of the flesh, nor of the will of man, but of God (John i. 13). Heresy must surely acknowledge itself to be overcome by this evidence, and be forced to desist from the vain attempt to make Scripture contradict itself by asserting—first, that Mary refused to sacrifice her virginity to become the Mother of God; and next, that she did sacrifice it to become the Mother of man.

No, those who thus interpret the Gospel have never understood its meaning. They do what they will with the letter, for the letter does not cry out when it is tortured; but the Spirit which dictated it, and which alone giveth life,[1] the Spirit promised by Jesus Christ to the universal and perpetual Apostolate, to the Church which is to teach "all days, even to the consummation of the world;"[2] the Spirit ever living in that teaching which He marks with His own token of unity, victorious over space and time;—the Spirit of truth Himself teaches us by the tradition of all ages that nothing ever touched the virginal integrity of Mary, as nothing ever diminished the purity of her spotless soul; that the curse which fell upon the first Eve reached not to the second; and that Mary brought forth without sorrow. He teaches us that the Second Adam, the Incarnate Word, who even during His mortal life assumed when He willed (as He showed upon Mount Tabor) the properties of a glorified body, awaited not His resurrection to enter the cenacle when the doors were closed, or to leave His tomb without breaking the sealed stone; but at His Incarnation in

---

[1] 2 Cor. iii. 6.   [2] Matt. xxviii. 20.

the womb of His Mother, and at His birth from that virginal womb, He went in and out of His temple, as He entered the cenacle and issued from the sepulchre, purer than the ray of light which leaves intact the crystal which it penetrates, and, far from sullying it, makes it shine with more refulgent light: *Qui natus de Virgine, Matris integritatem non minuit sed sacravit*[1] ("He who was born of the Virgin did not diminish the integrity of His Mother, but consecrated it").

In the presence of this harmony of the truth of Holy Scripture, and of the tradition ever living in the faith of the Church, how narrow, poor, and inconsequent does heresy appear! Would that it were nothing worse! But we have just seen that it is both sinful and delusive. Let us not confuse with it all those whom it has deceived. There are those among them who have never heard any other voice, and who are thus innocently in error. It is our part, then, to enlighten instead of judging and condemning them.

I was one day with a friend, who was passionately fond of flowers, in a room which commanded a view of his magnificent gardens, when we saw a poor man come in who began to walk backwards and forwards over the beds, trampling the choicest flowers under his feet. The owner went out in a tumult of indignation to punish the culprit, when he saw that he was blind. He was immediately touched with compassion, took him gently by the hand, and led him back into the path which he had lost. Let us do the same with regard to those blind souls who trample under foot the holiest, sweetest, and most sublime truths. Let us do still more, for their blindness is not incurable; let us show them the truth of that which they have been made to misunderstand, the greatness of that which they have been made to despise, and the divinity of that which they have been made to blaspheme.

[1] *Missa de Nat. B.M.V.*

Prayer.

Yes, my Saviour and my God, I will neglect no means to bring back Thy poor blinded children to the knowledge, love, and veneration of their Mother.

And thou, Mary, my sweet Mother, wilt obtain for me from God grace to speak of thee in a manner not wholly unworthy of thee.

I offer thee this good desire and resolution, and hope that they will obtain for me, who know thee too imperfectly and love thee but too coldly, the light which revealed to the Saints how much thou deservest to be loved, and the fire which inflamed them with the love of thee, a blessed light and a blessed fire which ascend continually unto the Heart whence they came forth, the Sacred Heart of Jesus; Who liveth and reigneth eternally with His Father in the unity of the Holy Ghost. Amen.

CHAPTER X.

THE MERIT OF MARY.

WE have now seen the matchless dignity of Mary, the equally unexampled grace which corresponded with that dignity, and the plenitude of grace which filled every moment of the life of the Mother of God; but we have hardly considered the fidelity of that life itself, which was far more meritorious than all the lives of the most faithful of Patriarchs and Prophets, Apostles and Martyrs, Doctors, Confessors, religious, hermits, and virgins,—of all Saints, in short, of all vocations and of all ages.

The merit of a life, as of a work, is its value before God in relation to the reward which God gives it in time by the increase of grace, and in eternity by the life of glory. But what is the measure of the merit of any work, interior or exterior, or of a life which results from the whole chain of actions offered to God from birth to death? Its merit is measured chiefly by the greatness of its charity. The degree of glory which awaits any man in heaven corresponds with the degree of love to God and his neighbour to which he has attained on earth. Why? Because love is the most excellent of gifts, the only one which implies the gift of *self*. God gives Himself only to the soul which has given itself to Him, or rather, which has given itself *back* to Him who created it; and He gives Himself in proportion to the fidelity of the soul in corresponding to the grace which has called forth that gift of itself. Nevertheless, though the degree of glory depends chiefly on the degree of love, it is not less true that the merit corresponds also to the proper value of the acts of virtue produced by charity, to the quality of the good works which spring from it, their number, and their difficulty. The least work performed with a great love of God is certainly of greater value before Him than the greatest performed with a lower degree of charity; but supposing the intensity of the love to be the same in both, martyrdom will certainly be more gloriously rewarded than a simple alms, a sacrifice repeated twenty times more than one offered once, and that which wrings forth tears of heroic suffering more than that which excites tears of joy.

All this is true; and yet it is also true that, when God finds in any heart a *true* will a thousand times renewed, by the help of His grace, to do and to suffer great things for Him, that will (if the opportunity of realising it has alone been wanting) will be accounted for as many works as it desired to perform. It is needless to say that, in order thus to merit divine and eternal rewards, the soul must necessarily be in a state of grace, and that it must do or suffer by an impulse of grace all that it does and suffers through love and in order to please God.

Now, from what we have said of the grace of Mary —a grace immeasurably superior to those which have been granted to all other creatures—we may doubtless at once conclude that the flame of love which arose from her heart was the purest and most intense which ever ascended to God either from earth or heaven. But shall we not find in the life of the Mother of God proofs of her fidelity to that grace above all graces, and thus of her love being also above all other loves?

They are there assuredly, many and manifold; but as we shall speak of them hereafter in treating of the life of our Mother, we will dwell here only on the chief of these proofs. We have seen that if merit is measured principally by love, it is because love is the first and most excellent of gifts—the only one which implies the gift of self on the part of him who loves. Is it not because love implies the gift of self that the love of God to us always infinitely surpasses our love to Him? When we give ourselves to Him by love, we give Him only a human heart; when He gives Himself to us by love, He gives us the Heart of God. Now, Mary is the only creature to whom it has been granted not only to give herself to God, but to give to God the gift of God Himself in the Person of the Incarnate Word. What a heart must that have been which was capable and worthy of offering such a gift to God!

Above all, what a heart must that have been which was able to offer It to God as He willed that It should be offered!

The Gospel tells us, by the mouth of the holy old man Simeon, when Mary offered in the Temple the Lamb of God who came to bear the sins of the world, " A sword shall pierce thine own soul."[1] But it reveals it more divinely still when it shows us Mary with that sword piercing the very depths of her soul: *Stabat juxta crucem Jesu Mater ejus.*[2] We suffer in proportion to our love at the sight of the sufferings of those we love. What, then, must have been her sufferings who beheld in the object of her love her Son and her God expiating

[1] Luke ii. 35.   [2] S. John xix. 25.

the sins of the whole human race! What must have been her sufferings, who, in union with the Divine Victim, offered Him to God with her whole heart, both for love of Him and for love of us?

There was never, therefore, love to be compared to the love of Mary, because no other love ever offered to God a gift like Mary's.

Again, no other love was ever to be compared with hers, because there was never heroism equal to that by which she triumphed over the greatest difficulties which love had ever to overcome. In their most painful sacrifices the Saints had always the consolation of suffering for God; but Mary had the unspeakable anguish of suffering with God made Man, and of sharing, as she alone has ever shared, the voluntary dereliction of the Man-God, the absolute privation of all consolation which He was pleased to endure in that human Heart which He assumed for us. Yes, Mary consented to that terrible dereliction, and thus bore, together with her Divine Son, as no other creature ever bore, the immense weight of redemption; having no support in that abyss of misery but the will of that Divine Son, which decreed that she should bring forth mankind in sorrow at the foot of the cross.

Lastly, to understand what must have been Mary's love, we must think not only of the incomparable gift which was offered, and of the heroism with which it was offered, but also of the continuity of that offering—from the Incarnation even to Calvary.

If every one of our acts of fidelity to grace merits an augmentation of grace, what must have been the spiritual wealth of Mary, upon whom so many graces had been lavished from her conception and her birth until the day of the Annunciation? Thus the Word of God judged her, then, to be fitly prepared to become His living tabernacle. We may judge, therefore, of the increase of grace and love in that soul, blessed above all other souls, by the continuity of the offering which she then made of the Lamb of God, whom she knew to be destined to the cross.

Let us judge also whether there was ever love but hers in heaven or earth, save only the substantial and personal love of God Himself, which could give God to God; if ever there was heart but hers, save only the Heart of her Son, which made to God a sacrifice so holy, so pure; if ever there was life but hers, save only the life of Jesus, which was one long oblation of such a sacrifice: *Quædam prolixitas crucis.* If such there has been, we may compare the merit of Saints or Angels with the merit of the Mother of God.

Prayer.

Mother of God! that name says every thing to a heart which understands and loves. It expresses, Blessed Mary, what belongs to thee alone, and that none has ever loved God as thou lovest Him. But I rejoice to be able to prove it to those who ask for proofs, of which thy children have no need. I rejoice to be able to say to all: Behold, if Mary was full of grace, she was full also of fidelity; and if her gifts were greater than any other creature ever received, far greater also were her trials. She had not indeed to sustain a degrading conflict with passion; but if she had not to overcome concupiscence, she had to overcome sorrow—sorrow long, terrible, and unequalled, to maintain her fidelity to the will of God.

Thy life, my Mother, was in all things the life of the spotless Lamb.

Thou wast truly the mirror of justice (*speculum justitiæ*); for there was not a suffering in the Life, Passion, and Death of the great Mediator of justice which found not an answering pang in thy soul. O purest, most humble, most loving, most afflicted of creatures, what a joy it is to know that, of all creatures, thou art also the most beloved, the most blessed, and the most glorified by God! I love thee as God would have thee to be loved, and as He loves thee Himself, with a like love of preference; and because of that love, I hope one day to share His love with thee, my Mother, without a fear ever to lose it. Pray for me, then, that henceforth I may never cease to love and suffer for thee, that so I may live eternally with thee in the bosom of the Father and the Son and the Holy Ghost. Amen.

CHAPTER XI.

THE GLORY OF MARY.

Mary glorified in body and soul.

WHEN a child remembers what he has cost his mother, when he thinks at the price of what suffering she has given him life, it is sweet to him to know that she has received consolation in proportion to her sorrow, and joy in proportion to her cross. *Secundum multitudinem dolorum meorum in corde meo, consolationes tuæ lætificaverunt animam meam*[1] ("According to the multitude of my sorrows in my heart, thy comforts have given joy to my heart"). The children of Mary rejoice to know with the certainty of faith that the happiness and the glory of their Mother are proportioned to the immeasurable superiority of her graces, her trials, her fidelity, her love when on earth, to all the graces, all the trials, and all the virtues of all Angels and of all Saints.

It was given to him who, after Jesus Christ, was pre-eminently the son of Mary, to S. John the virgin Apostle, the prophet of the New Testament, the eagle of the Evangelists, whose glance penetrated the depths of heaven, there to contemplate the Word eternally begotten in the Bosom of the Father, there to behold also the Mother of the Incarnate Word divinely glorified. Let us hear what he tells us in human language, let us behold the image which he gives us of it, the shadow of the glorious truth: *Signum magnum apparuit in cælo:*

[1] Psalm xciii. 19.

Mulier amicta sole, et luna sub pedibus ejus, et in capite ejus corona stellarum duodecim: et in utero habens, clamabat parturiens, et cruciabatur ut pariat[1] ("And there appeared a great wonder in heaven, a Woman clothed with the Sun, and the moon under her feet, and on her head a crown of twelve stars; and she being with child cried, travailing in birth, and was in pain to be delivered").

S. John does not separate the suffering from the glory, the merit from the recompense—the inconceivable sufferings of Mary in the spiritual childbirth of regenerated humanity from the inconceivable joy which was their reward. In the light of God he sees, like God, both at once. But why is Mary shown to him clothed with the Sun, with the moon under her feet, and crowned with stars? The moon represents the Church, because she receives her light from Jesus Christ, the Sun of Justice; and God shows to S. John, that Mary is the triumphant, as she was once the suffering, Queen of the Church. The stars, as we know from S. Paul, represent the elect, the Saints; and Mary is crowned with them because they are truly her crown, the fruit of her sorrowful maternity. The Sun represents Jesus Christ Himself, according to the well-known language of Scripture, and Mary is clothed therewith because the glory of her Son has become hers: *Mulier amicta sole.*

We should be ashamed to attempt to add to these words any which must fall below them; for no one can express like S. John, who seems to blend them together, the likeness of the glory of Mary to the glory of Jesus.

But is Mary, like her Son, already glorified in body and in soul? Or is her soul only glorified in heaven, and her body still awaiting in the tomb the resurrection of the dead?

Death has no part in the Mother of Life. This is the belief of the universal Church, and the Greek Church has not lost it in its fall into schism.

[1] Apoc. xii. 1.

The Council of Jerusalem in 1672 thus confirms the ancient faith of the East against the innovators of the sixteenth century: *Ipsa est procul dubio Virgo Sanctissima, quæ magnum in terra signum cum extiterit, eo quod Deum in carne genuit, et post partum integerrima permansit, recte etiam signum dicitur esse in cœlo, eo quod ipsa cum corpore assumpta est in cœlum. Et quamvis conclusum in sepulcro fuerit immaculatum corporis tabernaculum, in cœlum tamen, uti Christus fuerat assumptus, tertio et ipsa die in cœlum migravit.* Assuredly, since the Word became Flesh to suffer for us, since God became Man to die for us, it was fitting that she from whom He took Flesh should die, and that willingly, like Him. In her, and by her, Jesus was the Son of Adam, the Son of Man, and although He in no way participated in the guilt of mankind, He came upon earth expressly to expiate that guilt: *Deus Filium mittens in similitudinem carnis peccati*[1] ("God sending His own Son in the likeness of sinful flesh"), and that "He became like to us in all things, sin only excepted." *Non enim habemus pontificem, qui non possit compati infirmitatibus nostris; tentatum autem per omnia pro similitudine absque peccato*[2] ("For we have not a High-Priest who cannot have compassion on our infirmities; but One tempted in all things like as we are, yet without sin"). He, therefore, took for His Mother a daughter of Adam, like to us also in all things, sin only excepted, from which He preserved her, still with a view to the Incarnation, and by the grace of Redemption; for He would not that the second Eve should come into the world less highly privileged than the first, who was created in grace and original justice. It was consequently in the order of God's great purpose that Mary, like her Son, should share the punishment of sin, and yet have no share in the sin itself, and that therefore she should not be exempt from death, "the wages of sin" (*stipendia peccati mors*).[3]

But if it was according to the order of God's purpose

[1] Rom. viii. 3.   [2] Heb. iv. 15.   [3] Rom. vi. 23.

that Mary, like her Son, without sharing the guilt of sin, should share its punishment,—even death; it was also in the order of that Divine purpose that the Son of Mary, having by His death triumphed over death, and having willed that death should have no dominion over His body, willed also that the body of His Mother should be exempt from its power, and forbade it to detain her in the prison of the grave. This is the thought of S. Gregory the Great in that prayer for the Feast of the Assumption which appears in his Sacramentary, and which is partly taken from that of S. Gelasius: *Veneranda nobis, Domine, hujus diei festivitas opem conferat salutarem, in qua Sancta Dei Genitrix mortem subiit temporalem, nec tamen mortis nexibus deprimi potuit, quæ Filium tuum ae se genuit incarnatum.* Having been preserved from the stain of original sin, it was yet possible and fitting that Mary should die with Jesus, but it was neither possible nor fitting that death should retain the mastery over her, because her flesh is the flesh of Jesus: *Caro Christi, caro Mariæ est.*[1]

These are the words of the Divine sentence which gave death the victory over man: *Pulvis es, et in pulverem reverteris*[2] ("Dust thou art, and to dust shalt thou return"). It is in the grave that death finishes its victim. Death is but a sleep (*dormitio*), when it is stayed in its course; when it fails to attain its end—dissolution and corruption; when it is compelled to respect the tabernacle of the soul, until that soul returns to it. Therefore it is that our Lord said of Lazarus, although he was really dead, "Lazarus sleepeth, but I go to awake him out of sleep" (*Lazarus amicus noster dormit, sed vado ut a somno excitem eum*).[3]

Far less,[4] then, did He suffer Mary thus to die or sleep; for He Whose flesh could not be subject to corrup-

---

[1] S. Aug., *Lib. de Ass.*, ch. v.   [2] Gen. iii. 19.
[3] John xi. 11.
[4] The resurrection of Lazarus was not final, neither was his body respected by death, as was that of Mary.

tion—*Non dabis Sanctum tuum videre corruptionem*[1]— never suffered her from whom He took flesh to be subject to its power.

Never can the faithful Christian doubt that Mary, the living Ark in which Jesus dwelt, and of whom He vouchsafed to be born, remained ever incorruptible. When we read of the ark of the covenant, which imperfectly prefigured her, those words which are prophetical by the very type which they express: *Surge, Domine, in requiem tuam, tu et arca sanctificationis tuæ*[2] ("Arise, O Lord, into Thy resting-place, Thou and the ark which Thou hast sanctified"), we see and understand that, having exalted His body and soul to heaven, our Lord assuredly left not in the tomb the living Ark in which they had dwelt.

Far, then, from feeling the slightest difficulty in receiving the belief of the Church on this point, we should feel an invincible repugnance to admit any other, which would oblige us to lose sight of the divine harmony of the truth of the Assumption with the dogmas of revealed truth. Though it be not proposed to our acceptance as a dogma of faith, properly so called, yet the belief of the Church on this subject is in no way uncertain, and if the man who rejects it cannot be precisely held to be a heretic on that account, he must be at least considered rash, and to be suspected of heresy, in supposing that the Church could propose an error to the belief of Christendom. According to the words of Benedict XIV., *Card. Gottus*, part ii., tom. 4, "De Verit. Relig. Christ," c. 41, cap. 2, n. 40: "*Temerariam esse pronuntiat hanc propositionem, B. Virginem corpore et anima non esse in cœlum assumptam, et qui eam propugnaret, vehementer de hæresi eum fore suspectum, non quod Catholicæ fidei adversaretus, sed quod præsumi posset, falso eum judicare B. Virginis venerationem per errorem ab universali Ecclesia proponi.*"[3]

[1] Psalm xv. 10.   [2] Psalm cxxxi.
[3] Bened. XIV., *De Festis B. Mariæ Virginis*, ch. viii., "De Festo Assumptionis."

The Feast of the Assumption is the solemn profession of the belief of the Church, and the same learned Pontiff brings forward unanswerable testimonies and produces authentic monuments to show that it was celebrated by both East and West before the sixth century.[1] This fact alone would suffice to show that the belief which it embodies is, as S. John Damascene asserts, of apostolic tradition.

We are not, however, to expect to find that all the festivals of the Church date from her beginning. The Church is not a structure without life or power of development. As she has spread externally from nation to nation, she has grown also in her interior life; and the acts of her piety have grown also in number and in brightness. And again, although the Church carefully abstains from making any addition whatsoever to the deposit of faith which has been intrusted to her care, the Spirit Who was promised to her, and Who directs her "all days, even to the consummation of the world," helps her to fix the sense of truths on which questions may be raised by good men, or misinterpretations attempted by evil men, either by defining them as dogmas of faith, or by simply proposing them to our belief by her acts, her prayers, or her solemnities. Ignorance, doubt, and denial of truth have thus often given occasion for definitions of faith, the most solemn acts in which the Church expresses her belief. The Spirit of God thus develops in her both the understanding of dogma by the presence of error, and piety by the presence of impiety. *Etenim Ecclesia*, says Canisius,[2] *successu temporis auget sapientiam, ducequo Spiritu Sancto, a quo semper regitur et eruditur, e posterioribus Conciliis, majoreque consensu Doctorum illustriorum, veritatis lumen accipit et ostendit.* S. Vincent of Lerins gave utterance to the same truth, in those celebrated words on progress in the Church,

[1] Bened. XIV., *De Festis B. Mariæ Virginis*, ch. viii., "De Festo Assumptionis."
[2] Quoted by Benedict XIV., as above.

which have lately been called to the memory of the Catholic world by the Sovereign Pontiff Pius IX.:

"Progress exists there, and very great progress," says Pius IX., in his Brief of the 17th of March 1856, addressed to the Bishops of the Empire of Austria; "but it is the true progress of the faith, and not any change in the faith. It is necessary that in the intelligence, the science, and the wisdom of all, as of each one in particular, of the ages and centuries of the whole Church, as of individuals, there should be growth and progress, very great growth and progress; that what was at first more obscurely believed, should be afterwards more clearly understood; that posterity should be enabled to understand what antiquity venerated without understanding; in order that the precious stones of divine doctrine should be carefully wrought, exactly arranged, skilfully adorned, and thus become richer in grace, splendour, and beauty, but always in the same unity,—*i.e.* in the same doctrine, in the same sense, in the same substance; so that although new terms be used, it is not to express new things."[1]

The Church, then, changes not in her faith or in her love, but in the expression she gives to both she is inexhaustible; and the monuments of her piety, such as are her festivals, multiply like the monuments of her wisdom. Ever living and ever young, because immortal, she may continually grow in her intelligence of dogma even unto the end of the world. In her inexhaustible fertility she may continually bring forth new works of piety and charity, according to the necessities of the time, by the power of that Spirit Who was promised her for all times.

Thus, as we have already shown, though she has always known and believed Mary to be full of grace, blessed among all women, accounted blessed by all generations, she has, nevertheless, waited until these latter

[1] Brief of 17th March 1856 to the Bishops of the Austrian Empire.

days to define with authority the full sense of those divine words, by the proclamation of the dogma of the Immaculate Conception, which had always been held more or less explicitly by Christians in all ages.

The ancient Festival of the Assumption rests, in fact, on this belief; for if death was powerless to hold Mary under its dominion, it was because, after having been undergone by Mary, as by Jesus, it was to be finally overcome by the Mother as by the Son; it being impossible that the penalty of sin should have the mastery over her over whom sin itself never had power. The father of sin and of death, the murderer of the human race, might, indeed, lie in wait for the heel of the Woman whose coming he dreaded; but it was only to be crushed by the foot of the second Eve, in the might of her Son, the Conqueror of sin and death.

Prayer.

Thy soul was ever stainless, O my Mother, and thy most chaste body, the tabernacle of that soul, never saw corruption. When the soul was separated from the body, which was no longer able to endure its consuming flame of love, it was only quickly to resume it, and to communicate to it life, glory, and immortality. From the height of heaven, where thou reignest with thy Son, cast thy merciful eyes upon the poor child whom Jesus has given to thee, and whom thou lovest spite of his unworthiness. My soul also, O my Mother, must soon be separated from my body; but this soul, as thou knowest, has been very guilty, very ungrateful, very unfaithful to Jesus and to thee; and this body, before the great day of its awakening at the call of its risen Saviour, must be buried in corruption and turn into dust. Let it return to dust, since it has served us an instrument of sin; and let not my soul resume it till it shall have passed through the crucible of God's justice. But let my soul, O my Mother, be purified here, that it may be found worthy of the glory which it is to share with my body. Obtain for it the sorrow which alone purifies, the sorrow of love, indignant with itself at its own infidelities. I shall never have that true sorrow, O my true Mother, unless Jesus vouchsafes to grant to me once more the light, the grace, and the life which I have lost,—light to reveal to me the beauty, the love, the majesty of Him Whom I have offended; grace to touch and penetrate me; life which He will communicate to me by uniting me to Himself. I acknowledge with all my heart that I have rendered myself undeserving of all these gifts; but it is thy Mother's wont to obtain for us what we do not deserve: *Stella maris, succurre cadenti surgere qui curat populo!* Star of the wayfarer lost in the ways of sin, help me to arise from the gulf and to return to God! I feel a full confidence that my cry of distress will not be in vain; yes, a full confidence, for it would be the first sigh which ever failed to touch Thy Heart. *Memorare, O piissima!* Remember Thy love, remember my misery, that I may bless Thee for ever for thy motherly care.

CHAPTER XII.

MARY THE UNIVERSAL MEDIATRIX.

Unus enim Deus, unus et mediator Dei et hominum, homo Christus Jesus: qui dedit redemptionem semetipsum pro omnibus[1] ("For there is one God, and one Mediator of God and men, the Man Jesus Christ: who gave Himself a redemption for all"). As there is but one God, there is but one Mediator between God and men, the Man Christ Jesus; who gave Himself for the redemption of all men.

There is, therefore, and there can be, but one Mediator of justice or of redemption, because none but the Man Christ Jesus, the Man-God, could offer the reparation required by eternal justice for the offence offered by

[1] 1 Tim. ii. 5, 6.

human nature to the Divine Majesty. *Injuria est in injuriato, honor in honorante,* are the words of human law, and they express a great truth; for unquestionably the grievousness of an insult is weighed by the dignity of him to whom it is offered; and the value of an honour paid, and, therefore, of a reparation offered, is measured by the dignity of him who offers it. An offended God could, therefore, receive due satisfaction only from a Divine Person. But, behold! mercy triumphs over justice. God Himself becomes man in the person of His Word, and gives Himself for the redemptiom of all: *Superexaltat misericordia judicium*[1] ("And mercy exalteth itself above judgment").

Once more, then, the Word made flesh,[2] the Man Christ Jesus, God and Saviour,[3] is the only possible Mediator of *justice* between God and men. But every intercessor is evidently also a mediator. Of what nature, then, is such mediation, and by what name shall it be distinguished? What should I call your mediation, were you to intercede for me with any person in authority, in order to obtain any kind of favour for me?

When I say to you, *Pray to God for me,* and you charitably comply with my request, what kind of mediator are you for me?

When I say the same thing to the Angels, or to the souls of the Blessed, to my friends in heaven, to the friends of God Himself, what mediation do I implore of their love for my soul?

All these questions resolve themselves into one, and contain their own answer; for when we ask for prayers or intercession, we ask for the mediation of grace or prayer. It is, then, in the order of grace and of prayer, or in the mediation of intercession, that Mary, by the will of God Himself, is the universal Mediatrix of the human race.

But in what sense is she this universal Mediatrix? Is it in such a sense, that of all the graces of redemp-

[1] James ii. 13.   [2] John i. 14.   [3] 1 Tim. ii. 3.

tion, of all the graces which Jesus Christ alone has merited for men, He will grant none to their prayers unless they have had express recourse on each several occasion to the intercession of Mary? No; but in this sense, that no grace is ever granted to them for which Mary has not interceded in their behalf. "It is, in one word," says S. Alphonsus, "that God has been pleased that the charity of the Mother of the Redeemer should intercede for all those whom her Son has redeemed with the price of His Blood,—that Blood in which alone is salvation, resurrection, and life; and it is in the spirit of this doctrine," he continues, "that I have drawn up all the propositions of this book."[1] Mary is, then, far more a Mother to us than we are children to her; she thinks more of us than we think of her, and her mercy is far more ready to succour us than our misery to ask for aid. It is, nevertheless, true, as we shall see, that the oftener we have recourse in our prayers to the intercession of Mary, the more faithful shall we be to the divine order of the dispensation of grace, and the more sensibly shall we grow in the confidence which obtains it. The holy Fathers and other ascetical writers touchingly express this truth of the universal mediation of Mary, when they teach that all the graces which descend from heaven to earth by the merits of Jesus, pass through the hands of His Mother (*Hæc est voluntas Ejus qui totus nos voluit habere per Mariam*).

It is not necessary to remark that there is a figurative sense in these words. As it is by the hands that we draw from a treasure or a fountain, and as it is by prayer that we draw from the Heart of God, the treasury of all mercy, the inexhaustible fountain of all grace, the holy Fathers say that all graces pass through the hands of Mary, because it is her compassionate prayers which obtain them for us. Again, uplifted hands are in themselves the symbol of prayer, and for this reason it is said that the maternal hands of Mary distribute all graces to

[1] *Glories of Mary*: Advice to the Reader.

her children, because our Divine Lord, being pleased to grant them all to the prayer of His Mother, has thereby rendered her the dispenser of all the fruits of Redemption.

But is the mediation of Mary truly universal? Is it true that not one of all the graces which our Lord has purchased for us has been granted to us without the intervention of the Heart of Mary? Is not this a pious exaggeration of filial love?

No; it is no pious exaggeration, it has been the belief of the greatest men in all ages of the Church, the unquestionable feeling of the Church herself, and consequently a certain truth.

It is at the same time a magnificent truth, a truth in deepest harmony with the whole order of Redemption.

Which shall we undertake to demonstrate first,—its certainty, or its sublime beauty?

We think it best to excite a desire for its certainty by first bringing out its exceeding beauty, by showing its harmony and agreement with the whole great work of Redemption.

I. God has constituted all His works in a certain order or hierarchy. In the natural world, the first cause acts through second causes, which are themselves subordinate to one another. As soon as intelligent creatures appear on the great theatre of creation, we see them in their turn constituted in an order or hierarchy, superiors being charged with the support of inferiors both in domestic and public society. It is the same with the higher life, the life of grace. Here also God acts by second causes: *Ordo est divinitus institutus in rebus secundum Dionysium,* says S. Thomas, *ut per media ultima reducantur in Deum.*[1] God, then, enlightens, helps, and directs inferiors by means of superiors in the spiritual society, that divine society whose relations extend beyond the reach of time, and whose members, when they have won their crown of victory, intercede for their brethren who are still in the place of conflict or expiation.

[1] In 4 Sent., d. 15, q. 4, a. 1.

As in the kingdom of nature there is, therefore, an order or hierarchy, so also in the kingdom of grace. But the order of grace is no other than the order of the Divine action, the Divine assistance superadded to the gifts of nature; and it is by virtue of a Divine order, Divine also in its wisdom, that grace and prayer are correlative, that the one answers to the other, and that one hierarchy of grace corresponds with another hierarchy of prayer: *Constituit Deus ut inferiores ad salutem perveniant implorato superiorum subsidio.*[1]

Hoc divinæ legis ordo requirit, ut nos in Deum per Sanctos medios reducamur: et quia reditus noster in Deum respondere debet processui bonitatum ipsius ad nos, sicut mediantibus sanctorum suffragiis Dei beneficia in nos deveniunt, ita oportet nos in Deum reduci ut iterato beneficia ejus sumamus mediantibus Sanctis.[2] Now, who stands at the summit of the hierarchy of prayer?

Semper vivens ad interpellandum pro nobis[3] (Jesus Christ, " always living to make intercession for us"); the Sacred Humanity of the Incarnate Word. But in Jesus Christ suppliant human nature is not alone. "God also is in Christ, reconciling the world" (*Deus erat in Christo mundum reconcilians tibi*).[4] Who, then, is the purely suppliant creature, who stands alone next to Him at the summit of this hierarchy of prayer?

We have already seen and recognised Mary as the last, the highest link of the chain of creation, which ascends to God by Jesus Christ.[5] She is alone on that sublime summit. Above her, God alone, Incarnate in His Word; beneath her, all that is not God. Alone in her rank as the highest of all creatures in dignity, she is also alone as the highest in merit and in grace.[6] Is it, then, any matter of astonishment that, in conformity with the hierarchical order universally established by

---

[1] Contin. Tournel., *De Relig.*, p. 2, c. 2, a. 5, q. 1.
[2] *Loc. supra cit.* [3] Heb. vii. 25. [4] 2 Cor. v. 19.
[5] See Consideration iv., *supra*.
[6] Considerations v. and x.

His wisdom, God has been pleased that the prayers of men and Angels should be offered to Him by the supreme supplication of her whom He has placed alone so near His throne that nothing can reach Him without passing by her? Is it wonderful that for the same reason nothing should descend from heaven to earth, that no gifts should be bestowed upon His creatures by the love or the Heart of God, without also passing through the heart of her who stands alone, next to Jesus Christ, between heaven and earth, between God and all that is not God? Would it not rather be astonishing were it otherwise? There is nothing, therefore, to surprise us in the universal mediation of Mary,—the wonder would be were it not universal.

II. But it is not only by virtue of the holy hierarchy of hearts and of prayer, in which God has placed Mary alone in the foremost rank of suppliant creatures,—alone between Himself and all other beings; it is not only by reason of that supreme rank, that unequalled dignity and sanctity, that Mary is the universal Mediatrix of intercession; it is also, and above all, by reason of the very nature of her dignity as Mother of God that she has been constituted Mediatrix or Coöperatrix of the Divine mercy in the effusion of all graces. Was it not the will of God that Mary should coöperate with His love in the highest gift of His mercy, that gift which was the principal of all others—the Incarnation of the Word? Open the Gospels, and you will see that God willed the coöperation of Mary in that His highest gift to the world. What does the Son of God await to become man? The consent of Mary, the free coöperation of Mary, an act of her will, a movement of her heart, which submits, accepts, and asks,—*Fiat mihi* ("Be it done unto me"). It is then of faith that, according to the order decreed by God, Mary, by that act of her will, by that *Fiat* of her heart, by that most sublime prayer, freely coöperated in giving to us the Source of every good, the Principle of every grace. But if God is thus pleased that Mary should coöperate in giving to us the universal Principle of grace, is it not in perfect accordance with the order and the wisdom of His economy of redemption that, having decreed her coöperation in the gift of the very Principle of grace, He should have decreed it also in all those other operations which are dependent upon it ?[1] Instead, then, of being astonished at this harmonious unity in the Divine decrees, we should rather have reason for amazement did we fail to recognise it in the great work of Him who orders every thing in number, weight, and measure (*in mensura, et numero, et pondere*).[2]

III. But if it be wholly worthy of the wisdom of God to have decreed that Mary should be the universal Mediatrix of intercession, the suppliant Coöperatrix in all the operations of grace, in her character of Mother of Jesus Christ, it is equally worthy of that Divine wisdom to have decreed that Mary should coöperate by her love and her prayer in the communication of all graces, in her character of the most true Spouse of the Holy Ghost.

All souls, it is true, which are in a state of grace are the spouses of the Holy Ghost; but Mary is His Spouse in a special and singular sense, inasmuch as she is His Spouse, not only by the superior grace which unites her soul more closely than others to Him, but by a special and singular title, which belongs to herself alone, and in which no other creature participates even in the lowest degree. She alone contributed by her consent to the omnipotent operation of the Holy Ghost, which alone formed within her the Sacred Humanity of the Redeemer; she alone furnished the blood of which the "power of the Most High" formed the adorable Body of Jesus, which was conceived, not by the concupiscence of the flesh, but by the obedience of the spirit (*quem non concupiscentia carnis, sed obedientia genuit mentis*).[3]

---

[1] This is the idea of S. Bonaventure and Bossuet, whose words we shall read further on.

[2] Wisd. xi. 21.   [3] S. Augustine, Serm. 128, *App. E. B.*

She became, therefore, in the Incarnation of the Word, the most true Spouse of the Spirit of God, and by the light of this truth we discover the depth of those words of S. Bernardin of Sienna: *At empore quo Virgo Mater concepit in utero Verbum Dei, quamdam, ut sic dicam, jurisdictionem obtinuit in omni Spiritus Sancti processione temporali, ita quod nulla creatura aliquam a Deo obtinuerit gratiam, nisi secundum ipsius piæ Matris dispensationem*[1] ("Since the moment of the Incarnation, in which Mary was raised to the dignity of the Spouse of the Holy Ghost, Who is the substantial Love of the Father and the Son, the supreme Giver, the essential Gift, whence all other gifts flow, she has obtained, so to speak, a certain right over the dispensation of all the gifts of God, so that no creature receives them except through the hands of that Mother of Mercy").

And why? Because the fruits of grace which flow from that Divine union, which rendered Mary the one Spouse of the Holy Ghost, and the Mother of the Word made Flesh, must hereafter depend on the love and the will of the two Spouses. Is it not fitting that the bounty of a husband should be shared by a beloved wife, whose compassionate heart has no sweeter joy than to relieve misery, especially when it is the misery of her own children? But we have seen and understood that Mary is not only the true Mother of God, but the true Mother of men also; the true second Eve; the only Mother of the new life. We have seen that God, who does nothing imperfectly, has given her a Mother's heart. Can we, then, believe that to her who has suffered so much for us all, who at the foot of the cross bore the burden of our redemption, God has refused the consolation of participating by her love, by the prayer of her heart, in the effusion of all His graces, when she has participated in all the sorrows which purchased them for us?

Shall not those words, then, which are addressed to

[1] *Pro Fest. V.M.*, s. 5, ch. viii.

God by all faithful souls, be addressed to Him by Mary: " Thy consolations, O Lord, are proportioned to the multitude of my sorrows" (*Secundum multitudinem dolorum meorum in corde meo, consolationes tuæ lætificaverunt animam meum*)?[1] We must have lost the Christian sense of these words to suppose such a thing possible. *Da amantem et sentit quod dico*, would St. Augustine exclaim. Give me a heart that loves, give me, above all, a mother's heart, and it will understand.

IV. Yes; and give me a child's heart, and it also will understand.

By predestinating Mary to be the second Eve, the true Mother of mankind in the order of the new life, God, as we have seen, has made us all children of Mary. He wills, therefore, that we should all bear to her the hearts of children full of tender, filial love. And what more likely to increase this love, what more fitting to fulfil His purpose, than to make our Mother the inseparable fellow-worker in all His merciful designs for us? Is it not a sweet thought for a child to know that he has nothing that he does not owe to the love and the prayer of his mother? God, our Father, is the sole Master of His own gifts. He alone is their source; He alone bestows them upon us. But our Mother obtains them for us, and it is through her hands that we receive them. And do not imagine that this thought can in any degree lessen the supreme love which we owe to our Divine Lord alone. No; it will but enkindle it the more; for Jesus alone, who made our hearts, made that Mother's heart for us. Before He died, He gave us the most precious gifts He had to bestow—the Holy Eucharist, and Mary, with the last drops of His Blood, when He said: "Behold thy Mother." He gave us His own Heart in the Sacrament of love, as the inexhaustible source of all blessings; and the heart of His Mother, to encourage ours to approach it with invincible confidence.

[1] Psalm xciii. 19.

Prayer.

O my Mother, how often do I need that heart to save me from losing this confidence! When I remember the chain of mercies which thou hast obtained for me, and the chain of infidelities by which I have requited them, I am tempted to fear that by my sins I have dried up the fountain of Divine grace. Thy name then revives my hope, for I know that thou art more merciful than I am miserable; more powerful to obtain pardon for me than I to draw down justice on myself; more invincible in thy love than I in my ingratitude. I take refuge, then, in thy Mother's heart; and I hope from thy compassionate prayers for still greater graces than I have yet received; and, above all, for the continuation of thy prayers, even to the last moment of my life, that I may die in the love of Him whom I have so deeply offended, and to accomplish that Divine Will which I have so long resisted. But obtain for me before my death, and even now, my Mother, a deep repentance for my sins, a true change of life, and fidelity to grace even to the end. Grant that I may rather die than fill up, it may be, the measure of my sins by some new fall, which may separate me from God. Never, I implore thee, suffer me again to lose Jesus. By the union of thy heart with His adorable Will thou hast given Him to me as a Brother in the manger; as a Victim on the cross; as my nourishment in the Holy Eucharist. Thou wilt give Him to me one day as my reward in heaven, and He will not know how to refuse thy prayer, nor even mine; for I will then say to Him with all my heart: "Look upon me, O Lord, and have pity on me, and receive Thy Mother's poor child into thy kingdom" (*Respice in me, et miserere mei, da imperium tuum puero tuo, et salvum fac filium ancillæ tuæ*).[1]

[1] Psalm lxxxv. 16.

CHAPTER XIII.

MARY THE UNIVERSAL MEDIATRIX (*continued*).

WE have seen in what sense Mary is called the Universal Mediatrix, and how perfectly the universality of her mediation with regard to all men and all graces harmonises with the whole design of the work of redemption, how worthy it is of the wisdom of God, how beautiful as a scientific theory, and how consoling to the heart of the Christian.

This consolation, however, would not be perfect if it rested upon science alone; because science here, without authority, cannot give certainty. God has not left the science of salvation at the mercy of men's disputations, as He has left the science of this world; we must therefore inquire whether the authority which He has established to lead us safely to Himself,—whether the mother which he has given to the great human family, to nourish it with the pure milk of the truths of salvation,—authorises, embraces, and professes this belief in the universal mediation of Mary.

Now, she assuredly does authorise, embrace, and profess it.

I. She authorises it; for the most celebrated theologians of all ages have held it and taught it, which they could not have done with impunity had it been tainted with error. For the Church is never silent when error speaks to her children, though it be but by a single mouth. She protests, she warns, she threatens, and, if the error prove obstinate, she condemns its author. Her silence alone, then, would suffice to give authority to the teaching of a long chain of great men and great Saints. Nevertheless, after having examined some of the principal links of this chain, we shall see that the Church not only authorises their teaching by her silence, but has declared it to be free from error.

II. We shall see hereafter that she herself expresses

this belief in her public ritual, that she embraces and professes it in her admirable prayers.

1. The belief in the universal mediation of Mary has been the belief of the most faithful guardians of tradition in all ages of the Church; it is the common opinion of her doctors.

To attempt to enumerate them all would be too large an undertaking; but the children of Mary will rejoice and exult to hear the opinions of some of these great men, at every period of Christianity.

We will, then, read their names, as we ascend the course of ages; we will afterwards listen to their testimony.

In the last century, I choose as my witness my own father, S. Alphonsus Liguori; not because he is my father, but because the Sovereign Pontiffs who have governed the Church since the end of the 18th century have vied with each other in extolling the faith and the learning of that great Saint; and because one of them has pronounced him to be one of the brightest lights of the Church (*Fulget inter maxima Ecclesiæ lumina*).[1]

In the 17th century, I choose Bossuet. Though he sometimes failed in firmness in resisting the powers of the world, his piety was equal to his learning, and his genius was perhaps unparalleled.

In the 16th century, I choose Suarez, whose name is so great in theology, and of whom it was said that he would have given all his learning for the grace of a single "Hail Mary."

In the 15th century, I choose Gerson, the Chancellor of the University of Paris, and S. Bernardin of Sienna, the great apostle of his day.

In the 14th, S. Antoninus of Florence, the great theologian, who was so justly named the "Angel of the Counsels."

In the 13th, S. Bonaventure and S. Thomas of

---

[1] Gregory XVI., Brief of Jan. 13, 1840.

Aquin, names to which, even for the ears of the world, it is needless to add any epithet.

In the 12th, S. Bernard, the oracle of nations, and the counsellor of Popes and of kings.

In the 11th and 10th centuries, S. Peter Damian and S. Anselm, both Doctors of the Church; the former, one of the greatest philosophers of any age, and certainly the first of his own.

About the 9th century, S. John Damascene, the S. Thomas of the Greeks, whose right hand was cut off by the persecuting imperial power, because it wielded a pen mightier than the empire.

In the 8th century, S. Germanus, the Patriarch of Constantinople, whose works Photius himself was constrained to praise.

In the 7th, S. Ildephonsus, the illustrious Bishop of Toledo, the worthy disciple of his master, S. Isidore of Seville, and the triumphant vindicator of the virginity of Mary.

In the 6th, the celebrated Cassian, and S. Fulgentius, the illustrious interpreter of S. Augustine.

Lastly, after these great names of modern days, of the middle ages, and of that indefinite period which divides the middle ages from the primitive times of Christianity, I choose from among the Fathers of those early days, S. Augustine, the greatest authority among the Latins; S. Chrysostom, the greatest authority among the Greeks; and one of the most illustrious doctors of the East, S. Ephrem, whose works were read in the assemblies of Christians together with Holy Scripture.

Let us now gather together the words of these great men, who are unanimous in acknowledging and celebrating, as designed by God, the universal mediation of the second Eve; and, consequently, the necessity of her intercession in the order of grace, and in the dispensation of graces.

"There is," says S. Alphonsus, "a great difference between saying that God cannot, and saying that He will not, grant graces without the intercession of Mary. We have no difficulty, assuredly, in confessing that God is the Source of every good, the Sovereign Dispenser of all graces, and that Mary is but a mere creature, who can obtain nothing but what comes from God. But is it not, at the same time, most conformable to reason to believe that God, desiring to exalt to the highest degree possible that mere creature whom He had chosen for the Mother of His Son, our common Redeemer, has ordained, to her greater honour, that all the graces which He bestows upon us should come to us through her? We confess, assuredly, as we have already said, that Jesus is the only Mediator of justice—that it is to His merits that we owe the grace of salvation ; but we say, at the same time, that Mary is the Mediatrix of grace ; and that, although it be really by the merits of Jesus Christ alone that she obtains what she asks, it is no less correct to say, that all the graces which we receive come to us by the intercession of Mary.

"There is nothing in this contrary to the sacred dogma ; on the contrary, it is the doctrine of the Church herself, who, in the public prayers which she has sanctioned, teaches us to have recourse to that divine Mother, and continually to invoke her. Mary is there called the salvation of the weak, the refuge of sinners, the help of Christians, our stay, our life, our hope (*salus infirmorum, refugium peccatorum, auxilium Christianorum, vita, spes nostra*). Again, in the Office for her Feasts, the Church applies to her those words of the Wise Man, which teach us that all our hopes rest on her: 'All hope of life and virtue is in me' (*In me omnis spes vitæ et virtutis*); that all grace also dwells in her : *In me omnis gratia viæ et veritatis ;* and lastly, that in her we shall find eternal life and salvation: 'He who shall find me, shall find life, and shall have salvation from the Lord' (*Qui me invenerit, inveniet vitam, et hauriet salutem in Domino*). And again, 'Those who act by me, and with me, shall not sin ; and those who extol me, shall have eternal life'

(*Qui operantur in me, non peccabunt ; qui elucidant me, vitam æternam habebunt*). All this, as it seems to us, sufficiently proves the necessity of Mary's intercession.

"This is the teaching of a great number of doctors and theologians, who cannot be reasonably reproached with having fallen into hyperbolical or exaggerated expressions. To exaggerate, we must depart from the truth. Now, how can we suppose this is the case of men so full of the Spirit of God? and, if it were permitted to us to add our own opinion to the authority of so many great names, we should say, that to reject a view which tends to honour Mary, and which in no way contravenes the holy doctrines of the Church, is to show, to say the least, very little devotion to the Blessed Virgin. God forbid that either I or my reader should ever be found among the number of those who are lukewarm in the service of Mary! Far rather would I be found among those who believe firmly and who admit heartily all that can be admitted and believed of her greatness, without falling into heresy. According to the Abbot Rupert, who accounted faith in the greatness of the Blessed Virgin to be one of the most acceptable acts of homage that can be offered to her, *Ejus magnalia credere*. And, had we no other authority for this, that of S. Augustine would be sufficient, who tells us that all praise which can be offered to Mary will always fall below her deserts. Moreover, the Church herself tells us in the Mass of our Lady: 'Thou art blessed, O holy Virgin ; and all praise is beneath thy merits' (*Felix namque es, sacra Virgo Maria, et omni laude dignissima*)."[1]

That which the love and exquisite instinct of Catholic tradition taught the great Saint whom we have just quoted, was learned also by Bossuet, from the view of the whole Divine plan of Redemption. In his third Sermon on the Immaculate Conception, where he treats of the grounds of devotion to the Blessed Virgin, he gives,

[1] *Glories of Mary*, ch. v.

as one of these grounds, the coöperation of Mary in all the operations of grace, expressing himself thus :

"'No man,' says the Apostle, 'can lay any other foundation than that which is laid, even Jesus Christ.' That Divine Saviour is, therefore, the unchangeable foundation of our devotion to the Blessed Virgin, because it is impossible for mankind ever sufficiently to honour that Virgin Mother from whose blessed womb it received Jesus Christ. Raise your minds, my brethren, and attentively consider how great, how preëminent, is the vocation of Mary, by whom God decreed before all ages to give Jesus Christ to the world. But we must add to this, that God, Who called her to that glorious ministry, would not have her to be the simple channel of that ineffable grace, but a voluntary instrument, who should contribute to the great work, not only by the holiness of her soul, but by a movement of her will. Therefore did the Eternal Father send an Angel to announce to her the mystery which was not to be accomplished until her consent should be obtained ; so that, when God had resolved upon the accomplishment of that great work of the Incarnation, for which all nature had been waiting for so many centuries, it had yet to wait for Mary's consent ; so necessary was it for the salvation of mankind. As soon as that consent is given, the heavens are opened, the Son of God becomes Man ; and men have a Saviour. In a certain sense, therefore, the charity of Mary was the fertile source whence grace sprang forth to be shed forth in abundance over the whole human race. And, as S. Ambrose says, and after him S. Thomas, 'It was from her blessed womb that that spirit of holy fervour went forth in abundance, which, having been first poured forth upon her, afterwards overflowed the whole earth' (*Uterus Mariæ, spiritu ferventi qui supervenit in eam replevit orbem terrarum, cum peperit salvatorem*).[1] 'She received,' says S. Thomas again, 'so great a plenitude of grace, that she attained to a most intimate

[1] S. Ambros., *De Inst. Virgin.*, ch. xii.

union with the Author of grace, and merited to receive within her Him Who is full of all grace ; by bringing Him forth, she, in a certain sense, caused grace to be poured forth upon all men' (*Tantam gratiæ obtinuit plenitudinem, ut esset propinquissima Auctori gratiæ, ita quod eum qui est plenus omni gratia, in se reciperet, et eum pariendo, quodammodo gratiam ad omnes derivaret*).[1]

"It was necessary, therefore, Christians, that the charity of Mary should concur in giving the world its Deliverer. This truth is too well known to need further exposition ; but I will say a few words upon a consequence which follows from it, which you have not perhaps sufficiently considered ; that consequence is this, that God does not change the order of His purpose, by which He determined once to give us Jesus Christ by the holy Virgin,—'for the gifts of God are without repentance.'[2] It is and always will be true, that, having once received by her the Principle of all grace, we still receive by her intervention its application in all the different states which compose the Christian life. Her maternal charity having contributed so powerfully to our salvation in the mystery of the Incarnation, which is the principle of all grace, she will contribute to it eternally in all the other operations which are simply dependent upon this."[3]

The celebrated ecclesiastical historian, Noel Alexandre, brings out Bossuet's conclusion with great force and clearness, when he says that it is the will of God that we should look for all blessings from Himself alone, but by the intercession of the Blessed Virgin Mary (*Deus vult ut omnia bona ab ipso expectemus potentissima Virginis Matris intercessione impetranda*).[4]

Suarez had said before these remarkable words: *Sentit Ecclesia Virginis intercessionem esse sibi utilem ac necessarium.*[5] The Church teaches that the intercession

---
[1] S. Th. iii.   [2] Rom. xi. 29.
[3] Third Sermon on the Immaculate Conception.
[4] Ep. 50, *In Calce Theol.*   [5] *De Inc.*, q. 37, a. 4, d. 23, s. 3.

of Mary is useful, and *even necessary* to her, not by necessity of justice, like that of the mediation of Jesus Christ, but by necessity relating to the order which God has determined for the dispensation of His grace,—a Divine order, which, Suarez says again: *Inter sanctos non utimur uno ut intercessore ad alium, quia omnes sunt ejusdem ordinis; ad Virginem autem tanquam ad Reginam et Dominam alii adhibentur intercessores*[1] ("Among the Saints, we do not use the intercession of one with another, because they are all of the same order ; but in addressing the Virgin, who is our Lady and Queen, we use the intercession of others").

The words of Gerson are equally strong: *Maria Mediatrix nostra per cujus manus Dei ordinavit dare ea quæ dat humanæ creaturæ*[2] (" Mary is the Mediatrix through whose hands God has decreed that all His gifts should pass to all mankind"). St. Bernardin of Sienna, who has just now given us the deep reason of this dispensation of God, thus, in his turn, concludes:[3] *Per Virginem a capite Christi vitales gratiæ in ejus corpus mysticum transfunduntur*[4] (" It is by the Virgin that all life-giving graces pass from Christ, the Head of the Church, to all the members of His mystical Body").

S. Antonine had said the same: "By Mary all heavenly graces have been given to the world" (*Per eam exivit de cælis ad nos quidquid gratiæ venit in mundum*).[5] " To wish to obtain them without her," says he again, " is to attempt to fly without wings" (*Qui petit sine ipsa duce, sine alis tentat volare*).[6] The great theologian of Florence does not intend by these words that we can never obtain any thing from God without expressly invoking Mary whenever we pray, but that to desire to obtain graces independently of her intercession would be to set ourselves against the order established by God. Thus the more docile we are to that Divine

[1] *Loc. cit.*
[2] Serm., *De Ann. B.V.*
[3] Ch. xii., pp. 137, 138.
[4] *Pro Fest. V.M.*, s. 5, ch. viii.
[5] P. 4, tit. 15, ch. xx., s. 12.
[6] Ibid., ch. xxii., s. 9.

order, the more faithfully we follow it by taking the same way to go to Him which He took to come to us,— by the blessed medium of His Mother and ours,—the more shall we find our prayers increase in the confidence which renders them efficacious. As for us, say the Protestants, we go directly to God. But do we go less directly to God by going in company with His Mother? That which goes straight to the Heart of God, and, as He Himself tells us, infallibly obtains His grace, is "humility;"[1] and he who says to Mary: "Do thou, who art so pure and holy, supply for my unworthiness, come to God with me, and pray to Him for me," we may rest assured, goes more directly to God than all the Pharisees of ancient or modern times. The heavens will always be iron to the proud man, for "God resisteth the proud."[2]

Let us return to the great chain of faith which heresy has vainly attempted to break, and listen to the testimony of the Angel of the Schools.

"Mary," says S. Thomas, "is called full of grace for many reasons, but chiefly because she transmits it to all men. It is a great and glorious prerogative for a Saint to possess grace sufficient for the salvation of a great number of men; but 'the height and plenitude of grace would be to possess a sufficiency of it for the salvation of all men; and this is to be found only in Jesus Christ and in the Blessed Virgin,' for by her a soul may be delivered from all its dangers. Hence it is said of her 'that she is armed with a thousand bucklers,'—that is to say, with remedies against sin and with safeguards against peril. Hence also what she says of herself: 'In me is all hope of virtue and of life,' because it is from her that we receive help for the exercise of all virtue" (*Dicitur autem beata Virgo plena gratia, quantum ad tria. . . . Tertio quantum ad refusionem in omnes homines. Magnum enim est in quolibet sancto, quando habet tantum*

[1] "But to whom shall I have respect, but to him that is poor and little, and of a contrite spirit, and that trembleth at My words?" (Isaias lxvi. 2.)
[2] S. James iv. 6, ad 1 Peter v. 5.

de gratia quod sufficit ad salutem multorum, sed quando haberet tantum quod sufficeret ad salutem omnium hominum de mundo, hoc esset maximum, et hoc est in Christo et in beata Virgine. Nam in omne periculo potes salutem obtinere ab ipsa Virgine gloriosa. Unde (Cant. iv. 4): "*Mille clypei,*" *id est, remedia contra pericula,* "*pendent ex ea.*" *Item in omni opere virtutes potes eam habere in adjutorium; et ideo dicit ipsa* (Eccl. xxiv. 25): "*In me omnis spes vitæ et virtutis*").[1]

S. Bonaventure, comparing the life of fallen humanity to a gloomy night, borrows a consoling image from Holy Scripture when he says of Mary: "As the moon is placed between the sun and the earth, and transmits below the light which it receives from above, thus that Royal Virgin is placed between God and us, and transmits to us the influences of His grace."[2] "Since God has been pleased to dwell in the womb of the Holy Virgin," says S. Bernardine of Sienna, "I am not afraid to affirm that she has acquired a certain right over the communication of all graces which thus flow to us out of her bosom like rivers from the ocean of the Divinity" (*Cum tota natura Divina intra virginis uterum existiterit, non timeo dicere quòd in omnes gratiarum effluxus quamdam jurisdictionem habuerit hæc Virgo, de cujus utero, quasi de quodam Divinitatis oceano flumina emanabant omnium gratiarum*).[3]

'But we know no words on this subject at once so sublime and so sweet as those which S. Bernard addresses to man in order to lead him to God:

"Fix thine eyes on the Divine plan; mark well and recognise the purpose of wisdom, the purpose of love. Desiring to cover the whole earth with the dew of heaven, He first saturated with it that chosen *fleece*[4]

---

[1] *Expos. in Sal. Aug.*
[2] *Ap.* Spanner, *Polyanth.*, litt. M., lit. 6, c.
[3] *Pro Fest. Virg. Mariæ*, Serm. v. ch. viii.
[4] Judges vi. S. Bernard alludes to one of the types of Mary contained in Holy Scripture.

whence it was to be shed over all the world (*Cœlesti rore aream rigaturus, totum vellus prius infudit*). Having determined to ransom mankind, He deposited the whole ransom in the chaste bosom of Mary. Behold, then, and deeply ponder, with what affectionate devotion He would have us honour Mary, Who has thus deposited in her the fulness of every blessing; so that if we have any hope of grace and salvation, we have it by Mary, who has ascended full of grace and benediction to God (*Altiùs ergo intuemini quanto devotionis affectu a nobis tam voluerit honorari, qui totius boni plenitudinem posuit in Mariâ ut proinde si quid spei in nobis est, si quid gratiæ, si quid salutis, ab eâ noverimus redundare quæ ascendit deliciis affluens*). Let us, then, venerate Mary with all the powers of our soul and all the affections of our heart, because such is the will of Him Who has been pleased to give us all things by her (*quia sic est voluntas Ejus, Qui totum nos habere voluit per Mariam*).[1]

"Such, I say, is His will, and for love of us. Being full of compassion for our miseries, Mary consoles us in our fears, excites our faith, rekindles our hope, raises and supports us in our weakness and depression. Thou wast afraid after thy fall to go again to God thy Father; thou didst fly to hide thyself at the very sound of His voice (*solo auditu ad folia fugiebas*). But God Himself has given thee Jesus to be thy Mediator. Is there any thing which such a Son cannot obtain from such a Father? He will certainly be heard and His humble prayer be granted, for He is the beloved of His Father. Dost thou tremble also to go to Jesus?—He is thy Brother, He is thy flesh, he has been pleased to suffer all that man can suffer to convince thee of His mercy; and that Brother was given thee by Mary. But the Majesty of God which thou beholdest in Him perhaps still affrights thee; for though He has become man, He still remains God. Wouldst thou have an advocate to lead thee to Himself?—have recourse to Mary, in whom

[1] *De Aquæd.*

humanity is pure and alone,—pure not only from the stain, but pure also by the unity of that human nature which is alone in her. Doubt not that Mary also will be heard, and her humble prayer granted; the Son will hear the Mother, and the Father will hear the Son. My dear children, this is the ladder of sinners, this is the foundation of my greatest confidence, this is the whole foundation of my hope (*Filioli, hæc peccatorum scala, hæc mea maxima fiducia est, hæc tota ratio spei meæ*). What more can we desire? Let us seek grace, and let us seek it by Mary; for what she seeks, she finds, and she never prays in vain. But let us seek grace from God, for the grace of men is but a delusion (*Quæramus gratiam et per Mariam quæramus, quia quod quærit invenit, et frustrari non potest. Quæramus gratiam apud Deum, nam apud homines gratia fallax*)."[1]

S. Peter Damian also bids us to seek grace, and to seek it by Mary, because she is the universal Mediatrix of grace, and has all the treasures of the Divine Mercy in her hands: *In manibus tuis sunt thesauri miserationum Dei.*[2]

S. Anselm points out more formally this universal mediation when he says to Mary: "Whatever the Saints can obtain by their intercession *united to thine*, thy intercession can obtain alone without the assistance of their prayers."[3]

This explains that invocation of S. John Damascene, which could be only addressed to God, or to her whom God has invested with the power of universal intercession: "Ever pure and immaculate Queen, save me and deliver me from eternal damnation" (*Regina immaculate et pura, salva me libera me ab æterna damnatione*).[4] Again, S. Germanus thus addresses the Blessed Virgin: "No one is saved, O holy Mother of God, except by thee; no one is delivered from dangers, but by thee; no one receives a grace from God, but by thee, who art

[1] *De Aquæd.*
[2] *De Nativ. B.V.*
[3] *Orat.* 46, ed. Migne.
[4] *Paracl. in Deip.*

full of grace" (*Nemo est, O sanctissima, qui salvus fiat nisi per te, Dei parens; nemo liber a periculo nisi per te, Virgo Mater; nemo donum Dei suscipit nisi per te gratiâ plena*).[1]

The words of S. Ildefonsus, the great Bishop of Toledo, are no less clear than those of the Patriarch of Constantinople: "O Mary," he cries, "all the blessings which the Divine Majesty has determined to bestow upon men, He has been pleased to place in thy hands, so that all the treasures and gifts of grace have been intrusted to thee" (*Omnia bona quæ illis summa Majestas decrevit facere, tuis manibus voluit commendare; commissi quippe sunt tibi thesauri et ornamenta gratiarum*).[2]

Cassian had before him expressed the same thought, and feared not to affirm that the salvation of the whole world lies in Mary's maternal charity and multitude of graces: *Tota salus mundi consistit in multitudine favoris Mariæ*.[3] S. Fulgentius, in his turn, shows Mary to be inseparably united with the mediation of Jesus Himself: *Facta est Maria scala cœlestis, quia per ipsam Deus descendit ad terras, ut per ipsam homines ascendere mererentur ad cœlos* ("Mary is the ladder to heaven; for by her God descended to earth, and by her men ascend to heaven").[4]

Lastly, unless God had decreed the universal mediation of the second Eve, S. Augustine could never have invoked Mary as the *only* hope of sinners: *Spes unica peccatorum;*[5] nor S. Chrysostom, as the advocate who obtains the pardon of our sins: *Per hunc peccatorum veniam consequimur;*[6] nor S. Ephrem, as our *only* hope: *Nobis non est alia fiducia quàm ad te Virgo sincerissima.*[7]

If there be any one thing certain, it is that the belief in the suppliant and universal mediation of Mary has been the belief of all those great men whom the Church has regarded in different ages as her most faithful children, and as the truest organs of all her teaching. Now, I ask,

---

[1] *In Dorm. Deip.*, Serm. 2.   [2] *De Cor. Virg.*, c. 15.
[3] Apud S. Alp. Esp., *Salve Regina.*
[4] *De Laud. B.V.*   [5] Serm. 194, *App. E.B.*
[6] *Offic. B.M V. per Annunt.*   [7] *De Laudibus Dei Genitricis.*

if this belief had contained the shadow of an error contrary to faith—if it had been in the slightest degree open to reprehension—would the Church have tolerated it thus long and thus continuously? Have we not seen that, if error speaks though but by a single mouth, the Church does not keep silence, but protests, warns, threatens, and condemns? Her prolonged silence, as we have seen, would suffice to authorise the teaching of a succession of great men and of great saints. But the Church does not only authorise by her silence their belief in the universal mediation of Mary; she declares it to be blameless, and *professes it herself.*

She declares it to be blameless; for works in which this belief is laid down, explained, defended, and vindicated—as it is, for example, in those of S. Alphonsus—have been declared free from blame by the Holy See.

It is true, to be held blameless in this sense, it is sufficient that a doctrine should contain nothing against faith and morals; but when a doctrine is held by a multitude of Saints and holy men without being opposed by equivalent authorities, or without being opposed at all, except by a few isolated voices here and there of those who have misunderstood it, it is evident that such a doctrine becomes certain, especially when it is consecrated by the language of the Church herself.

Now, the doctrine in question has been thus consecrated. It is impossible on any other belief to explain the prayers which the Church addresses to Mary alone in her public offices. Has she ever said to Saint, Angel, Archangel, to the whole society of Saints, or to the united choirs of Angels, what she says to Mary, and as she says it to Mary, when she addresses to her those general invocations which ask all things for all men?—" Health of the sick, refuge of sinners, comforter of the afflicted, help of Christians" (*Salus, refugium, consolatio, auxilium*).[1] Has she ever said to any other creature whomsoever, on earth or in heaven, *Succurre cadenti surgere qui curat populo*[2] (" Help

[1] *Litan. Loret.*   [2] *Antiph. post Compl.*

thou thy tottering people, and be thou their strength")? Has she ever said to any other but Mary: "Thou art not only the root of all blessing, the gate from whence the light hath issued forth for us" (*Salve radix, salve porta ex quâ mundo lux est orta*),[1] " but thou remainest ever the gate of heaven for us" (*Quæ pervia cœli porta manes*)?[2] How could Mary be the gate of heaven to us, unless all the graces which conduct us thither were granted to us through the prayers of her motherly love? Is not the same belief in the universality of Mary's intercession the inspiration of the *Salve Regina?* " Children of Eve, exiles from our country," says the Church to the second Eve, the Mother of mercy, " to thee do we cry from the depth of this valley of tears, for thou art our life, our hope, our consolation" (*Mater misericordiæ vita, dulcedo, spes nostra, salve*). " Cast thy compassionate eyes upon us, and after this our exile show us Jesus, the blessed Fruit of thy womb" (*Illos tuos misericordes oculos ad nos converte, et Jesum benedictum fructum ventris tui nobis post hoc exilium ostende*). Once more: have we ever heard the Church say to any but Jesus and His Mother, " Thou art our life, our hope"? Assuredly not; and why? Because Jesus Christ alone is the Source of grace, and Mary alone is its universal channel by her prayer as the Mother of God and the Mother of men—the true Mother of man's new life.

Prayer.

Yes, this is thine office, blessed Mary; and my consolation is increased and my gratitude towards God redoubled by the conviction that this belief, which I have seen to be so beautiful, so sublime, so fully in harmony with the whole order of redemption,[3] is a certainty, because it is the belief of the Church itself.

What must be thy happiness, O most loving of mothers, in having thus a share by thy prayers and thy love in all the gifts which God bestows on thy children!

[1] *Antiph. post Compl.*   [2] Ibid.   [3] Ch. xii., *supra*.

And what a happiness it is to me to know that I have never received, nor ever shall receive, any grace which thy maternal and virginal heart has not contributed to obtain for me!

Now that I know thee better, I will think of thee as thou dost think of me, and, after the example of holy Church, I will begin and end all my prayers with a word of love and confidence addressed to thy Mother's heart. I shall thus faithfully observe the order established by God for the diffusion of His gifts, since I shall no longer forget by whose prayer all ours are perfected and offered unto Him. The confidence that I shall be heard will also increase in my soul, because my poor prayers, being mingled with thine, will become all-powerful in their weakness. I will say, "Hail, Mary, full of grace;" and the poorer I feel myself to be, the greater shall be my hope in thy abundance, because thou art my Mother, and because there is no mother whose tenderness and compassion equals thine. And then, when the sight of my sins troubles me and tempts me to despair—when the long array of my infidelity and ingratitude rises to discourage me—I will remember that thou art the advocate of the whole human race, that thou carest for the vilest and most unworthy, and that God has appointed thee to intercede for all; and I will say to thee, with S. Thomas of Villanova: *Eia ergo advocata nostra, officium tuum imple* ("Sweet advocate of sinners, fulfil thy merciful office").

Lastly, when I am sad at the thought of my slothfulness in the service of God and my neighbour, and tremble at the memory of the souls which I have not aided, which I have not raised, which I have not supported, which I have not edified, which I have perhaps scandalised,—I will say to myself that God beheld beforehand the tears which I now shed, and that thou, my Mother, who art in the enjoyment of the light of God Himself, who beholdest face to face Him Who beholdeth all things, and before Whom all time is but a point, didst then offer to Him my prayers of to-day for those poor souls and for my own, imploring mercy for us all: *O Domine, quia filius Ancillæ tuæ !*

CHAPTER XIV.

THE CULTUS OF MARY.

The cultus of hyperdulia—Tokens of this cultus in the sanctuaries, offices, and festivals of the Church.

I. By cultus (or worship) in general we understand the honour which is paid to any person by reason of a certain perfection or superiority belonging to him in power, dignity, or merit.

We must distinguish between the civil cultus and the religious or sacred cultus.

The cultus is civil when the greatness or superiority of its object is simply human or natural.

The cultus is religious, or sacred, when the superiority of its object is supernatural.

Both the civil and the sacred cultus may be either absolute or relative. The cultus is absolute when it is paid to a person on account of his own excellence or superiority; as that, for instance, which is paid to a king on account of his royal dignity.

The cultus is relative when it is paid to a person or a thing, not on account of its own excellence, but on account of that which is represented by that person or thing. Thus a legate, an envoy, or an ambassador receives civil homage on account of the power which he represents. Thus also we pay honour to the statues of princes, heroes, and celebrated men, and a religious honour to the images and relics of the Saints, the image of Mary, the cross, or the image of Jesus Christ, on account of the excellence or supernatural perfection of the Saints, the sublime dignity of Mary, and the Divine Majesty of Jesus.

II. The sacred cultus is also manifold, and is thus subdivided into the cultus of latria, of dulia, and of hyperdulia. The object of the cultus of latria is the Divine, Infinite, and Uncreated Perfection; it is consequently due to God alone. Sacrifice, which is the distinctive act of the cultus of latria, can be offered to God alone. We invoke Mary, the Angels, and the Saints during the Holy Sacrifice, but we offer it to the Divine Majesty alone. The cultus of latria is synonymous with adoration properly so called. In the ancient, and in some modern languages, the word 'adoration' bears different significations, standing sometimes for Divine adoration in its proper sense, sometimes for simple veneration, according to the object to which it relates; but in our language custom has reserved its use for the cultus of God alone. The language of the passions only has profaned it by its application to the miserable cultus or idolatry of the flesh.

The object of the cultus of dulia is a perfection or excellence which is supernatural, but finite and created. This is the cultus which we owe to the Angels and the Saints. The honour which we pay to men during their lifetime on account of their supernatural perfections, the veneration excited by the sanctity which springs wholly from the grace of God, belongs therefore, in reality, to the cultus of dulia.

When the supernatural and created perfection which is the object of this cultus is not only eminent in its degree, but alone of its kind, and superior to all others, it is the object of the cultus of hyperdulia, *i. e.* of a cultus superior to that of dulia, and this is the cultus which is due to the Blessed Virgin.

It is true that if the relative, though not the absolute, cultus of latria may be offered to the Cross, according to the teaching of S. John Damascene, S. Bonaventure, S. Thomas of Aquin, and a number of other theologians,[1]

---

[1] Other theologians object to the direction of even the *relative* cultus of latria to the Cross, because, they say, this cultus

in reference to the Man-God who died upon its arms, and bathed it in His blood. Such a relative cultus might with still greater reason be paid to Mary, who not only carried the Man-God in her arms, but in her bosom, who brought Him forth, nourished Him, and thus bestowed on Him the very blood by which we were redeemed; but though it may be theoretically true that this relative cultus might be more fitly rendered to the Mother of Jesus Christ than to His Cross, the Church does not practically authorise it, lest the faithful should be exposed to the danger of confounding the absolute with the relative cultus; the Mother of God being a living creature, worthy by her own greatness to be honoured by an absolute cultus, which is not the case in the instance of the adoration of the Cross.

It is of faith that the absolute cultus of latria is due to God alone. It was not, therefore, simply an abuse, but an absolute heresy, on the part of the sectaries called Collyridians to honour the Blessed Virgin by this cultus. On the other hand, there would be a certain want of exactness in affirming of the cultus of hyperdulia which we pay to Mary, that it is only the cultus of dulia in its highest degree. This would be true were its object only the degree of grace or glory belonging to the Mother of God, because Mary's grace and glory, although immeasurably superior to the grace and the glory of all the Saints, constitute, nevertheless, only an eminent perfection in the same species of greatness. But the foundation of the cultus of hyperdulia is not only the sanctity, the grace, and the glory of the most holy Virgin Mary, but also her dignity as Mother of God, a dignity which borders immediately on the Hypostatic Union, and is intrinsically related to it, as Suarez[1] has shown

should never be paid to creatures, far less to inanimate creatures, and because the same homage is never paid to an image as to its original. The former theologians reply that, just for these two reasons, the cultus in this instance is simply relative.

[1] Ch. iv., *supra*.

us. "It *alone* touches the confines of the Divinity" (*Propria operatione attingit fines Divinitatis*),[1] according to the words of Cardinal Cajetan; and it thus proposes to the cultus of hyperdulia an object *formally* distinct from that of the ordinary cultus of dulia. That object indeed comprehends the grace and glory of Mary, or her incomparable sanctity; but as that sanctity is incomparable only because it corresponds with a dignity which has never belonged to any but herself alone, it is still true that the cultus of hyperdulia is a cultus apart, infinitely inferior to Divine cultus, but immensely superior to the cultus of the holiest of creatures, as the dignity of Mary, with the grace and the glory which are proportioned to that dignity, constitute together an order of greatness apart, in which other creatures have no share.

We have no intention to condemn the language of those who consider the cultus of hyperdulia to be simply that of dulia in its highest degree, because this is true in a certain sense, the greatness of Mary being only created greatness, but as that greatness is of an order to which no other creature has ever been raised, we prefer the language of those who understand by the cultus of hyperdulia, not only the supreme degree of the cultus of dulia, but a cultus superior to it.

III. Cultus in general comprehends two things: the honour rendered to a person of exalted power or merit, and the invocation of his assistance. This is true both of the civil and sacred cultus. The honour paid to one who is exalted by dignity, power, or virtue is not, indeed, inseparable from invocation, but the one leads to the other. The poor honour the rich, and ask their assistance; the lowly honour the great, and ask their favour; the weak honour the strong, and ask their support; sinners honour the just, and ask their prayers.

We ask the prayers of each other here below, according to the counsel of the Apostle, and the "Pray for me" from one Christian to another amid the trials of the

[1] Cajetanus.

Church militant, is always an act of legitimate hope: *Orate pro invicem ut salvemini: multum enim valet precatio justi assidua.*¹ And that hope becomes necessarily stronger when we invoke our brethren of the Church triumphant, and ask the intercession of the Angels and of the souls most closely united to God in glory. If the invocation of Saints be useless, it must follow that they cannot do for us in heaven what we can do for each other on earth, which would be an absurdity; or that they cannot know our needs and our miseries, nor offer our supplications together with their own, which is at once contrary to Holy Scripture and to the belief of all Christians in all ages. In Holy Scripture, in fact, we find the Saints after their departure from this world interesting themselves no less than the Angels² in the true happiness of those whom they have left behind, praying assiduously for their brethren,³ and offering their prayers to God.⁴

Moreover, the Bible has never been the liturgical book of Christians. It is evident that when the Apostles and Evangelists wrote the New Testament, they had no intention of composing a book of prayers. It was by word of mouth and by their own practice that they regulated the public worship; and the liturgies⁵ of all the Apostolic Churches agree in proving the "communion of Saints" in the act of prayer which ascends from earth to heaven, and passes from heaven and earth to the place of expiation, thus combining in one family the Church militant, the Church suffering, and the Church triumphant. "Let us not fear," says S. Gregory the Great, "that the Saints are ignorant of our prayers: are they not in the light of God, do not they see Him Who sees all things, and Who gives them the enjoyment of Himself? Is it not a far greater thing to enjoy the vision of God, than to behold in God what is not God?"

The early Christians knew by faith in the Old and

---

¹ James v. 16. ² Luke xv. 7-10. ³ 2 Macc. xv. 12 *et seq.*
⁴ Apoc. v. 8. ⁵ Syriac, Greek, Latin.

New Testament, and by the faith and preaching of the Apostles, that distance no longer exists for spirits who are living by the life of God. Never shall we forget the act of faith in prayer which we once read on a stone in the Catacombs. Beneath the symbols of martyrdom hastily carved, we found these words: "Holy Martyr, pray for the sculptor and for his departed ones, that they may rest in peace." These few words contain all: the invocation of the Saints by the living for the dead. There we find the three worlds of prayer, or rather prayer penetrating at once into its three spheres.

Now, at the summit of the ladder of these three worlds, the great hierarchy of prayer, we have already seen the universal Mediatrix of intercession,[1] who holds in her hands the hearts of all who pray and of all the choirs of Angels and Saints. The cultus of hyperdulia which we pay to Mary is therefore a cultus apart, not only with regard to veneration, but also with regard to invocation.

The Holy Church points this out to us by the manner in which she prays to the Blessed Virgin, as well as by the way in which she honours her. At the beginning of all her offices she unites the Angelical Salutation to the Lord's Prayer, and she finishes them all by one of those fervent antiphons in which she offers all her prayers to Mary, that the universal Mediatrix of intercession may offer them herself to God. And behold how she honours her; in all her temples, in all her basilicas, in her most humble churches, we find an altar consecrated to God, under the invocation of Mary; the altar of Mary thus leading the faithful to the High Altar where dwells her Divine Son, ever living with us until the consummation of the world. In every Catholic Church the patron Saint has his altar; but Mary, the Patroness of the whole Church, has hers in every consecrated place, in every church in Christendom. Generally speaking, also, the principal church in great cities,

[1] Ch. xii. et xiii., *supra*.

and especially in episcopal towns, is dedicated to God, under the invocation of Mary; and the greater number of cathedrals bear the name of our Lady. Lastly, instead of honouring the Blessed Virgin on one day of the year, as she honours each Saint on the day of his festival, the Church honours Mary by a succession of feasts, which embraces the whole year, because it embraces the whole life of her who is the Mother of the new life, and the model of our own.

Prayer.

I understand now, O Lord, the dying words of S. Teresa, "After all, O Lord, I am a child of the Church!" She felt an overflowing joy in death at the thought that she was dying in the great family of Thy children, which bears the threefold mark of its Father's inheritance, the mark of Thy Divine unity, by its perpetuity, its universality, and its indefectibility in all places and through all time. In that thrill of joy in death, she felt within her the ineffable life which Thou dost communicate to Thy family by Thy Holy Spirit, the Spirit of prayer: *Spiritus gratiæ et precum.*[1] Thou hast said, O Lord, "My house is a house of prayer;"[2] and by Thyself I swear that the Catholic Church is truly Thy house, because it is the true house of true prayer. Man indeed prays every where, unless he has suffered the last spark to be extinguished of that fire which Thy breath continually seeks to rekindle in our souls; but that fire does not wholly consume them except in the Church, whither thou callest us all. How many have I known who have returned to that home, and have found there that of which they have felt the need elsewhere, and found hardly a trace! It is Thy Spirit, O my God, which enkindles the prayers of the sacred solemnities in our temples, those sublime prayers of Thy assembled children which the spirit of man never dictated, and the force, the unction, and the sublime sim-

[1] Zach. xii. 10.   [2] Mark xi. 17.

plicity of which he is powerless to imitate. It is Thy Spirit also Who inspires the prayers of the souls who speak to Thee in secret (*in abscondito*),[1] and repeat to Thee in a thousand different ways the prayer which Thou hast taught them, the " Our Father," that *Abba, Pater*,[2] which enfolds in its supernatural depths all their desires, which suffices to the weakest among them, and expresses the full meaning of the strongest of those who are most closely united with Thee in recollection, and even in the highest contemplation. Lastly, it is Thy Spirit Who quickens all the members of the Church militant, triumphant, and suffering, making of them one body, of which that Spirit is the soul; and by it the prayer of the souls in triumph brings grace to the souls still in the conflict, and consolation to those in the place of expiation. O my God, how sweet it is to know that by the Communion of Saints we are united to all who pray upon earth, to the holy souls who pray in purgatory, to the Saints who pray in heaven, to Mary, the Mother of all, who offers the incense of that universal prayer in the sacred thurible of her heart to her Divine Son, the only Mediator of Justice, by Whom all things come to us from God, and by Whom all return to Him!

My Mother, the grain of incense which I bring thee is very poor and insignificant, but it will not burn alone in the fire of thy heart; and as "I am a child of the Church," and desire to live and die a child of the Church, I shall have my share in life and death in those graces which are brought down from heaven by the prayers of all, and above all by thine, which completes and perfects them, and I have a full confidence that I shall one day bless thee in heaven for having obtained for me on earth, by the merits of our Lord Jesus Christ, faith, hope, repentance, love, and perseverance, and for having watched over my soul unto the end, to deliver it from the arms of death into the bosom of the Father, of the Son, and of the Holy Ghost. Amen.

[1] Matt. vi. 6.   [2] Gal. iv. 6.

CHAPTER XV.

THE FESTIVALS OF MARY.

The life of Mary the light of ours—Feast of the Immaculate Conception—Fidelity to grace.

AT the end of the last consideration we pointed out, as one of the signs of the superiority of the cultus which the Church pays to Mary over that which she renders to the Saints, the chain of Festivals celebrated in honour of the Blessed Virgin,—a chain encircling the whole year, because it embraces the whole life of her who is the Mother and model of souls. It is true, that in order to lose nothing of what the Gospel reveals to us of the life of Mary, and of what the Church commemorates in her Festivals, we must never separate the Feasts of the Son from those of the Mother, so divinely united was the life of the Mother with that of the Son. If, however, we cast but a glance at her principal Feasts, we shall find sufficient proof that the life of our Mother is the model offered for our imitation.

These Feasts are those of her Immaculate Conception, her Nativity, her Presentation in the Temple, her Annunciation, her Visitation, her Purification, her Compassion, or her Dolors, and her glorious Assumption. The ecclesiastical year does not, indeed, arrange them in this order, because the Church has fixed them on the anniversaries of those days on which those mysteries actually took place which form the links "full of grace" of the whole life of the Mother of God. The first of these links was the mystery of her Immaculate Conception. We have already explained[1] what we mean when we say that Mary was conceived without sin; *i.e.* that at the very moment when the soul of the second Eve was created and united to her body, God clothed and adorned it with sanctifying grace, as He did that of the first Eve, not willing that she who was blessed among women, and destined to be-

---

[1] Chap. vi., *supra*.

come the Mother of the Saviour of mankind, should enter into this world soiled with the stain of original sin, or devoid, like the other children of Adam, of the light and the splendour of grace; but, on the contrary, that she should appear from the very first worthy of Him whom she was to bear, and endowed from the first moment of her life with the merits of Jesus Christ, the gifts of the Son of God, who willed to become her Son.

Holy Scripture teaches this when it calls Mary "full of grace;"[1] grace having so filled the life of Mary, as it filled her soul, that not the smallest portion of either was left devoid of its sanctifying power.

The Church teaches us the same truth in the prayer for the Feast of the Immaculate Conception: *Deus, qui per Immaculatam Virginis conceptionem dignum Filio tuo habitaculum præparasti* (" O God, Who, by the Immaculate Conception of the Virgin, didst prepare for Thy Son a habitation worthy of Him").

The Immaculate Conception was, then, the first grace bestowed on Mary to prepare her for her divine vocation. It was the first act of God's Providence executing in time the design which He had formed regarding her from all eternity.

What is there in this to recall us to ourselves, and make us look into our own hearts?

It is, that each one of us has a divine vocation, and is called by Providence to attain to God by a way divinely appointed from all eternity; that each one of us has received gifts and graces proportioned to that end, beginning from our birth and our baptism;[2] and that if we faithfully recall to mind that chain of graces, we shall find an abundant occasion for gratitude, love, repentance,

---

[1] Luke i. 28.

[2] There are three kinds of baptism: the baptism of water, the baptism of blood or martyrdom, and the baptism of desire—*i.e.*, according to S. Thomas Aquinas, the grace to will to obtain salvation by fulfilling the will of God, a grace which He never refuses even to those who, from invincible ignorance, as yet know not the true Church.

and filial fear lest we fill up the measure of our ingratitude. Lastly, it is that which holy Church makes us ask of God, through the intercession of Mary, and by the merits of Jesus Christ, in the prayer for this very Feast: *Ut cor et corpus nostrum immaculatum tibi, qui eam ab omni labe præservasti fideliter custodiamus* ("Grant us faithfully to keep our hearts and bodies immaculate for Thee, Who didst preserve her from all stain").

Prayer.

Yes, Lord, Thou hast willed to do me good, and that the highest good, from all eternity. Thou hast prepared for me a way to attain to Thee, and I desire ever to remember those first rays of light which revealed it to me, and every additional illumination which Thou hast since bestowed upon me. Who is like unto Thee, O my God, in goodness and love? Who has loved me as Thou hast loved me, and who has ever given me equal proofs of love? But if nothing is like unto Thy love, O Lord, what is like to me in blindness and ingratitude? I deserve nothing more from Thee, or rather, I deserve all Thy chastisements; and yet I trust that Thou wilt give me tears, because they are due to Thee, because Thou lovest justice, and because I love it too, notwithstanding all my sins.

Mary, my Mother, thou who art so pure and so beautiful in the eyes of God, look upon thy child; and since the tears of repentance can alone render me precious in thy sight, thou wilt obtain them for me, because thou art my Mother, and wilt never cease to love me.

Grant, then, O Lord, to Mary that which she asks for me,—*ut cor et corpus immaculatum tibi fideliter custodiam*,—that I may faithfully keep my heart and body immaculate for Thee—this heart and this body which Thou hast given me—so that, at the moment of my death, my soul may fly to my Mother and to Thee, and my body await in the tomb the glorious resurrection of Thy children. Amen.

CHAPTER XVI.

THE NATIVITY.

A sign foreshadowing the revival of grace.

Attinget a fine usque ad finem fortiter, et disponit omnia suaviter[1] ("She reacheth from end to end mightily, and ordereth all things sweetly"). These words of Holy Scripture are perfectly verified in the birth of Mary. The promise of redemption, made to our first parents after their fall, was renewed two thousand years before the Incarnation to the father of that race of which the Messias was to be born; a thousand years later, God reiterated it to David, manifesting to him that the Christ was to spring from his family. And notwithstanding the revolutions of empires, notwithstanding the great powers which successively enslaved and carried into captivity the chosen people, notwithstanding their own infidelities and those of their kings,—spite of time, spite of the world, spite of all the powers of earth and hell,—behold at length, on the day marked out by the irresistible Providence of God, that woman promised from the beginning appears upon earth,—the Virgin of Isaias, the Daughter of David, the Child of Abraham, the second Eve, the Mother of the new Adam; and she appears not amid the delights of Eden, but in the humble and sublime poverty which befitted the God of the manger, the Mother of the voluntary Victim of the sin and pride of man.

Nativitas tua gaudium annuntiavit universo mundo; ex te enim ortus est Sol Justitiæ, Christus Deus noster, says the Church in her chants ("Thy birth gave joy to the whole world; for from thee is sprung the Sun of Justice, Christ our Lord"), even as the sun rises from the bosom of the dawn. The appearance of Mary was at first as little regarded as that of her Son, but she was no less the true dawn of the great day of redemption.

[1] Wis. viii. 1.

For the same reason, the Church invokes Mary as the Morning Star (*Stella Matutina*), because she was truly the mild planet which preceded that great day of the Lord.

But what the birth of Mary was to the human race in general, such is the birth or revival of her love in the hearts of each one of us in particular—it is a sign announcing the rising or the return of the Sun of Justice in our soul. It is not wonderful that Jesus, having willed to give Himself to the world through His Mother, should will also to give Himself to each one of us by her. Experience has decided this point; for all to whom God has revealed the secrets of the consciences of men will attest, that never has filial piety towards Mary remained long alone in a soul,—it has ever been the harbinger of the return of God, by leading the soul itself back to His love, and that because a loving confidence in Mary is in itself the commencement of correspondence with grace, and an act of faith in the order established by God for the communication of His graces.

When the name of Mary is sweet to a poor sinner, and restores hope to his enslaved heart, the chains of the captive are about to be quickly broken. When a poor soul loves to repeat, "Hail, Mary, full of grace," it will soon obtain from that plenitude of grace, which is the fulness of light and of life, a ray of life to dispel its darkness, and a drop of heavenly life to quench its thirst for happiness and peace.

Prayer.

O Mary, my Mother, how greatly do I need that light, and how ardently do I thirst after that life! I know indeed that here below we can but enjoy the divine reflection of the true light, the divine germ of the true life; but obtain for me at least to enjoy them both; obtain for me sufficient light and strength to enable me, by perseverance in prayer and the frequent reception of the Holy Eucharist, to follow even to the hour of my death that road whose light and eternal life.

I understand now, my Mother, why the Church, which celebrates thy birth, does not celebrate even those of the most heroic of her children, saving him only whom Jesus sanctified by thy word whilst yet in his mother's womb; and I understand also why she calls the day of our death *natalis dies* (the day of our birth); it is because when we leave the womb of our mother (the first world we inhabit), we do but break the bands of that dark prison, to enter into a new darkness and to fall into new chains. But when we shall leave this our land of captivity, when we shall emerge from the bosom of that second Mother who shall also bring us forth in pain, our soul will then break her last ties to enter into possession of the perfect " liberty of the children of God," in the true abode of light, of life, and of peace (*in locum refrigerii, lucis, et pacis*).

I hope for thy presence at that hour of death, that beginning of true life, O divine Mother of Him Who suffered death that He might give us life. In that hour may the remembrance of thee, and the faithful invocation of thy name, be to me the star to guide me into port, the dawn of the eternal day! Amen.

CHAPTER XVII.

THE PRESENTATION.

The great law of grace, which obliges all men to give themselves wholly to God.

WE must not confound the Feast of the Presentation of Mary with that of the Presentation of our Lord Jesus Christ. The Infant Jesus was presented in the Temple by His holy Mother on the day of her Purification, according to the law of Moses; and the child Mary was presented there by her blessed parents, S. Joachim and S. Anna, not in virtue of the law of Moses, which related only to the first-born son of a family,—*Omne masculinum ad aperiens vulvam sanctum Domino voca-*

*bitur*¹ ("Every male opening the womb shall be called holy to the Lord"),—but in accordance with the custom of the Hebrews, to consecrate to God (either in fulfilment of a vow, or for some other pious motive) one or more of their children, who then received a holy education in the school of the Temple itself. Historical tradition assures us of this fact, and it is confirmed also by the writings of the Old Testament. It was this custom which enabled Josaba, the daughter of King Joram, and sister of Ochozias, to rescue the young Joas, the son of the latter, from the fury of Athalia, and to keep him "for six years hid in the house of the Lord," as we read in the 11th chapter of the 4th Book of Kings, and the 22d chapter of the 2d Book of the Paralipomenon. The Gospel also refers to this custom when it speaks of Anna, the prophetess, who lived in the Temple, *quæ non discedebat de templo*² ("who departed not from the Temple"); living there as Josaba had doubtless done: devoting her time to the education of the children consecrated to God.

And, truly, this holy place was well suited for the early abode of her whom God had not only chosen for His own Temple, but to be the living Ark of the Holy of holies in the New Testament.

The Feast of the Presentation of Mary offers us a lively and touching picture of the perfect fulfilment of two great duties: one of which belongs to parents; the other, to every child of man.

Whatever, in truth, may be the destiny or vocation of their children, parents should never forget that God wills to have these children for His own, and that the different states of life to which He calls them are but so many roads which lead to that one true end of man. We ought to belong to God because we came from God. The mother of the Machabees reminded her heroic children of this truth when she said to them: "I know not how you were formed in my womb; but the Creator of the

¹ Luke ii. 23. ² Luke ii. 37.

world, who formed the nativity of man, and found out the origin of all, He will restore to you again, in His mercy, both breath and life, as now you despise yourselves for the sake of His laws."[1]

All are not called to the sacrifice of martyrdom; but all are called to a life of sacrifice, and, sometimes, to the martyrdom for duty's sake, which is always the sacrifice of love. S. Augustine exclaims, in reference to this: *Da amantem et sentit quod dico* ("Give me one who loves, and he will understand me"). The royal Prophet thus loved when he said to God: "Thy hands have made me, and formed me; give me understanding in the way of Thy commandments." As if he said: "I came from Thee alone, O my God; teach me to understand this truth, that I may, in like manner, live to Thee alone" (*Manus tuæ fecerunt me, et plasmaverunt me: da mihi intellectum, et discam mandata tua*).[2]

This is the truth of truths, the great law which concerns all men — the law of love and of justice; because love is evidently due to God — the heart to Him who made it: *Hoc est maximum et primum mandatum*[3] ("This is the first and great commandment").

We know not a more striking proof of the injury inflicted on human reason by the fall of our first parents, than the difficulty which men experience in discerning any thing so clearly evident as the obligation which rests upon them of belonging solely and entirely to God.

This difficulty is less in childhood, when our passions have not yet cast their gloomy shadows over baptismal grace. Who does not remember the facility with which he then realised the thought of God? Who does not recollect the reality and the sweetness of the first glimpses of God? Who speaks so plainly to the hearts of the innocent? As time goes on, God speaks to us in a different language, and reiterates the great law of love in other terms: "If any man will come after Me, let

---

[1] *In Joan.* tr. 26.   [2] Ps. cxviii. 73.   [3] Matt. xxii. 38.

him deny himself."[1] If these words seem hard to us, it is because we have become blind; for the abnegation which they require from us is still but love and justice. How can we belong to God, if we only follow the vain caprices of our own will, instead of desiring the accomplishment of the Divine will—of that holy law which would make justice and truth to reign within us? When we love, we will only what he wills whom we love. If our love be evil, we shall sacrifice our will to falsehood; but if our love be good, if we love God, and what God would have us love, we shall find verified in the sacrifice of obedience the promise of the Living Truth Himself: "My yoke is sweet, and My burden light."[2] He who, to please God, embraces the cross of obedience and love, does not creep, but runs in the way of the commandments and of conformity to the Divine will, which is itself that Divine cross to which we nail our will, that it may be reformed, and on which it dies, only to live again.

Mary, as we have seen,[3] unlike the other children of Adam, had not to overcome concupiscence, God having worthily prepared her to be the Mother of the New Man; but she had to overcome sorrow, and her life was in fact the most heroic of all lives. Having been called to a degree of virtue of which we cannot even form an idea, fidelity to grace required of her a fortitude and a courage far above the fortitude and courage of all the Saints. God prepared her in the Temple for this life of ineffable sacrifice: it was there that she began the ascent of those steps of love and sorrow which were to conduct her even to the heights of Calvary: *Ascensiones in corde suo disposuit, in loco quem posuit.*[4] It was in the Temple, also, that she accumulated those interior treasures which were soon to draw down upon her the salutation from on high: *Ave, gratiâ*

[1] Matt. xvi. [2] tt. xi. 30. [3] Ch. x.
[4] Ps. l. ke i. 28.

Prayer.

Thou, Lord, didst say: "Suffer the little children, and forbid them not, to come to Me, for the kingdom of heaven is for such." I have no difficulty in believing this, O my God, for I can still recall the blessed days of childhood; and I know that Thou dost speak more often to lowly souls than to the great and proud. Thou dost bestow on children those lights and attractions which, in after life, we should be but too happy to recover; when, alas, vain learning has inflated our intellect without filling it. Why are we not always as reasonable as we were when on the threshold of life, when Thy Divine word showed us the great end, the inevitable term of our existence? Then Thy Name, alone, O Jesus, my Saviour and my God, shed a ray of light on my soul; to love Thee and to obey Thee then seemed easy and pleasant. How well did I know by experience that prayer is the life of the soul—of that divine being destined to live the very life of its Father! How fully did I realise that Thou wast my Father, when I said to Thee: "Our Father, Who art in heaven"! And how earnestly did I desire to be where Thou art!

O my God, how is all now changed! I have strayed far, very far from Thee, my Lord; and I have desired the life of those who seemed to live, but who were in reality dead in Thy sight. Father, I have sinned against heaven and against Thee. But my Mother has prayed for me, and behold me weeping at Thy feet: *Redde mihi lætitiam salutaris tui et spiritu principali confirma me* ("Restore unto me the joy of Thy salvation, and strengthen me with a perfect spirit"). Yes, restore to me the joy and the spirit of my childhood—that spirit which came from Thee, and which I have lost by my fault. Hear Mary, who asks it for me; grant that I may, indeed, receive it never to lose it again.

Holy Virgin, my Mother, intercede for me, that I may die that death,—which is but the death of an hour, the death of an instant,—rather than die again by sin that death which shall be eternal.

CHAPTER XVIII.

THE ANNUNCIATION.

Humility.

THE Feast of the Annunciation of Mary may also be called the Feast of the Incarnation of the Word. He Who gave Himself visibly to the world, on the day of His Nativity, which the Church celebrates at Christmas, had already given Himself in reality to the human race, when He gave Himself to the new Eve on the day of the Annunciation. At Christmas, the Church shows us God, answering to that cry of man: *Aperiatur terra et germinet Salvatorem* ("Let the earth be opened and bud forth a Saviour"); but on the Annunciation she shows Him answering to that other sigh of humanity: *Rorate, cœli desuper, et nubes pluant Justum* ("Drop down dew, ye heavens, from above, and let the clouds rain the Just"). On this day was accomplished in reality what had been prefigured when the dew which was to cover the whole earth, at the prayer of Gideon, the liberator of Israel, fell first only on the hidden fleece, from which it was to spread over the rest of the world.[1]

The day of the Annunciation thus became that of the greatest act of Providence, the greatest of the works of God. The creation which brought into being that which was not, was, doubtless, an act of infinite power, since there is an infinite distance between nothing and being. But the Incarnation of the Word, which consummated the personal union between the Creator and the creature, was an act of equal power; for if infinity separates nothing from being, it equally separates created

[1] Judg. vi.

from uncreated being. For this reason the Apostle St. Paul gives to the Incarnation the name of exinanition, because there is no term in human language which so fully expresses the infinite abyss which the Word had to cross when He became flesh: *Semetipsum exinanivit formam servi accipiens, in similitudinem hominum factus*[1] ("He debased Himself, taking the form of a servant, being made after the likeness of men"). The Creation and the Incarnation, then, equally manifest the omnipotence of God. Both are, also, manifestations of His love; but if the love of God is manifested in the gift of existence which He bestowed upon us, it is manifested in a far more glorious degree in the gift which He has bestowed upon us of Himself: *Apparuit benignitas et humanitas Salvatoris nostri Dei* ("The goodness and kindness of God our Saviour appeared"). It is, above all, in becoming man, and the Saviour of man, that the love of God has manifested itself to mankind. It is, then, true that the day of the Incarnation or Annunciation was the great day of God, the especial day of His power and goodness.

It is the day of mercy promised to our first parents, and which they foresaw in the distant ages as the day of their future deliverance. It is the day which from that moment was universally expected, because it was to be that of the "Desired of all nations."[2] It is the day prefigured by the types of the Old Testament, and announced by all the Prophets. It is the day pointed out by Daniel, with a precision fatal to incredulity,[3] in its relation with the history and with the end of the empires of force which pass away, and the commencement of that spiritual empire which shall never pass away.[4]

We have already heard a voice from heaven an-

---
[1] Phil. ii. 7. [2] Agg. ii. 8.
[3] *Vide* ch. ix. of Daniel, and the explanation of that prophecy in *The Christ and the Antichrists*, p. 1, ch. ii.
[4] See ch. ii. and vii. of Daniel, and their explanation, ibid.

nouncing to the world the establishment of that kingdom which shall have no end.[1] We have already listened to the words of the heavenly messenger, by whom God treated concerning our salvation with the second Eve; as the enemy of the human race had treated concerning our ruin with the first. We have learnt, also, all that the Gospel reveals to us of the Incarnation and of the incomparable greatness of Mary,[2] as well as of her invincible determination to remain a Virgin;[3] but we have not yet fathomed the depth of that humility which it unveils to us in the soul of the second Eve. The pride of the first involved the head of the human race in her fall; the humility of the second drew the Saviour of renewed humanity into her bosom. Her virginity rendered her pleasing to God, and she would never have been the Mother of Christ, if she had not determined to remain a Virgin;[4] yet it was humility which made her a Mother: *Placuit ex virginitate, ex humilitate concepit.*[5]

Let us see how the Gospel reveals to us the exceeding beauty of Mary's humility, before it manifests to us its power: it does not say that Mary was troubled by the apparition of the Angel, but at his saying: *Turbata est in sermone ejus.* It was because those words full of praise saluted her as "full of grace," and humility shrinks from all praise save that of God. Thus Mary asked what this language could be, and the heavenly messenger reassured her by declaring that if she were full of grace, she owed it utterly and entirely to God alone: *Ne timeas, Maria: invenisti enim gratiam apud Deum* ("Fear not, Mary, for thou hast found grace with God"). She then listened fearlessly to him, who left her in her own nothingness, and became the Mother of God by declaring herself to be His handmaid, and at the very moment when He was raising her above all: *Ecce Ancilla Domini; fiat mihi secundùm verbum tuum* ("Be-

---

[1] *Vide* ch. viii., *supra.*   [2] *Vide* ch. iv., *supra.*
[3] *Vide* ch. viii., *supra.*   [4] Ibid.
[5] S. Bernard, *De Laud. V.M.*, Hom. 2.

hold the handmaid of the Lord; be it done to me according to Thy word"). God only builds on nothingness, and it was because Mary knew herself to be nothing, and faithfully rendered to God alone all the glory, that He willed that she should coöperate so largely in the greatest of all His works. He who made us without us, will not save us without us, and willed not to redeem human nature without the assistance of Mary.

Redemption was a work of justice as well as of love; the offended Majesty of God demanded a satisfaction worthy of it; and, consequently, the victim of expiation was to be at the same time Divine and human,—human, to expiate; Divine, to give to that expiation the infinite value required by Almighty God. Yes, it was His sacred humanity that the Word asked from our nature, when he asked it of Mary; and it was the *fiat* of Mary which gave to the human race the Lamb of God, Who bears and Who takes away the sin of the world. The *fiat* of God drew all things out of nothing, and the *fiat* of nothing (the *fiat* of the humility of Mary) drew God out of Himself to give Himself wholly to us. The most profound humility thus became the free and voluntary instrument of the greatest work of Omnipotence. God is ever the same; He never does any thing really great, be it in the heart of man or by the hands of man, but in proportion to man's obedience and humility. The works of the proud are only great in appearance; they vanish as a mere sound: *perierunt cum sonitu.*[1] That which lasts and which lives, derives its life and its strength from God alone. He only is the source of those virtues which render a soul great in His eyes; and He only is the origin of those human designs which triumph over time and themselves. Now, it is humility which alone drinks at that source,—the humility of those who found works truly living and durable, and who alone drink at that Divine fountain, the life in which they live and the strength by which they endure.

[1] Ps. ix. 7.

If we are wanting in grace to construct the interior edifice of virtues, and if we are without strength and fruitfulness to perform exterior works with success, it is because we are wanting in humility. Humility will produce in us magnanimity, and inspire us at once with a distrust of ourselves and a confidence in God. Pride, on the contrary, after having inflated the heart, leads to discouragement, because we cannot find in ourselves that for which we were vainly seeking. Happy, then, is he who, seeing himself such as he really is, says to God from the depths of his misery: *Cognovi, Domine quia æquitas judicia tua: et in veritate tuâ, humiliasti me Fiat misericordia tua, et consoletur me*[1] ("I know, O Lord, that Thy judgments are equity; and in Thy truth Thou hast humbled me. Oh, let Thy mercy be for my comfort"); for all my hope is in Thee, and I trust to Thy word, according to that Divine promise: *Quoniam in Me speravit, liberabo eum: protegam eum, quoniam cognovit nomen Meum*[2] ("Because he hoped in Me, I will deliver him: I will protect him because he hath known My name").

Prayer.

By the inspiration of Thy Spirit, I hear, O my God, Thy faithful Apostle say to me: "What hast thou, that thou hast not received? Why dost thou then glory, as if thou hadst not received it?"[3] And by the light of that truth I see that pride is but an injustice and a lie. I see it clearly, O my God; and yet that injustice has penetrated like a hurtful oil through all the faculties of my soul, and that lie has become identified with my whole being. There is something in me which endeavours to snatch from God the glory which belongs to Him; something which would make myself the centre of every thing, would refer all things to myself, *i. e.* would, by a monstrous disarrangement, reverse the order of truth and love, which refers all to God: a vain and

[1] Ps. cxviii. 75, 76.   [2] Ps. xc. 14.   [3] 1 Cor. iv. 7.

foolish attempt; but its futility, O Lord, does not render it the less hateful. Give me, at least, my God, a detestation of that pride which I bear within me, since the hatred of evil is the beginning of good, and the hatred of pride the first step on the road to humility. Guide me along that road, O holy Mother of the Lamb of God, that I may at last come whither thou art. Yes, I have a firm confidence that Thou wilt take pity on me, and that Thou, so full of grace and yet withal so humble, wilt not permit me, Thy child, to remain so poor, and yet so proud. Thy Divine Son, I know, "resisteth the proud, and giveth grace to the humble."[1] Ask Him, then, to bestow on me humility and all things which will enable me to acquire it. I do not forget that in praying thus I ask for the bitter remedy of humiliation; but I know that the bitterness of that chalice soon changes into sweetness, because it infuses grace, love, and peace into our soul. Poor, fallen, blind, rebellious, and ungrateful nature causes me to fear humiliation as death, but Thou wilt not listen to that fear, but will show a Mother's love for thy child, by obtaining his cure, spite of his own resistance. Amen, Amen.

CHAPTER XIX.

THE VISITATION.

The mystery of faith, charity, humility, grace, and consolation.

IMMEDIATELY after the narrative of the Annunciation, we read in the Gospel:

"And Mary rising up in those days, went into the hill country with haste into a city of Juda.[2] And she entered into the house of Zachary, and saluted Elizabeth. And it came to pass, that when Elizabeth heard

---

[1] James iv. 6; 1 Peter v. 5.
[2] To Hebron, the priestly city where Zachary dwelt.

the salutation of Mary, the infant leaped in her womb. And Elizabeth was filled with the Holy Ghost:[1] and she cried out with a loud voice, and said: Blessed art thou among women, and blessed is the Fruit of thy womb. And whence is this to me, that the Mother of my Lord should come to me? For behold as soon as the voice of thy salutation sounded in my ears, the infant in my womb leaped for joy. And blessed art thou that hast believed, because those things shall be accomplished that were spoken to thee by the Lord. And Mary said: My soul doth magnify the Lord. And my spirit hath rejoiced in God my Saviour. Because He hath regarded the humility of His handmaid; for behold from henceforth all generations shall call me blessed. For He that is mighty, hath done great things to me; and holy is His name. And His mercy is from generation to generations, to them that fear Him. He hath showed might in His arm: He hath scattered the proud in the conceit of their heart. He hath put down the mighty from their seat, and hath exalted the humble. He hath filled the hungry with good things; and the rich He hath sent away empty. He hath received Israel His servant, being mindful of His mercy. As He spoke to our fathers, to Abraham and to his seed for ever."

What a scene is this! The ancient covenant in the last of its Prophets, in him who was "more than a Prophet," thrills at the approach of the new, and the benediction promised to our first parents, the benediction promised to the father of believers, both for his own nation and for all the nations of the earth,—" And in thy seed shall all the nations of the earth be blessed" (*In*

---

[1] She was filled with the Holy Ghost at the same time, or rather after, S. John the Baptist, as plainly appears by comparing the 15th with the 41st verse of the first chapter of S. Luke. The first of these verses says of S. John the Baptist: " He shall be filled with the Holy Ghost, even from his mother's womb;" and the second says: " The infant leaped in her womb, and Elizabeth was filled with the Holy Ghost."

semine tuo benedicentur omnes gentes),[1]—begins to be shed abroad by the Incarnate Word, by means of the Woman blessed among all women; the Woman promised from the beginning, whose Canticle has just sounded in our ears, in thanksgiving for the mercy shown to all generations. Eve had been the instrument of malediction; Mary, the chosen instrument of benediction, returns thanks to God in the name of the whole human race, for which she has received Him, for which she bears Him enclosed in her living tabernacle, and communicates the first fruits of that blessing to him who was to make known to the world the presence of his Saviour. Yet a little while, and the grace of the Deliverer of Israel, still hidden in the bosom of the second Eve, like the dew in Gideon's fleece, shall cover the whole earth, and then the Canticle of Mary shall become the song of all mankind, which shall echo even to the consummation of all things.

Let us not be content, however, with simply gazing upon the glory of this divine scene; let us carefully study the lessons which it contains.

The first is a lesson of charity. Mary, whom the Angel of the Lord had found in her solitude, and whose faith, purity, and humility had drawn down the Word of God from heaven; Mary, who had been full of grace before the Incarnation,—was from that moment full of God Himself. The world was no longer any thing to her who possessed God; and the silence of contemplation, which had ever been her delight, was henceforth the only life of her life. Nevertheless, God wills that she should leave it, God wills that she should leave herself to communicate to others something of her fulness, and that she should do so without delay, a short time only after the Annunciation; for we read in the Gospel that it was at that very time that Mary arose in haste to go to the mountains of Juda: *Exurgens autem Maria in diebus illis abiit in montana cum festinatione in civitatem Juda.*

[1] Gen. xxii. 18.

She knew the good which God purposed to work there; she knew that it was the will of her Divine Son to sanctify His Precursor, who was to receive grace "at her voice," announcing the approach of the Word: *Ut facta est vox salutationis tuæ in auribus meis.* Mary, therefore, tears herself from the delicious repose of contemplation, to fly to the hill country: *Abiit in montana cum festinatione.* All the Saints who have been filled with the Spirit of God have had an ardent thirst for prayer, silence, and solitude; and all those who have been destined to convey to others the graces which have been lavishly bestowed upon themselves, have thirsted no less ardently to overcome themselves by forsaking interior joys for the love of their brethren. But what a difference is there between the grace of the Saints, and the plenitude of Mary's grace! What a difference between the love of the Saints, and the love of Mary for silence and contemplation! What a difference between the sacrifice made by the Saints in breaking the Divine repose of the soul in obedience to the voice of charity, and the sacrifice which Mary must have made in leaving the heaven within her heart to tread the rough, hard ways of this world! But it was the sacrifice of charity, the sacrifice of the love of souls, and she hesitates not a moment; she hastens whither the will of God calls her: *Viam mandatorum cucurri dilatasti cor meum.* She remains also with Elizabeth as long as it is the pleasure of the Word that she should abide there; Who willed that she should continue, as she had begun, the sanctification of the greatest of the Prophets.

To this example of charity Mary joins another of which we all stand greatly in need,—the example of the most profound humility in the highest exaltation. Elizabeth, enlightened by God, and full of confusion at the honour conferred upon her, says to Mary: "And whence is this to me, that the Mother of my Lord should come to me?" She says but the truth when she calls Mary "happy," and "blessed among all women;" but

Mary, more enlightened still, says nothing more than the truth when she refers all praise to God alone, the only Source of all good, of all grace, of all greatness: *Omnia ex te, et ideo in omnibus es laudandus;* and cries: " Thou praisest me, and I praise the Lord" (*Magnificas matrem Domini, sed magnificat anima mea Dominum*). Thou praisest me for the greatness to which thou seest me raised, but it is the Almighty alone Who has done these great things in me, and Who has been pleased to cast His eyes on the lowliness of His handmaiden. Mary thus reveals to us the two sources of humility: the knowledge of God, and the knowledge of ourselves; and teaches us that the most profound humility is ever the deepest truth.

Lastly, the mystery of the Visitation is a mystery of consolation, because it recalls to us most sensibly the order established by God for the communication of His graces, that order of which we have already spoken at length,[1] and of which the Visitation of Mary is the living image. All graces come from God: *Omne datum optimum et omne donum perfectum de sursum est, descendens a Patre luminum.*[2] But all graces come to us by the merits of Jesus Christ, the only Mediator of Justice between God and man, because He alone has reconciled us with God, and redeemed us by the price of His Blood. It is, nevertheless, His will that we should ask Him for these graces, and that we should also ask them for one another: *Orate pro invicem ut salvemini; multum enim valet deprecatio justi assidua,*[3] and, consequently, that the mediation of prayer or intercession should be added to the mediation of justice. Now, it is in the order of intercession that we have seen Mary to be constituted the universal Mediatrix;[4] and it is this office of love, so truly worthy of her Mother's heart, which we see her fulfil when she communicates by a word from her blessed mouth the first grace of the new covenant to the last

[1] Ch. xii. and xiii., *supra.*
[2] James i. 17.
[3] James v. 16.
[4] Ch. xii. and xiii., *supra.*

Prophet of the old. This order ordained by God has prevailed in every age; for as all the graces which have been granted to the world, have been granted to it for the sake of the merits of Jesus Christ, they have been also granted to the prayers of His Mother, and, as it were, at the voice of the second Eve, the Mother of our new life.

Prayer.

My God, I bless Thee for this order of Thy dispensation. I am full of gratitude and joy at the thought that Thou art pleased to grant me all things for the merits of Jesus, and at the prayer of Mary. My poor prayers, then, can never ascend alone. My Mother will perfect them and offer them, especially if I faithfully invoke her with childlike confidence, to obtain grace to overcome myself, and to become pleasing in Thy sight. I know, O Lord, that Thou hast prepared grace for us, to enable us to become like unto Thee by the accomplishment of Thy Divine Will. I shall certainly obtain it if I desire it for that end, if I ask it for that end: *Fiat voluntas tua.* I will ask it, then, by the "Our Father," the prayer of Thy Divine Son, to which I will always add the "Hail Mary," the sweet prayer of the universal Church, that Mary herself may offer the Lord's Prayer to Thee for me, with the perfect devotion of her own heart. Thou wilt have me, O Lord, to resemble Jesus, as Mary resembles Him; to be humble, chaste, charitable, obedient: *Fiat voluntas tua.* May Thy holy will be done in me now and always, and at the hour of my death (*nunc et in hora mortis nostræ*). Amen.

CHAPTER XX.

THE PURIFICATION OF MARY AND THE PRESENTATION OF JESUS IN THE TEMPLE.

The Mosaic law—The primitive law—The fulfilment of prophecy.

LET us open the Gospel, that we may fully receive what is there revealed concerning the mystery of the Purification and the Presentation. "And after eight days were accomplished, that the Child should be circumcised, His name was called Jesus, which was called by the angel, before He was conceived in the womb. And after the days of her purification, according to the law of Moses, were accomplished, they carried Him to Jerusalem, to present Him to the Lord. As it is written in the law of the Lord: Every male opening the womb shall be called holy to the Lord. And to offer a sacrifice, according as it is written in the law of the Lord, a pair of turtle-doves, or two young pigeons. And behold there was a man in Jerusalem named Simeon, and this man was just and devout, waiting for the consolation of Israel; and the Holy Ghost was in Him. And he had received an answer from the Holy Ghost, that he should not see death, before he had seen the Christ of the Lord. And he came by the Spirit into the Temple. And when His parents brought in the Child Jesus, to do for Him according to the custom of the law, he also took Him into his arms, and blessed God, and said: Now Thou dost dismiss Thy servant, O Lord, according to Thy word in peace; because my eyes have seen Thy salvation, which Thou hast prepared before the face of all peoples: a light to the revelation of the Gentiles, and the glory of Thy people Israel. And His father and Mother were wondering at those things which were spoken concerning Him. And Simeon blessed them, and said to Mary His Mother: Behold this Child is set for the fall, and for the resurrection of many in Israel, and for a sign which shall be contradicted. And thy own soul a sword shall pierce, that, out of many hearts, thoughts may be revealed."[1] The better to understand this passage of the Gospel, we must recall to mind those two precepts of the old law to which it refers.

By the first, every woman who had given birth to a son was forbidden to approach the sanctuary for forty days (in the case of the birth of a daughter, the time was prolonged to eighty); at the expiration of that time, before being admitted into the Temple, she was to offer a lamb as a holocaust, and a young pigeon or turtle-dove as a sin-offering. If the woman were poor, the was to offer two pigeons or doves, the one as a holocaust, the other as an expiation.[2] This positive law reminds us of the truth of which we all bear the evidence within us, the truth of our original corruption, and is founded on the natural law of the propagation of our race by generation, in virtue of which human nature is transmitted *as it is*, and thus passes from age to age, like the waters of a river which bear with them the pollution of their source. The second positive law of the old covenant referred to in the Gospel of the Purification, is that by which mothers were commanded to offer their first-born son to God and to redeem him,[3] in memory of the first-born of Israel, who were preserved by the blood of the lamb from the sword of the destroying Angel, when he struck the first-born of Egypt to overcome the obstinacy of Egyptian tyranny, and set free the first-born people of God. The consecration to God of the first-born is, however, of still higher antiquity, for they had been already destined to the priesthood under the law of nature by the primitive revelation :[4] God thus requiring the offering of the first fruits

---

[1] Luke ii. 21-35.   [2] Lev. xii.   [3] Exod. xiii.
[4] The law which is called the law of *nature*, to distinguish it from the *written* law, or the Mosaic revelation, and from the law of *grace*, preëminently so called, or the Christian revelation, is not the *purely natural* law, which would have corre-

of all things, that man might never forget the great duty of gratitude and love so well expressed in these words of the Saint: *A te recepi, recipe.* But under the written law, or by the Mosaic revelation, in the place of the first-born of all the Jews, God had made choice of the tribe of Levi from amongst the twelve, that all its male children should be consecrated to the service of the Temple. The first-born sons of the other tribes were to be presented in the Temple, and the sovereign dominion of God was to be recognised in the act of their redemption.[1]

The respective texts of the Old and New Testaments prove to demonstration that the Blessed Virgin was free from the obligation of the first of these laws. In fact, the Gospel clearly reveals to us that Mary would rather have sacrificed the privilege of the Divine Maternity than have purchased it at the price of her virginity;[2] and that when she became a Mother, she still remained a Virgin. God Himself formed the second Man by His

sponded to the state of pure nature, which might have been, but never was, the state of mankind. The real, positive state of mankind has been, first, the state of nature in its integrity and of original grace, corresponding to the supernatural destiny of man positively willed by God. In the next place, it has been the state of nature fallen and corrupt,—*corruptæ*, in the words of S. Thomas,—and mercifully restored to its original end by the grace of redemption, and that even from the beginning,—for the sacrifice of redemption was accepted in the purpose of God from the beginning of the world: *Agnus occisus ab origine mundi.* The primitive revelation, the Mosaic revelation, and the Christian revelation, are but phases of the same revelation of the Word, from His dawn until His meridian day. God spoke to our first parents and to the Patriarchs; He spoke to Moses and the Prophets; He spoke by His Son, His Incarnate Word Himself: *Multifariam, multisque modis loquens Deus patribus in prophetis, novissimè locutus est nobis in Filio quem constituit heredem universorum, per quem fecit et sæcula,* says S. Paul. Therefore our Lord Jesus Christ says in the Gospel that He did not come to destroy the Divine law, but to fulfil it: *Non veni solvere, sed adimplere.*

[1] See *Le Nouveau Testament, traduit par le P. Lallemant.*
[2] *Vide* ch. viii., *supra.*

own immediate agency in her womb, as He had formed the first man by His own immediate agency from the bosom of the earth. Mary, therefore, conceived without concupiscence by the operation of the Spirit of God alone, and brought forth without pain Him who, like a ray of light, penetrated the chaste womb of His Mother as He penetrated the door of the cenacle and the stone of the sepulchre. Now, the law of Purification, as the text of the Old Testament expressly declares, was binding upon all women who had conceived and brought forth after the manner of the other daughters of Eve.[1] It had no reference to the second Eve.

Why, then, did Mary subject herself to it?

For the same divine reason which led Jesus to subject Himself to the Mosaic law, to the rite of Circumcision, to His Precursor's Baptism of Penance, to the Presentation in the Temple, where He vouchsafed to be ransomed like the other children of Israel, and, lastly, to the sacrifice of the Cross, where He did penance for the whole human race: *Oblatus est quia ipse voluit.*[2] He Who had come down from heaven to perform that perfect and universal penance, in which we have only to partake by His grace, assumed for that purpose the likeness of a sinner: *In similitudinem carnis peccati.*[3] He declared this in answer to S. John the Baptist's exclamation: "I have need to be baptised by Thee." Jesus said: "It becometh us to fulfil all justice."[4] He became subject to the law, says S. Paul, that He might redeem them that were under the law, and bear the penalty of all our sins: *Christus nos redemit de maledicto legis, factus pro nobis maledictum.*[5]

The innocent and spotless Virgin, therefore, beholding her Son arrayed in the garb of a sinner, as the last and lowest of men (*novissimum virorum*), desired, in imitation of the Lamb of God, to subject herself, like the

---

[1] Lev. xii.   [2] Is. liii. 7.   [3] Rom. viii. 3.
[4] Matt. iii. 15.   [5] Gal. iii. 15.

last and lowest of women, to all those humiliating precepts which had no reference to her.

Jesus and Mary had another reason also for submitting to the law of presentation or redemption of the first-born. Jesus came to establish the priesthood of the New Covenant,—that perfect priesthood which was to replace the priesthood of the law of nature and of the written law,—and to be Himself the sole Source of that priesthood; the First-born of every creature,[1] the Eternal Priest according to the order of Melchisedech,[2] He willed to be offered by His Mother in the Temple, as a sign of His future oblation on the Cross, as He wills now to be offered perpetually by another Mother, even our Mother the Holy Church, on every altar in the world, in memorial of the same oblation offered once after a bloody manner on Mount Calvary.

Lastly, there was a general reason, arising from the Divine plan of redemption, for the fulfilment by Jesus and Mary of all the precepts of the law. The redemption by the Word made flesh was not to be fully manifested to the world until it should be accomplished by the life, passion, death, and resurrection of the Son of God. Until the victory of Christ over death (*Qui mortem nostram moriendo destruxit*), until His triumph over hell, which has now no power over the souls "who have a will to be set free," the mystery of salvation was to remain buried in darkness and silence, and to be revealed only to some few souls chosen by Divine Providence to be the blessed but still hidden seed of the universal Church. Thus the Divinity of the Incarnate Word and the virginity of His Mother were veiled by the virginal marriage of Joseph and Mary; thus the birth of Jesus at Bethlehem, according to the prediction of the Prophets, was indeed glorified by the Angels in heaven, by the three privileged Sages from the East, by the simple Shepherds of Palestine; but how soon was all this forgotten by the multitude, lost in the tumult of the world,

[1] Coloss. i. 15. [2] Ps. cix.

and in the pomp and pride of the Roman Empire, which was so soon, however, to be overthrown by " the stone cut from the mountain without the hand of man," to be replaced by that spiritual Empire which will have no end. Thus, on this day of Mary's Purification and of the Presentation of Jesus in the Temple, we see indeed two divinely illuminated souls, the holy old man Simeon and Anna the Prophetess, who recognised Jesus to be the Child of promise, the Glory of Israel, the Desired of nations ; but all the rest of the people in the Temple and out of the Temple beheld with supreme indifference those three poor peasants, Jesus, Mary, and Joseph, submitting to the law, and, as it were, veiled by the law ; never suspecting that Joseph, the son of David, was in reality what Joseph the Patriarch, the son of Jacob, had been but in figure, the guardian of the " Living Bread" which was to satisfy the hunger of the world ; that Mary, the daughter of David, was the Woman revealed from the beginning, the Virgin of Isaias, the Mother of Emmanuel, of God made Man ; that Jesus was the Incarnate God, annihilated for the love of us, the true Paschal Lamb, the Victim of the human race, the Light, the Salvation of nations. The time was not yet come when these nations, having been called to the faith by the Apostles of the risen Jesus, were to repeat in their chants the holy Simeon's cry of joy (*Lumen ad revelationem gentium*), and to go forth with the torch of faith in their hands, as if to greet the second Advent of Jesus.

Neither was the time yet come when all should see the full light of that truth, to which the Jews were so marvellously blind, and which the wilfully blind can alone still fail to see, that our Lord, by appearing in the Temple, which had been rebuilt after the captivity of Israel and the destruction of the Temple of Solomon, fulfilled the prophecies of Aggeus and Malachy as to the time of His appearing. " Be comforted," said Aggeus to the old men, who were comparing the second Temple with the first ; " be comforted ; for the glory of this second Temple shall be greater than the glory of the first; for in it shall the Desired of all nations appear.[1] "The Lord whom you seek," added Malachy, "and the Angel of the testament whom you desire, shall come to His temple."[2] Now, the Romans destroyed the second Temple, as the Chaldeans had destroyed the first. According to the prediction of our Lord, the second Temple was razed to the ground in punishment of the Deicide of Israel, as had been already foretold by Daniel, and this at the very time of the Incarnation of the Son of God, and as is attested at this day in the Roman Forum by the monument which paganism raised, as it supposed, to the glory of Titus, but by which it bore unconscious witness to the glory of primitive, Mosaic, and Christian truth. The Jews, therefore, ought either to deny Moses and the Prophets, or to point to the Messias who visited the second Temple, and confess that this Messias can be He alone Who not only so declared Himself to be, but Who died according to the prophecies in attestation of His mission and His Divinity; Who confirmed His word by His miracles and by His glorious accomplishment of all the ancient oracles in His person; Who promised to rise again on the third day, and Who thus arose from the tomb victorious over death, striking terror into His guards by the apparition of His Angels; Who appeared to His Apostles and Disciples, conversing with them forty days on the kingdom of God and on His Church; Who transformed poor and timid fishermen into teachers of the nations, sending forth His apostolate throughout all ages to gather together His scattered children into the bosom of the great spiritual family which adores Him, and which shall never pass away.

Yes, it is Christ, the Anointed of God, Who enters this day into His Temple; it is the Son of God, the Son of Eternity Incarnate in time; the First-born of every creature in His humanity, because He was the first decreed in the plan of Divine Providence;[3] the Lamb

[1] Agg. ii. 8.   [2] Mal. iii. 1.   [3] *Vide* ch. ii., *supra*.

without spot, of Whom the other was but a figure; the Victim of Whom all other victims were but the shadows; the Eternal Priest, of Whom all other priests were but the image, and are but the organ. He it is Who offers to-day the sacrifice which He will consummate on the Cross.

Prayer.

Lumen ad revelationem gentium! My Lord and my God, I have offered to Thee all these prayers in my name and in the name of my brethren; but suffer me now to speak to Thee alone, and to give Thee thanks for the recollection of these words, heard long ago, on the Feast of Thy Presentation, in one of the most ancient churches in Western Christendom, in the basilica which for nearly a thousand years has been the glory of the old Roman city of S. Helena, the city of Clovis, the first Christian king of the Franks; the church of Our Lady of Tournay, where I laid aside the garb of the world to assume the vestments of the sanctuary. Two hundred Levites came forth to meet Emmanuel with tapers in their hands, and the old temple reëchoed with the sound *Lumen ad revelationem gentium.* O my God, grant that the light may ever shine as then in mine eyes; grant that I may ever be consumed as then with a thirst to shed it abroad, to enlighten therewith those who know not that all the lights of earthly science are but as shadows in comparison with its glory!

And thou, my Mother, who didst lead me to the temple where I was to find thy Divine Son, remember the petition I then made to thee to offer this prayer to Him for me: *Unam petii a Domino, hanc requiram ut inhabitem in domo Domini omnibus diebus vitæ meæ.*[1] I have but one desire, one thing only do I implore—fidelity in life and death to the service of God, and to the souls for whom He died. Amen.

[1] Ps. xxvi. 1.

CHAPTER XXI.

THE PURIFICATION OF MARY (*continued*).

Humble obedience.

WE have seen the laws to which Mary submitted, and why she submitted to them. Let us now inquire what lessons she has left us by that submission, and whether we are faithful to those lessons.

The first is a lesson of humility. Our Divine Mother seems to say to us: "Why do you refuse to pass for what you are—poor sinners, deserving humiliation—when I was willing to pass for what I was not?" The chalice of humiliation is thus presented to us by our Mother's hand. Let us accept it willingly, that we may become truly humble, *i. e.* true and just; for humility is too often an empty sound when it is not tested by humiliation. *Ille est humilis*, says S. Bernard, *qui humiliationem convertit in humilitatem*[1] ("He is humble who converts humiliation into humility"). It is true we do not always deserve the humiliation for the actions on account of which the mistaken world inflicts it upon us; and it is often the effect of the injustice of men. But in such cases the injustice of men is frequently the instrument of God's justice, who permits it for the expiation of faults of which the world knows nothing. "If the world knew me as God knows me," says S. Teresa, "it would treat me far worse than it does." It is an appointment of the wisdom and the goodness of God, when a humiliation has fallen upon us which we have not directly deserved. And why? Because if this chalice had been given us to drink when we were in a state of sin, we should perhaps have interiorly rejected it, and so we should have tasted its bitterness without any merit, being destitute of grace to receive it aright; whereas, when the chalice of humilia-

[1] *In Cant.*, Sermon 34.

tion comes to us after our return to God, though not then deserved, it is lovingly accepted, and, by the aid of Divine grace, avails to expiate old faults for which we have not done sufficient penance. There is no more dreadful spectacle than a sinner in this world without the Cross; it is but too evident that justice awaits him in the next. Justice in time leads us to mercy, and restores to us by repentance the white robe of innocence: but in order to this, it is necessary that the justice of God, which is exercised externally, should be united in us to humility, the true foundation of that interior justice which we inflict upon ourselves.

The second lesson which Mary teaches us in her Purification is a lesson of obedience.

If humility is the foundation of the spiritual building in this sense, that it makes and prepares a place within us for the grace by which it is constructed, obedience is its crown, for it is charity in action: *Vos amici mei eritis, si feceritis quæ ego præcipio vobis.*[1] Obedience to the law of God is very meritorious when that law commands what order requires, and when it forbids all that is disorder, although it then commands and forbids only what we are bound to do or to leave undone, irrespective of the law; order being itself good, and the source of happiness, and disorder being evil, and the source of misery. But when God commands us something which is not obligatory of *itself*, He then seems to say to each one of us, *Amas me?* ("Do you love Me?") and will you do it for Me? Obedience then becomes wholly an act of love, and acquires an especial merit of its own. What if that which God requires of us is an heroic action, or a painful sacrifice? It will then bear some resemblance to the obedience of Mary, from whom God required, at the moment of the Presentation, the oblation of the Lamb of God, the offering of her own heart on Calvary!

This resemblance will become more perfect if no glory attend the sacrifice, if it is offered in obscurity

[1] John xv. 14.

and silence, and is unnoticed by the world. We have seen Mary perform a sublime act in the Temple, when she appeared in the sight of Heaven, the greatest, the most exalted of creatures, because God vouchsafed to choose her from among them all to be associated with Himself in offering to His justice, for the salvation of the world, the Son who was one with Himself. An ineffable greatness, which caused S. Bonaventure to exclaim: *Sic Maria dilexit mundum!* No glory attended that sublime action; it passed unheeded of men. How happy are we, therefore, when we are called to do any thing to please God unknown to the world, and for God alone! A comparison may serve to show you the value of actions thus hidden and buried in a divine and holy obscurity.

You have sometimes made use of a pair of compasses, or you have seen others make use of them. You know that by this means we draw around the same centre circles, which on that account are called concentric, and which we multiply by enlarging them. The first of these circles—the smallest, and the nearest to the centre in which we are—is called earth; the others represent the spheres which extend throughout immensity. We hear no noise except in this poor little circle of earth; there is concentrated all that men call glory and reputation. In the eyes of the Angels and Saints, that reputation and that glory are but an imperceptible point in space, an insensible moment in time, a drop of water in a shoreless ocean. If, then, you act only for this world, accounting nothing to be great and glorious but that which makes a noise here below, you are manifestly the dupe of vanity and falsehood,—you lose your time and your labour. But if from the centre of the present life, where God has placed you for your trial, you direct your thoughts, your desires, your soul, like the Divine ray which returns to its Principle through all the spheres of creation, caring nothing for the vain-glory of the day, and the noise made by the drop of water which we call

Time as it falls into Eternity,—then this time will not be lost to you, and your labours and your works will not be in vain; for God alone remembers eternally what has been done for Him, and for the love which we have given Him, as we pass through the world, He will give His own, which will not pass away: *In memoria æterna erit justus.*[1]

Do you now understand that a good intention—that is, the desire of the soul to please God by its actions and its sufferings, even the least of them—is the heavenly alchemy which changes the most trifling things into the gold of Divine love? Do you understand that the true greatness of the soul consists in its elevation above all the vain tumult of time? Do you understand the love of the Saints for the hidden life, and their anxiety to conceal as much as possible from the eyes of men the works which God does not require to be performed in the full light of day, like those which are imposed upon all by the common law, or upon each by the obligations of his state?

While Mary and Joseph, the daughter and the son of David, were offering in the Temple Him whom the inspired Psalmist had saluted as his Lord[2] a thousand years before, the city of Herod was going its usual course, and the Roman power was filling all things with the tumult of its name. No one paid any heed to the three poor peasants who were fulfilling prophecy in the Temple, and offering beforehand that sacrifice which was to be consummated on the Cross, to overthrow the pagan empire, and to change the whole face of the world. Do you think that Mary and Joseph felt the slightest pain at being accounted as nothing, or the slightest desire of being known for what they in reality were,—the confidants and the ministers of the greatest of God's works? Their soul soared far above that pain or that desire. It rose above all the spheres of creation to the throne of the Eternal God, and united before Him that contempt

[1] Psalm iii. 7.   [2] Psalm cx. 1.

to the humiliations of the Passion, having no hope but in God, and no confidence except in Him. When shall we learn to love to be despised and to be forgotten by the world? When shall we know God by His true light, the light which He grants to all who ask Him for it, and which He keeps ever burning in the hearts which ask for it day by day?

We have all continual occasions of acting and suffering for God, and of thus preparing ourselves by our lives to die also for Him. Let us not lose any of these opportunities afforded us by Divine Providence; but if opportunities of imitating the hidden life of Mary be offered to all, they are offered in a preëminent and special manner to every truly Christian mother. Her work— *i. e.* the early education of her children—is at the same time sublime and obscure. It is sublime, for God has bestowed a special honour upon mothers, by appointing them to foster, to water, and to develop the souls of their children; the germ which is to become the tree of a whole life, fruitful in good or evil for generations to come.

It is obscure, for this great work is carried on in the secret recesses of a sanctuary into which the world enters not; but if the world comes not thither, God abides therein. He regards the Christian mother as His fellow-labourer in the work dearest to His Heart, and prepares for her a heavenly and eternal reward for all that she does for Him, and for the souls created to His image.

Prayer.

Holy Virgin of virgins, thou art also the Mother of mothers; have compassion on those who know not their own greatness, or who miserably misplace it! Deliver from vain-glory the souls who are called to form other souls. Pray for them, that they may love to be unknown to the world, but to be known and loved by God. Obtain for them the respect of their children; courage never

L

to flatter the weaknesses or vices of the young souls intrusted to their care; an ardent desire to render those souls pure, chaste, laborious, and faithful; a confident hope that their prayers, their tears, and their labours will be blessed by God, though they may have to wait many long years before they see it, with the invincible patience of the great Augustine's holy mother.

Think of us also, most holy Mother of God, and obtain for us a contempt of the world and of ourselves; a contempt of every thing which can hinder the growth of true greatness of soul, and impede the love of God. Ask thy Divine Son to make us taste the joy and peace which abide in humility and obedience: in humility, which draws down grace; and in obedience, which fills our actions and our sufferings with grace by conformity to the will of God. Yes, ask Him for this, and cease not to ask it until thou beholdest us, thy children, no longer proud and rebellious, but humble and docile, now and always, and at the hour of our death. Amen.

CHAPTER XXII.

THE PRESENTATION OF JESUS IN THE TEMPLE (*continued*).

Jesus a sign to be spoken against—The sword of Mary—Faith and incredulity.

THE ruin of the first Eve began by doubt. She was attracted by curiosity to listen to the flattering promises of the spirit of falsehood; and, suffering her faith to be shaken by his audacious contradiction of the word of God,—*Ne quaquam morte moriemini*[1] ("You shall not die the death"),—ended by disbelieving and aspiring to a knowledge independent of the Divine wisdom: *Eritis sicut dii scientes*[2] ("You shall be as gods, knowing good and evil"); and thus fell into the deepest darkness.

[1] Gen. iii.   [2] Ibid.

As it was by doubt that evil entered into the world, and ignorance together with it, so it is by faith that the Supreme Good has reëntered the world, bringing light with it; for it was by believing the word of God that the second Eve gave to us the Saviour, and thus restored grace and truth to all ages: *Vidimus eum plenum gratiæ et veritatis.*[1]

Let us not be astonished at the spiritual fruitfulness of her faith, or rather at the Almighty benediction which rendered it thus divinely fruitful. Was it not by faith in the fulfilment of the promise of God, notwithstanding Sarah's age and barrenness, and against all appearance of probability, that Abraham received the blessing which made him the father of the faithful, the father of generations faithful to the belief in God their Creator, in the midst of idolatrous nations, and through the long ages of heathenism? The faith of the second Eve was incomparably more fruitful, because it was incomparably more heroic. Mary became, in fact, the Mother of the children of God in all ages, because she believed in the Divine word, which promised to render fruitful, not barrenness only, but virginity.

Therefore does the Gospel declare Mary to be blessed, because she believed: *Beata quæ credidisti.*[2]

But if her faith was thus the cause of her blessedness, one of the causes of her affliction (*Et tuam ipsius animam pertransibit gladius*[3]) was the incredulity of those among her people to whom Jesus was to be a sign to be spoken against (*in signum cui contradicetur*),[4] and the incredulity of those who to the end of time should resist the light of faith.

And this because the loss of faith or its voluntary extinction, amongst those who reject the light of Divine revelation, is the greatest of human misfortunes. If a man has lost all other virtues, he may yet find them again by the light of faith, because by faith he will dis-

[1] John i. [2] Luke i. 45.
[3] Luke ii. 35. [4] Luke ii. 34.

cover motives for loving them and means to acquire them. If hope languishes and dies within me, faith will rekindle it by reminding me of the power, the mercy, and the goodness of God towards sinners, and of His fidelity to the promises made to the prayer of those who seek before all things the kingdom of God and His justice—even the accomplishment of the Divine Will. If sin deprives my heart of grace, and with it of the life of Divine love, faith teaches me to find it again in the tears of penance, and to find those tears themselves in the sincere confession of the heart, which lays itself open in obedience to Jesus Christ. If the vanity of this world, which passes away; if the frivolity of the things which are soon to disappear; if the chain of deceptions which we call life; if this life itself, which is but a lingering death,—casts me into despondency, or overwhelms me with sadness, faith alone can console me, because faith alone can show me that all is not vanity upon earth; because in the least of the works which we offer to God, or in the lightest of the sufferings which we endure for Him, are hidden true seeds for eternity, true sources of endless life and joy. If my resignation fails under the weight of sorrow which will sometimes crush us all, faith points to the cross of redemption, and, kneeling at its foot, teaches me to embrace it, and to find there Jesus Himself, and with Him every blessing,—hope, love, repentance, peace, perseverance, and heaven. Above all, faith shows me where to find love—that heaven begun on earth. Yes, faith alone can show me where to find the only love which never deceives; the only love which disappoints not; the only love which gives infinitely more than we have ever looked for. Faith is thus the source and the root of true life (*Radix et fundamentum omnis justificationis*),[1] because to live is to love, to live well is to love well, and because he who loveth not, abideth in death (*Qui non diligit, manet in morte*).[2]

Therefore, if all the virtues and all the joys of life

[1] *Conc. Trid.*   [2] John iii. 14.

have been extinguished one after another, like the lights in a church after some glorious festival, let only faith, which is the lamp of the sanctuary, still remain alight, and its flame will suffice to rekindle them all in their former splendour.

But when that last light, that last solitary lamp, is at length extinguished, what deep and mournful darkness falls upon the soul! and by what means shall it be dispelled?

We see, then, why it is that the Gospel, having shown us Jesus as a sign to be contradicted by unbelief, immediately afterwards points to the heart of Mary transfixed by the sword of sorrow. It is because that holy Mother is afflicted, not only by the Passion of her Divine Son, but by the misery of men, who refuse to acknowledge Him as their Saviour; and if the heroism of her faith was a source of divine joy to her (*Beata quæ credidisti*), the incredulity of men was also a bitter cause of sorrow. By that joy and by that sorrow Mary has purchased the privilege of being for ever the protectress of the faith of God's children, of aiding by the might of her prayer every Christian soul in its warfare for the truth, and of giving victory to the Church over all errors, even to the end of time: *Gaude Maria Virgo cunctas hereses sola interemisti in universo mundo.*[1]

The faith has been attacked in every age, and, though in manifold ways and by various weapons, always in the same spirit. We have shown elsewhere[2] that the spirit of pride, rebellion, and falsehood is always a spirit of division. From the very beginning he has been the master of all those who have since practised that maxim of cheats: "Divide and reign." But as he cannot divide the truth in itself, his continual endeavour is to divide it in the minds of men; and it is by mutilating it, and giving it out to them in shreds and patches, that both before and since the Incarnation he has produced every

[1] *Off. B.B.V. per an.*
[2] *La Divinité de Jesus Christ, ou Le Christ et les Antechrists.*

kind of false doctrine. Being incapable of creating any thing, he has been driven to build up the structure of error out of the fragments of truth. We shall not repeat what we have said elsewhere on this subject, but shall refer our readers to one of our previous works, thus following the example of our father, S. Alphonsus, who, in his *Practice of Love to Jesus Christ*, a work more exclusively ascetic than this, has referred his readers to his apologetic writings,[1] that, according to the recommendation of the Prince of the Apostles, the faithful might be enabled to render a reason for their faith and hope.[2]

Nevertheless, if we refrain from reproducing here a picture of all the errors which have attacked the faith in ancient or modern times, we must not omit to warn the faithful against the great error which assails the faith in our day, and, consequently, endangers its existence in their souls.

That error is no longer a simple heresy, *i.e.* a doctrine which chooses between Divine truths, embracing one to reject another. It is far more than this, it is more than the doctrine of division between revealed truths; it is the doctrine of division between reason and revelation, it is the doctrine which rejects all revealed truths at once by rejecting revelation itself.

This is the error of our day. It assumes the plausible name of rationalism, because it maintains that in religion, as in all other things, man's reason is a sufficient guide; that he has no need of the Word of God; that Divine revelation is, therefore, useless to him; and that, moreover, that revelation has, and can have, no existence.

Great need, therefore, have Christians carefully to apply themselves to the study of the truth which confutes this falsehood; and to master it in a sufficient degree to enable them to defend themselves effectually from the

[1] *Prat de l'Amour envers J. C.*, ch. xv. *Charitas omnia credit.*
[2] 1 Peter iii. 15.

seductions of this doctrine of pride, as well as to defend the Divine truth of the faith against its assaults. Why should they imagine themselves incapable of this undertaking? Children, who have just finished their Catechism of perseverance, are able to give a reason for their faith. Can men of the world, then,—above all, men of the literary world,—pretend that they have neither time nor opportunity to study the subject? How little study, properly so called, is needful for the conviction of the truths necessary for all men to receive!

Is it not just because religion, the great law of human life, cannot be a privileged subject reserved for the knowledge of learned and studious men; is it not just because it cannot be left to philosophers alone, and abandoned exclusively to their laborious, and often fruitless, researches; is it not just because it must be accessible to all men,—that God, the Father of the great human family, has divinely instructed His children in its truths, thus undertaking the care of their education Himself, and carrying it on by means of a teaching authority, which bears the visible marks of a commission from Himself? Is it not on this account that religion is not only useful, but necessary to man?[1]

We have elsewhere demonstrated that in the matter of religion, the mind of man has need of a revelation from God, and of the authority to whose keeping He has intrusted it.[2]

[1] As S. Thomas shows, ii. 2, q. 2, a. 4; *Confr.* 1, q. 1, a. 1; and i. 2, q. 109, a. 2; and *Sum. Cont. Gent.*, l. 1, c. 4. . The thesis of the necessity of revelation is not the demonstration of revelation, it is but a preparation for it; it is useful, not indispensable.

[2] On the necessity of revelation, we have followed S. Thomas, vide *Quest. Relig.*, ch. i.-iii., of which the titles are as follows: "There is necessarily a certitude for the reason with regard to religion—On what conditions?—Solution by facts—Are these facts true?" We do not only find these facts in history, but each one of us finds them in himself; and these facts, which are attested by the answer of each man's conscience concerning them, are not only vague aspirations of the soul, as

But we have, moreover, proved that this revelation, continually subsisting by the authority which perpetuates and manifests it, is a living, speaking, and glorious truth, proving its own Divine origin, and proving it by its own characteristics, which it shows to be evidently supernatural to the eye of reason, by the light of reason, or according to the principle of reason itself.[1]

In this demonstration by facts, far from intending to disparage the ordinary method of demonstration by facts called motives of credibility, we have only desired to simplify it, or rather to show it as simplified by Divine Providence. We have shown, in fact, that this maternal Providence anticipates our researches, seeks us first by the authority of which it has made us feel the need, and which it has marked with its own signet; thus giving to all a motive of credibility, or a seal of the revelation quite within the reach of the simplest, and no less needful to the most learned. We had at first intended to give a short abstract here of what we had elsewhere established on this point; but we refer our readers to our former writings, because the most concise abstract must break the thread of these recollections and prayers.

Prayer.

What need, O Lord, of so many arguments to prove to the children of men, *Thy* children, that Thou hast not sent them into the world without telling them why, and without impressing upon Thy revelation a visible

---

some French writers have supposed, but facts of the most positive nature. See the chapter on the *Quest. Relig.*, and our *Lettres à l'Ami de la Religion*, pp. 71-82, 190-195, 295-297, " Des Lett. Théolog."

[1] S. Thomas, *Quest. Relig.*, ch. iv., of which the following is the title: " Is it difficult for reason to discern the true religion ?" We there see the fact of revelation demonstrated to reason to be divine, according to the principles of reason. This has always been the practice of Christian apologists, after the example of our Divine Master, Who Himself said, *Operibus credite.*

character of authenticity? O my God, I believe that Thou didst speak to our first father; that Thou didst converse with the Patriarchs of old; that Thòu didst rebind the chain of primitive tradition by the second primitive family, by the fathers of the three great races in which mankind lived anew after the deluge. When the nations lost faith, and broke the tradition of patriarchal authority, Thou didst raise, as a divine protest against their defection, a living monument of the primitive revelation and the original promise, in a people placed by Thy merciful Providence at the centre and the confluence of the great empires of the earth. Thence were uttered those prophetic sounds which were heard by all the nations,—by Egypt and Assyria, by Persia, Greece, and mighty Rome,—until He came of Whom the prophets spoke, and Whose kingdom shall never pass away: *Multifariam, multisque modis loquens olim Deus patribus in prophetis: novissime, diebus istis locutus est nobis in Filio, quem constituit hæredem universorum, per quem fecit et sæcula.*[1] Then it was, O Lord, that, becoming Incarnate in the midst of time, Thou didst repeat and fulfil that primitive word which the world had often forgotten, but which had never forgotten the world.

Yes, my God, Thou hast spoken to us in all times, and Thou hast made Thy word to pass, as Thou makest life to pass, not immediately from Thyself to each one of us, but from father to son, from generation to generation; thus transmitting the truth, not as a secret to the initiated, but as the public heritage of all Thy children. Thou spakest to the father of the whole race, Thou spakest to the Patriarchs, Thou spakest to Moses and the Prophets, and Thou didst come according to Thy promise to speak to us Thyself, intrusting to the perpetual Apostolate the word spoken for all nations and for all times. Thou hast never left us since without that life-giving word, of which the world stands in con-

[1] Heb. i. 1.

tinual need. Thou didst say to the word which was to live for ever: "As My Father hath sent Me, I send thee" (*Sicut misit me Pater et Ego mitto vos*).[1] And why? *Prædicate evangelium omni creaturæ*[2] ("to teach the Gospel to every creature"); to teach all nations by word of mouth (*Docete omnes gentes*).[3] But for how long? All days, even to the consummation of the world.[4] And with what power? With Thine, O Lord, with Thy Divine power, assured for ever, and without interruption, to the divine teaching authority always, even to the end: *Ecce Ego vobiscum sum omnibus diebus usque ad consummationem sæculi.*[5]

Yes, I recognise Thee, O God of love and truth! well do I recognise Thee in this Thy work. When blind incredulity bids me listen to myself alone as to what awaits me in the invisible and eternal future, I have but to listen to it to know that it lies: for no sooner do I cast my eyes upon the awful abyss of the future life, than my sight fails, and this cry breaks from my soul: "Speak to me Thyself, O Lord" (*Loquere, Domine, quia audit servus tuus*).[6] When the multitude of sects would send me to Holy Scripture, saying: "Read, compare the translations with the original, and then compare the translations together; examine the thousand different ways in which we have interpreted them; and then judge for yourself,—it is the only way of salvation,"—I know at once they lie, for they ask me to do what is impossible, and I see by the same evidence which proves to me the existence of God that this is not His way of saving man. No; Thou hast not abandoned our souls to our disputations, O Lord, as Thou hast left the world. The world goes on without us, and recks not of our errors; but, lest we should go astray, we have need, O Lord, that Thou shouldst enlighten us Thyself: *Lucerna pedibus meis verbum tuum.*[7] We have need of Thy

[1] John xx. 21.   [2] Mark xvi. 15.   [3] Matt. xxvi. 19.
[4] Matt. xxviii. 20.   [5] Ibid.   [6] 1 Kings iii. 9.
[7] Psalm cxviii. 105.

living word, that the dead letter in the hands of our ignorance become not to us a labyrinth and a snare. Yes, I know, apart from all disputations, by my own misery, and by Thy goodness, that a word which leads only to questions, and which comes not to me with power to resolve them (*sicut potestatem habens*[1]), cannot come from Thee. But how plainly do I recognise Thy presence in Thy Church, when I behold her and listen to her! What other authority upon earth can go back to the origin of time, and show me the chain of her great history from age to age? What other authority upon earth bears on its forehead Thy true signet, the mark of that supreme unity which is mistress, not only of time, but of space and events; passing, always the same, through the troubled waves of human thought and passion? What other teaching authority speaks truly to all nations, waters with the blood of her Apostles the word which she sends forth through the two worlds, offers the Eternal Sacrifice in every region under heaven, and chants the symbol of her faith in every language of mankind? When did paganism ever attempt to proselytise us to its teaching? It knows not even the name of the love of man, and counts every foreigner to be an enemy. When did Islamism come to convert us to the Koran? It slays, indeed, to establish its empire; but where are its martyrs for truth and for the love of souls? I find barbarism, O Lord Jesus, wherever Thy word is rejected. But where, even according to the judgment of the world, are light and life, save only where Thou art adored? What other teaching than Thine, what other doctrinal authority than that of Thy Church, unchangeable and undecaying, ever ancient yet ever new, remains ever younger than all that passes away, because it alone is immortal? What other spiritual power can tell me what I am; can teach me whence come suffering and death, and what is their source; whence comes the evil that is in me, and what is its remedy? Above all,

[1] Matt. vii. 29.

what other power can give us with that remedy the assurance of its efficacy, and say to us, *Taste* (*Gustate*), see (*videte*), behold its effects in the *life* and the *works* of them who receive it?

I affirm in Thy presence, O Lord, that wert Thou not here, Thou wouldst be nowhere in this world; and if the Catholic Church were not Thy work, Thou wouldst have deceived us by suffering Thy authority to be usurped by a lie, and letting it work wonders in our eyes, which Thou only canst do, and which no power of man could effect.

But I believe in Thee, my God; and because I believe in Thee, I recognise and acknowledge Thee in Thy Church.

And thou, Mother of the Universal Church, because thou art the Mother of the " Author and Finisher of our faith;"[1] Mary, ever " blessed because thou didst believe," pray for me that I may live and die in this Catholic faith of the Patriarchs and the Prophets, the Apostles and Martyrs, the Confessors, Virgins, and Saints of all ages. Amen.

CHAPTER XXIII.

THE FEAST OF THE COMPASSION OR THE SORROWS OF MARY.

Faith, hope, love, sorrow, patience, conformity to the will of God.

THE Church celebrates this Feast on the Friday which immediately precedes Holy Week, as if to prepare us to compassionate together with Mary the Passion of her Divine Son. But as if she feared that we should be prevented by the exercises of holy Lent from fixing our attention and our memory fully and faithfully upon the sorrows of the Blessed Virgin, she commemorates them a second time upon the third Sunday in September,

[1] Heb. xii. 2.

when she says to all her children, "Forget not the tears and sighs of your Mother" (*Gemitus matris tuæ ne obliviscaris*).[1]

The children of Mary will not, therefore, be surprised that, having already spoken of the nature, the greatness, and the unapproachable intensity of their Mother's sorrows,[2] we now recall them again, and speak to them once more of that Mother who is no less Queen of Martyrs than Queen of Virgins : first Rose of martyrs, first Lily of virgins (*martyrum prima rosa, virginumque lilium*).[3] The memory of the sorrows of Mary, if they faithfully cherish it, will prove to them a certain source of great and innumerable graces.

First, it will be to them the source of faith, of that unchangeable faith of which Mary is the most heroic example. The Apostles had been terrified, crushed by the Passion of Jesus. S. John, Mary of Cleophas, and Mary Magdalen—virginity, fidelity, and the second innocence which is restored by the baptism of tears—alone bore Mary company at the foot of the Cross.

The other disciples had fled, and doubt had glided into their saddened hearts. All the lights of their soul had gone out at the storm which fell upon them in the death of their Master. They remembered no more His Divine lessons, or His almighty power, or the multitudes whom He had healed by a word or a sign, or the dead who had been awakened by His voice, or the prophecies which He had just fulfilled, or the Cross which He had Himself predicted, or the promises of the victory and eternal triumph which were to follow His death. But John, Magdalen, and Mary Cleophas were faithful to Jesus because they did not separate themselves from Mary. No sorrow was ever like to the sorrow of that Divine Mother, nor did such bitter tears ever fall from any human eye as those which she shed when she gazed at her Son upon the Cross, suspended between heaven and earth for the reconciliation of the world

[1] *Off. Sept. dol. Dom.*, 3 Sept. [2] *Vide* ch. x., *supra*.
[3] *Off. Sept. dol. Dom.*, 3 Sept.

("*Deus erat in Christo mundum reconcilians sibi*") ;[1] and when she heard from the mouth of the great Victim that cry which revealed at what cost He had redeemed the world: *Deus, Deus meus, ut quid dereliquisti me ?*[2] ("My God, My God, why hast Thou forsaken Me?") If the Disciples, who were so discouraged by the Passion as to say one to another, "We hoped that it was He Who should have redeemed Israel,"[3] had heard that cry of utter desolation, what would they have thought of their Master? Yet Mary heard it, and her faith remained firm, immovable; standing, as it were, erect in her soul, as she herself stood at the foot of the Cross (*stabant juxta crucem*).[4] She heard that cry of suffering Humanity, yet she ceased not to adore as God the Word Who for our salvation had come down from heaven into her womb; and she believed that if the Divinity of her Son abandoned His Sacred Humanity in its punishment, it was in order not to abandon the human race in its fault: *Est derelictus in pœnis, ne nos derelinqueremur in culpis*.[5] Far more enlightened than Moses and all the Prophets, Mary had seen the accomplishment in herself of that word from heaven which realised all promises and all prophecies; Mary knew herself to be the Woman blessed among all women, the Virgin of Isaias, the ever-Virgin Mother of Immanuel,—God made man. But as her faith was enlightened above the faith of all others, it was tried also above the measure of all others, and it remained, nevertheless, firm and immovable. She is our model. God will never permit our faith to "be tried above our strength;"[6] but He will, perhaps, permit it to be tried in proportion to the light which He bestows upon us. Let us remember those Divine illuminations "in the hour of darkness"[7] and of "the power" of falsehood; let us remember that "in God there is not Yes

[1] 2 Cor. v. 19.   [2] Matt. xxvii. 46.
[3] Luke xxiv. 21.   [4] John xix. 25.
[5] Simon de Cass., *De Gest. Salv.*, l. 13, c. 116.
[6] 1 Cor. x. 13.   [7] Luke xxii. 53.

and No, but unchangeable truth;"[1] and with a faith standing steadfast under the interior cross, let us repeat with firmness and confidence: I believe in Jesus Christ, "my Lord and my God."[2] I believe all that is taught me by the Church, which He has sealed with the inimitable signet of His Divine authority and His Divine unity. Yes, let us repeat this with victorious constancy; for the Church is no less manifestly marked in our eyes by the seal of her Divine mission than Mary was marked in her own eyes by the seal of the Divine promises and their fulfilment.

But the Mother of Sorrows is not only a source of faith to us in the Passion of her Son; she is also a fountain of tears. An ancient writer bids a child, still too young to feel its misfortune, at least to weep in imitation of its mother:

> "Si tua nondum funera sentis,
> Matris fletus imitare tuæ."

These tears will be at first tears of compassion, but they will soon become tears of contrition and love; as in Mary also they were tears of love and of bitter sorrow at the sight of the sins of mankind which required such an expiation, and of the sickness of our souls which called for such a remedy. Mary, transfixed for us by the sword which made her the Queen of Martyrs, will teach us to read in the Wounds of Jesus,—torn and broken for our sins, nailed to the Cross, crowned with thorns, dying desolate and forsaken,—the blackness of the stain which covers us, which could be effaced only by the Blood of God; the depth of our corruption, which could be fathomed only by the hand of God, the hand of the Author of nature—which He created by His power, but which He came to heal by His weakness. Mary will teach us to love Him Who vouchsafed thus to bear the sins of the world, and to weep over our offences against

---

[1] 2 Cor. i. 18-20.
[2] *Dominus meus et Deus meus!* (John xx. 28.)

a God thus infinite in love, in greatness, in tenderness, and in majesty.

She also will teach us patience, the true virtue of virtues, because it is the crown of them all: suffering being, after all, the true mistress of life, and its inevitable end. If this miserable life of ours could not be offered in expiation,—if it could not be offered by love and rendered meritorious by patience,—it would have indeed no meaning, it would be but a grotesque mystery. But Mary at the foot of the Cross, the second Eve standing upon Calvary, bids us read in Jesus the meaning of that mysterious life, teaches us to suffer with Him and for Him, to bear our crosses in a spirit of penance, with a full faith and entire confidence in their divine fruitfulness; nay, to embrace them with love, in memory of the spotless Lamb Who suffered so bitterly for us, and of our Immaculate Mother, who shared all His sufferings.

Lastly, constant devotion to the sorrows of Mary will bring down upon us a last benediction at the hour of our death. The most holy Virgin is the Mother of a good death, because she witnessed the death of the First Fruit of the elect. She is the Mother of a good death, because it was at the moment of the most bitter death of Jesus that the sword of sorrow pierced through the depths of her soul. She is the Mother of a good death, because when she gazed upon Jesus voluntarily forsaken in His last agony, she obtained for those who invoke her the grace never to die forsaken, but to breathe their last sigh in faith, love, penitence, and hope.

Prayer.

Mother of love and sorrow, I hope to obtain of Jesus, by thy prayers, a true contrition for my sins. I will renew this act by asking it of Him daily for thy sake, but especially when I approach the Sacraments, that I may confess my sins with a truly humble and contrite heart.

" Eia Mater, fons amoris,
Me sentire vim doloris
Fac, ut tecum lugeam."

Yes, my Mother, thou wilt teach me to say to Jesus in spirit and in truth :

My God, who is like unto Thee? Who has loved me like Thee? Who desires, like Thee, the love of my heart? Art Thou not my Creator and my Father? Art Thou not my Brother by Thy Incarnation, the Victim of Thy love for me by Thy Divine Passion, the true Spouse of my soul in the adorable Eucharist? O God of my childhood, only Light of my life which has never deceived me, only Love which has never betrayed me, how can I have ever forgotten the days passed in the liberty of Thy children,—days of innocence, grace, and peace,—to go far from Thee (*in regionem longinquam*) to become a slave? Why did I forsake Thee, the source of living waters, to quench my thirst in broken and polluted cisterns? Father, I have sinned, sinned against heaven and before Thee; for thy fatherly eyes have been ever fixed upon me. I have slighted Thy greatness, I have insulted Thy Majesty in Thy very presence, I have resisted Thy will, I have despised Thy love by preferring that of vile creatures before it, I have lost Thy grace, I have polluted my heart,.I have made myself hateful in Thy sight; and yet, O Lord, Thou hast borne with me, Thou hast waited for me, Thou hast recalled me. Thou hast said to me over and over again, "Return, return, and I will not reject thee." Behold me, then, my Father and my God—behold me weeping at Thy feet and loving Thee still. But grant that I may love Thee as I did in times past, that I may love Thee more than in times past,—that I may love Thee more and more; and that, having recovered Thy love, I may never again return to the mire from which I have been delivered by Thy grace, nor fall again into the abyss whence Thy omnipotence has drawn me forth. And thou, Mary, Mother of true and holy love (*Mater pul-*

chræ dilectionis),[1] obtain for me this love which I desire, and without which I cannot live.

> "Fac ut ardeat cor meum
> In amando Christum Deum,
> Ut sibi complaceam."

Obtain it for me, that, after having wounded the Heart of God and caused the sufferings of Jesus, I may thirst to suffer in my turn for Him Whom I have so deeply offended.

> "Sancta Mater, istud agas,
> Crucifixi fige plagas
> Cordi meo valide.
> Tui Nati vulnerati,
> Tam dignati pro me pati,
> Pœnas mecum divide."

Grant, above all, that, as I have caused His death by my evil life, I may find my true life by dying for Him, and as He died, patient and resigned, accepting and desiring death as an expiation for my sins, and for the accomplishment of the will of my Father and my God.

> "Fac ut portem Christi mortem,
> Passionis fac consortem,
> Et plagas recolere."

And Thou, my Saviour and my God, Who wouldst die forsaken, but not by Thy Mother, because her presence at the foot of Thy cross was to Thee an increase of agony, and caused her to share with Thee the burden of my redemption,—I beseech Thee, by virtue of Mary's presence at Thy death, that she may be present also at mine; and that, having obtained for me the grace to live in union with Thee, she may obtain for me, also, to die in union with Thy death,—both to expiate my sins, and to accomplish the will of my Father and my God.

Mary, Mother of grace and mercy, thou wilt then protect me in the last conflict with the enemy of my soul,

[1] Eccles. xxiv. 24.

and wilt receive that soul to present it thyself before its Judge.

"Maria Mater gratiæ,
Mater misericordiæ,
Tu nos ab hoste protege,
Et hora mortis suscipe. Amen!"[1]

CHAPTER XXIV.

PREPARATION FOR THE FESTIVALS OF MARY.

WE have seen that the Festivals of Mary recall to us the principal events of her life, and thus become the light of ours, because they reveal to us the dispositions of her soul, and her fidelity to all Divine graces, throughout the hardest trials and the most cruel sufferings. Thus her true children are careful to prepare themselves for her Festivals, in order to obtain, by their Mother's intercession, the grace to follow her example. Each will follow herein his own attraction; for it is not of one virtue only that Mary is, after Jesus, our most perfect pattern.

It has been said that the Gospel is reserved with regard to Mary. It is so in words, because the Sacred Text respects the great work of God, whose glory was all interior here below; but that reserve is no less full of meaning and of revelations of the mind of God. In the narrative of the Annunciation, the humility of the Blessed Virgin is shown to be no less profound than her love of virginity is invincible; and her magnanimity equals them both; for Mary knew well at what price she was to give to the world the Victim of our redemption.

In the Mystery of the Visitation, charity and humi-

---

[1] THE ASSUMPTION.—For the Festival of the Assumption, see chapter xi. "The glory of Mary: Mary glorified in body and in soul."

lity vie with each other. The one brings grace to earth, and the other returns all the glory of it to Heaven, by that incomparable Canticle of the ecstatic humility of the Mother of God, which shall reëcho in the songs of the Universal Church even unto the consummation of all things.

In the Mystery of the Purification, we know not which is the most touching,—the poverty of the daughter of kings, or her entire submission to laws which had no relation to her; 'that perfect obedience which asks not the reason of a command, but accomplishes it for the love of God, Who gives it, and Whose will alone it desires.

In the Mystery of her Compassion, the faith of the Queen of Patriarchs, Prophets, and Apostles shines forth in equal glory with the patience of the Queen of Martyrs, the confidence, firmness, and heroic love, the tearful constancy, of the Queen of all Saints, the Mother of all penitent sinners.

From her Immaculate Conception, in which God prepared her to become in time the Mother of His Eternal Son; from her Nativity, when her fidelity to the grace of her vocation began to appear; from her Presentation in the Temple, when the second Eve gave herself for ever to God; until her Assumption, when God removed her from earth to clothe her in heaven with the very glory of her Son—*Signum magnum apparuit in cœlo, mulier amicta sole*[1]—her whole life was a mirror of the life of Jesus Christ—*Speculum justitiæ*—and a living model of our own; not in the sense that we shall ever equal it—God forbid that we should have such a thought! —but in the sense that we should endeavour to copy it according to our vocation, and according to the grace which God prepares for us; a grace which is always far above our power to comprehend.

Let us, then, resolve so to prepare for the Festivals of Mary, that we may obtain, through her, grace to

[1] Apoc. xii. 1.

imitate those among her virtues which God especially requires of us.

This preparation has been to many souls the source of the most signal graces and illuminations. We could quote many examples of this truth; but let each of our readers try to prepare for the Festivals of Mary, and he will have the consolation of attesting it by his own blessed experience. To encourage him the more effectually to make this trial, we will relate a fact, of which we are as certain as if it had happened to ourselves.

A young man, who had just finished his studies, had begun to write in the journals of the day. It was in 1830 and 1831; a troubled time, when kingdoms were unmade and remade, to be unmade again. Our young man was full of faith, and proud of his faith. He mingled the defence of Christianity with that of the interests which had then possession of the press; but he was naturally unable to do it with the knowledge and maturity necessary to the promotion of so great a cause. His temptation, however, was to remain in public life. He had not shaken it off, when he happened to be present, on the 21st of July 1831, at the entry of a king into his capital. As he stood upon a balcony, he saw the sovereign pass, amid the enthusiastic applauses of his people; the crowd following the monarch like the waves of a roaring sea. Silence and solitude soon fell upon the deserted street, and the young politician re-entered a brilliant drawing-room, where his grave and thoughtful air excited the raillery of the guests. He was saying within his heart: "I will devote myself to an eternal cause, and to a King who passes not away."

In the following year he was at the Seminary, in obedience to an attraction to which the fascination of politics had caused him for a time to close his ears. He found in the sanctuary the peace and cheerfulness which he had lost, and learned that when we leave the world for God, we find in God what we seek in vain in the world. The more serious studies helped to excite his love for a more simple piety; and amongst the books which he used, there were two which shared his preference with the *Imitation;* the first was S. Alphonsus Liguori's *Practice of Love towards Jesus Christ*, and the second the *Glories of Mary*, by the same holy author.

In the latter he had learned to prepare for the Festivals of the holy Mother of God. The Feast of the Visitation had been especially dear to him ever since his ordination to the diaconate. He desired the grace fruitfully to proclaim the Word of God; and he beheld, in the Visitation of Mary, Jesus Christ sanctifying His Precursor by the voice of His Mother, and thus preparing him for the sublime ministry to which he was called: *Et tu, puer, propheta Altissimi vocaberis: præibis enim ante faciem Domini parare vias ejus: ad dandam scientiam salutis plebi ejus, in remissionem peccatorum eorum.*[1] He prepared himself, then, for this Feast, in order to obtain the grace which he desired,—to spread the knowledge of Jesus Christ, and to win souls to Him. To that end, he made use of the Novena of S. Alphonsus on the Litanies of the Blessed Virgin, which is so full of sweetness and unction. On the seventh day—the 29th of June, the Feast of SS. Peter and Paul—he read the Meditation, the third point of which explains this invocation, "Gate of Heaven" (*Janua cœli*). Most assuredly he had neither vision nor ecstasy; nevertheless, an hour or two of that day's Festival elapsed at the feet of our Lord in the Blessed Sacrament, without his perceiving how the time had fled. What he did clearly perceive, when the bell recalled him to himself, was, that the life of religion, combined with the life of the priesthood, was to be to him the way of salvation and the gate of heaven. In the Meditation and Prayer of S. Alphonsus there was not the slightest allusion to that vocation; yet the seminarist—who, on his part, had no thought of the kind—had seen, felt, and tasted nothing but this.

[1] Luke i. 76, 77.

He spoke of what had passed to the director of his conscience, and received this reply: "The confidence which you have reposed in me obliges me to tell you that it is the intention of your bishop that you should follow the course of higher studies just organised. You will be ordained priest in the following year, in the new establishment; and if, after that year of trial, you persevere in your resolution, you will be free to follow it." He passed that year in the place whither he was sent. The passion for knowledge had not stifled the voice which had spoken to him at the foot of the tabernacle; but it had in some degree weakened its echo within his soul, and cooled his desire to follow it; when, on the Feast of the Conversion of S. Paul, the young priest, after having offered the Holy Sacrifice, became conscious of his tepidity, and besought the Apostle to obtain for him that the knowledge which puffs up should never obtain the mastery in his heart over the knowledge of God. As he left the chapel in which he had celebrated the Holy Mass, he saw the director of the college coming towards him with a book in his hand. "Have you ever," said the good priest, " read any thing more beautiful than this?" and he read to him in the Life of S. Alphonsus these words, addressed by the Saint to the first companions of his apostolical labours, when he delivered to them the rules of his institute on occasion of their first taking their vows, 21st of July 1752, after the first Vespers of S. Mary Magdalen, the patroness of sinners:

"You are called to follow the footsteps of Jesus Christ, and to carry on His sacred ministry among men. After the example of S. Paul, whose apostolate you are to share, you must be able to show yourselves as the imitators of your God, and the models of the highest Christian perfection; henceforth you must embrace, without hesitation, the most generous sacrifices. It was to save souls that Jesus Christ offered Himself as a Holocaust to His Eternal Father. As you also desire to save these souls redeemed by the price of His adorable Blood, offer yourselves in like manner to the Lord; offer all that you are and all that you have: your body, by the vow of chastity; your mind, your heart, your will, your liberty, by the vow of obedience; all your earthly possessions, by the vow of poverty; sacrificing even the hope of any possible return to the world or its pomps by the vow of perseverance, and thus renouncing all its vanities. Die to the world, die to yourselves; live for God alone, and take Him truly for the only portion of your inheritance, by vowing to observe the holy rules which I present to you in His name, for His glory, and for your own, and for that of a multitude of elect souls throughout eternity. Stript thus of yourselves and of all that is earthly, you will have less to fear, in the course of your apostolic labours, from your own weakness and the corruption of the world. Being truly men of God, because you will belong wholly and of your own free will to Him, you will be invested with a divine power for the conversion of the nations; and you will behold the miracles of the days of old renewed at your voice in the souls of men. Yes, you will thus save a multitude of souls, and you will save your own; for no means are so mighty for your own salvation as the vows which I bid you pronounce. Oh, if you did but know their value, with what joy and eagerness would you make them! The vows are a divine buckler in the hands of the religious against the assaults of the devil; a buckler given to him by God to shelter his vocation from his natural inconstancy, and to secure his perseverance in the service of the Lord; they are a salutary anchor cast into the harbour: though the tempest be unchained, though the sea foam in its fury, he shall never be wrecked. Fixed by his vows in tranquil confidence in God, the religious will have little to fear from the storms and dangers of life."[1] S. Paul had replied directly to the prayer which had been addressed to him,

[1] *Vie de S. Alphonsus,* par Jeanend, 3me. partie, ch. i.

and the effect of that reply, so divinely to the purpose, was to restore the desire of our young priest for the religious life to all its original fervour. He wrote then to his Superiors, and received a reply which was at first unfavourable,—a last trial, which did not disturb him; for he had no sooner finished reading his letter than he opened the Epistles of S. Paul at the passage to which his daily studies had brought him, when his eye fell at once upon this passage:

Currebatis bene: quis vos impedivit veritati non obedire? Persuasio hæc non est ex eo, qui vocat vos[1] (" This cometh not from Him Who calleth you").

Having compared the rules of different religious institutes, and consulted various ecclesiastics, both secular and regular, in obedience to that rule of Christian prudence which bids us test our interior attraction by mature reflection, the young theologian set out, at the end of the year of probation, for the novitiate of the Order which he had always preferred.

He arrived there about nine o'clock on a summer's evening; which corresponded perfectly with the happy and tranquil state of his soul at reaching the long-desired haven. As he waited for the porter to answer the bell, the young traveller had time to look about him. But his eyes sought nothing further when they had read this old inscription, carved on the stone of the convent-gateway:

"Mater Dei,
Sis intranti,
Janua Cœli!"

(" Mother of God, be thou the Gate of Heaven to him who enters here!")

He had a struggle to restrain his tears, that he might not appear sorrowful when his heart was overflowing with joy. Mary had, then, long ago chosen the hour when he was invoking her as the Gate of Heaven to

[1] Gal. v. 7, 8.

draw him to the haven where she would one day show him that he had not invoked her in vain; and that it was indeed her own hand which had brought him safely thither.

That loving Mother was not content with showing him this double mark of tenderness, which she had reserved for her child who had kept faithfully to himself the secret of the "Gate of Heaven," and she bestowed it upon him on the day of his religious profession. He was listening attentively that day, in the midst of his religious brethren, to a passage of the *Glories of Mary*, a few lines of which are read in the institute he had entered, at the beginning of the evening meal, before the lecture from Ecclesiastical History or from the Lives of the Saints. The lines were as follows:

"Oh, what strong reasons have the servants of Mary for believing in their own predestination! The Church herself encourages this belief when she puts into the mouth of Mary these words from Ecclesiasticus: 'I have sought my rest on all sides, and I abide in the inheritance of the Lord' (*In omnibus requiem quæsivi, et in hæreditati Domini morabor*). Cardinal Hugo says in his Commentary: 'Blessed is he in whom Mary shall find rest' (*Beatus in cujus domo B. Virgo requiem invenerit*). So great is Mary's love for men, that she seeks to implant her love in the hearts of all; but there are many who refuse to receive it, or care not to preserve it. Blessed is he who receives and preserves it. 'I will abide in the inheritance of the Lord' (*Et in hæreditati Domini morabor*); 'that is,' says Pacciuchelli, 'in those who are the inheritance of the Lord' (*id est, in illis qui sunt hæreditas Domini*). Devotion to Mary is persevering in all those who are the inheritance of the Lord; that is, who shall belong to Him for all eternity. 'He who created me,' continues Mary, in the passage just quoted from Ecclesiasticus, 'has vouchsafed to come and rest in my bosom, and has ordained that I should come and dwell in the heart of all His elect (of whom

Jacob was a figure, and who are the inheritance of the Virgin); and He has decreed that all the predestinate should put their trust in me, and should be my servants' (*Qui creavit me, requievit in tabernaculo meo, et dixit mihi: in Jacob inhabita, et in Israel hæreditare, et in electis meis mitte radius*).

"Oh, how many souls, now in the enjoyment of the blessedness of heaven, would never have attained it without the intercession of Mary! 'I have made an eternal light to shine from heaven' (*Ego feci in cœlis ut orietur lumen indeficiens*). Cardinal Hugo interprets this passage of Ecclesiasticus by saying, that Mary has made to arise as many eternal lights in heaven as she has servants there; adding, that there are many Saints in heaven who would never have entered it but for her intercession: *Multi sancti sunt in cœlis intercessione ejus, qui nunquam ibi fuissent nisi per eam.*

"S. Bonaventure says, that all those who trust in the intercession of Mary shall behold the gate of heaven opened to admit them: *Qui sperabit in illa, porta cœli reserabitur ei.* S. Ephrem has called the devotion to the Blessed Virgin the key of paradise: *Reseramentum cœlestis Jerusalem.*[1] And the pious Louis of Blois says to Mary: 'O my Queen, to thee are intrusted the keys of the treasure-house of heaven' (*Tibi regni cœlestis claves thesaurique commissi sunt*).[2] We ought, therefore, to repeat to her continually the prayer of S. Ambrose: 'O Mary, open to us the door of paradise, of which thou hast the keys' (*Aperi nobis, O Virgo, cœlum cujus claves habes*); but art not thou thyself the door, according to the words of Holy Church: *Janua Cœli?*"

Our young religious wanted nothing more to enable him to recognise with superabundant clearness the hand of his Mother in the whole course of the interior history of his vocation; and from that hour he has been accustomed to say to the Blessed Virgin: "Once more, my

---

[1] *Orat. de Laud. Virg.*
[2] *Par. an. Fid.*, p. 2, end; 1 *ad Mar.*

good Mother! once more! for if thou dost not come to me again at my last moment, thou wilt not be truly the Gate of Heaven to me. Finish, then, thy work, and suffer not thyself to be overcome by my ingratitude. Faithful Virgin, be more faithful than I. Mother of Mercy, be more merciful than I am miserable. I wait for thee, then, Mary; I wait for thee at the hour of my death."

Prayer.

O my God, there are truly more things in heaven and earth than the blind ones of this world believe; and if we were all more like children, we should find Thee to be still more our most loving Father. But Thou hast not contented Thyself with being our Father by creation, and by Thy providential care; Thou hast vouchsafed also to become our Brother in Redemption, to become even the Spouse of our souls in the Sacrament of Life. And to encourage us to come to Thee with confidence, Thou hast given to us a Mother, whose spotless heart supplies all that is wanting to our prayers to render them effectual with Thee. Which of us has ever had recourse to that heart, which is Thy work, O my God, without quickly feeling that he has been heard? Who has ever said to Mary, Pray for me, but has speedily known that her maternal prayer has ascended for him to Thee, and has not ascended in vain? Oh, if we did but pay attention to all which passes within us and without us, by the action of Thy Providence! if we had but the memory of the heart, how many anniversaries should we all have to keep in memory of the long chain of Thy mercies to us! Suffer me not, O Lord, ever to be of the number of those who ungratefully forget Thy favours; and make me ever to remember that the name of Mary has been mingled with all Thy mercies to me.

I remember it, O my Mother; and do not thou forget me! Amen.

CHAPTER XXV.

SATURDAY: MARY'S DAY.

ACCORDING to a very ancient custom, the Church renders an especial homage to the Mother of God on Saturday.

Ecclesiastics recite on that day a special Office of the Blessed Virgin, priests celebrate the Holy Mass under her invocation, and the faithful also sanctify this day to their Mother by some work of piety, charity, or penance.

In the tenth century, S. Peter Damian speaks of this custom as anciently established; and, as it would be difficult to assign a period for its origin, it is probable that Saturday was considered as Mary's great day from the earliest ages of the Church.

And for what reason?

The holy doctor whom we have just cited sees no reason for astonishment that the day of the Creator's rest should have been consecrated to Mary; "for it was in her," says he, "that the Divine Wisdom rested when He came to restore His work" (*Sabbathum enimvero, quod requies interpretatur, satis congruæ Beatissimæ Virgini dedicatur, nam sapientia in ea per humanitatis assumptæ mysterium velut in sacratissimo lectulo requievit*).[1]

The idea of S. Peter Damian suggests to us another, which simply carries it out. The Incarnation is the crown, the true end of the works of God. By it, the Word, Who freely gave being to all creatures, freely gives Himself to His creature, comes to rest in His work, and to cause His works to rest in Himself, by the Hypostatic Union, the Tabernacle of which was the chaste womb of Mary. The day of the supreme rest of God, and of the rest of creation in God, is therefore truly the day of Mary.

Other writers prefer other reasons, and think, for

[1] B. Petrus. Dam., Opusc. 33, ch. iii. and iv.

example, that this day was consecrated to the Blessed Virgin because on the Saturday which intervened between the Death of Jesus and His Resurrection, Mary alone preserved in her heart a full and unchangeable faith in her Son's Divinity. We could not, however, affirm that the faith was absolutely extinct in the souls of the Apostles and disciples; it is impossible, at least, to doubt that it still lived in the heart of S. John and of S. Mary Magdalen, according to the observation of Bellarmine, and of the learned Pope Benedict XIV. But it is by no means necessary to suppose the extinction of the faith in the hearts of the disciples of Jesus to understand the reason of the consecration of the Saturday to the remembrance of the victorious faith of the Mother of God. It is undeniable, in fact, that in every heart but the heart of Mary, the faith was either shaken, as in the case of several of the Apostles and disciples, or depressed and troubled, as with Mary Magdalen herself, who said in her anguish, as she stood by the empty sepulchre, "They have taken away my Lord, and I know not where they have laid Him."[1] She showed thus that in her trouble she had forgotten Christ's promise of His Resurrection. The Mother of God made Man alone awaited with divine certainty the Resurrection of the Man-God. It is true, then, that the full, living, and perfect faith of the Church was on that day hidden in the heart of Mary, as the germ of the Divine Tree which was to overshadow the whole earth.

This reason alone would suffice to account for the homage which Christendom pays on Saturday to the Blessed Virgin.

But there is another, no less urgent. The Saturday of the great week of our redemption was the chief day of Mary's sorrow. It was not the day on which that sorrow was most bitter; but it was the day on which it was most profound. Mary suffered more cruelly at the foot of the Cross; but she was there bringing forth the

[1] John xx. 13.

human race to a new life. She saw her Son suffer and die; but she heard the voice of Him Who thus redeemed the world: *Dimitte ! quare dereliquisti ? Consummatum est.*[1] And that voice descended sweetly upon her, to declare her the Mother of mankind: *Ecce, Mater tua !*[2] Every thing changes from the evening of that great day and the approach of the Saturday.[3] The Word of God, it is true, never ceased to be united both to the Soul and the Body of that nature which He had assumed in His love. But the Soul of Christ was separated from His Body, and the Son of Mary was no longer living in His Human Nature. Life was in death,—the life of God in the death of man for the expiation of the sins of the world, to restore to man that Divine life which he had lost, and to purchase for him even the immortality of the body by the resurrection of the flesh. It was on this day alone, therefore, that Mary could say in her heart, " My Son is no more !"

It was on this day that the Soul of Christ, united to His Divinity, descended into hell (*descendit ad inferos*)[4]

[1] Luke xxiii. 34; Matt. xxvii. 46; John xix. 30.
[2] John xix. 27.
[3] The Sabbath commenced on the Friday evening.
[4] By hell, in this place, we are not to understand the place of eternal separation from God, which is the state of men who have died in obstinate and final resistance to the Spirit of grace and mercy. Hell, properly so called, with its eternity of punishment, is reserved, says a holy Father, for those souls in whom the eye of God has foreseen an eternity of sin. But the hell here spoken of in the Creed is the abode of souls who do not yet enjoy the intuitive vision of God, who do not as yet behold Him face to face, who do not yet enjoy Him in the close union of glory, but who are in a state of expiation or expectation. In this world expiation is not alone, for earth is the special place of trial and of merit. Purgatory is the place of expiation. The souls in purgatory are more closely united there to God than we upon earth ; for if the expiatory suffering is greater there, love is there without alloy. We are, therefore, ordinarily speaking, lower on the ladder which ascends to God on earth than in purgatory. We give the name of limbo to the place of those souls whose state is rather that of expectation than of expiation. This was the state of the Saints before

to console the ancient Church. We see Him there appearing in His glory to the first man and the first woman, the father and mother of the human race, with that greeting waited for during forty centuries: "Behold Me;" behold the salvation promised from the beginning. We see Him visiting the multitude of souls saved by the very ruin of the old world, poor souls which had at first been incredulous of the words of Noah, but who afterwards believed and expiated their crimes in the shipwreck of the human race (*Christus semel pro peccatis nostris mortuus est, justus pro injustis, ut nos offerret Deo, mortificatus quidem carne, vivificatus autem spiritu. In quo et his, qui in carcere erant, spiritibus veniens prædicavit: qui increduli fuerant aliquando, quando expectabant Dei patientiam in diebus Noe, cum fabricaretur arca*).[1]

We see Him going back through expecting ages and generations—generations not only of the people whom He had chosen to serve as a monument of the primitive faith in the midst of idolatry—but manifesting Himself to all those who had believed in God and in

---

the death of our Lord. Limbo was that prison of which S. Peter speaks, in which the souls of the just were still held captive, because they were still detained far from the vision of God. On the other hand, that expectation was not without joy, because it was without fear, and because the union of these souls with God was more intimate than that which is enjoyed on earth, and free from the conflicts of our earthly probation. Many holy and illustrious theologians are of opinion that the state of the souls of infants not regenerated to the life of grace by baptism has some resemblance to this, not in the enjoyment of the supernatural blessedness of grace, but in the happiness of a natural union with God, a happiness which is exempt from the desire of a higher blessedness, of which these souls know nothing, and exempt also from the perils and conflicts of the world. See on this point the words of S. Thomas, and of the great Pope Innocent III., quoted in *Le Christ et les Antichrists*, tom. ii. pp. 298-300. God owes nothing to any one, because He owes being to no one. Every several degree of life and happiness is always, therefore, on His part, a gift of free love to His creatures.

[1] 1 Peter iii. 18-20.

His justice; who had believed God, and observed the natural law,[1] by the help of that grace which God offers to all men: *In veritate comperi, quia non est personarum acceptor Deus; sed in* OMNI GENTE, *qui timet eum, et operatur justitiam acceptus est illi*.[2] We behold Him filling them with joy by the first-fruits of that glory, the plenitude of which they will enjoy when He ascends into heaven with the multitude of just souls of all ages in His company. But while the Church, which is soon to be triumphant, is in joy, the Church militant is in sorrow; and this is the great day among all days on which the Church, sheltered in the heart of her Queen and Mother, mourns in deed and in truth.

"And yet," exclaims S. Bernard, "men say, Did not Mary know that Christ was to die?—Most assuredly she knew it. Did she not hope for His approaching resurrection?—Yes; and that faithfully. And yet she wept when she saw Him crucified, and beheld Him in the arms of death?—Yes; and that bitterly. And who, then, art thou, my brother, and whence cometh to thee this manner of wisdom, which marvels not at the Passion of the Son, and yet marvels at the sorrowful compassion of the Mother? Thou believest of Him that He could truly die the death of the body, and thou believest not of her that she could truly die the death of the heart, or suffer in the heart an anguish bitter as death."[3]

The Saturday which intervened between the great day of the immolation of the Man-God and the great day of His Resurrection was, then, in truth, the only day when Jesus Christ lay in death, the one great day on which His Mother could say to Him, "O my Son, Thou art no more!"

---

[1] See, in the theology of S. Alphonsus: *De credendis explicite necessitate medii* (*Hom. Apos.*, 1, 4, c. 1). His words apply also to all those who, since the Incarnation, have been invincibly ignorant of the Christian revelation. See, in the *Entretiens sur la Demonstration Catholique*, the words of S. Bernard there cited (*Entret.*, 3d edit. p. 243).

[2] Acts x. 34, 35.   [3] Serm. *In Signum Magn.*

What wonder, then, that all true Christians bear it in mind; that they commemorate it with grateful hearts by prayers, sacrifices, and good works?

We shall soon return to this point when we come to treat of the practices of piety by which the children of Mary honour their Mother in the secret of their hearts; but we will not omit to mention here the public practice of the Church in the law of the Saturday abstinence,[1] which is binding on us all, and which we cannot, unless lawfully dispensed, infringe without a grave fault.

A gross and voluntary ignorance prevails in our days on the nature and obligation of the laws of the Church. Her disciplinary laws, it is true, are not Divine laws, in the same sense, for example, as the laws of the Decalogue, or those which affect prayer, sacrifice, and Sacraments. But disciplinary laws are the decrees of an authority divinely established. The Apostles did not confine themselves to the preaching of a doctrine; they enacted laws, and, in particular, laws of abstinence,[2] in the name of the Holy Ghost,[3] Whose organs they were. Now, the Apostolate of Jesus Christ was not established by Him for one age, but for all ages; for it is evident that Christ constituted the apostolic or teaching authority to be perpetual, promising to be with it "all days, even to the consummation of the world;"[4] and saying of it to all ages, "He who heareth you, heareth Me; and he who despiseth you, despiseth Me."[5] How could it have been otherwise? Is religion nothing but an idea, a sentiment, a solitary opinion of some random dreamer? Is it not, on the contrary, the soul of the religious society of men with God, and of men among themselves in order to union with God? It is the soul of the religious society; it has never been any thing else than this. If, then, religion and the religious society are correlative terms, of which one implies the other, there is a religious authority divinely established by God to lead men to

---

[1] Obligatory in France.—*Translator's note.*   [2] Acts xv. 29.
[3] Ibid.   [4] Matt. xxviii. 20.   [5] Luke x. 16.

God, since there can be no society without authority, and the relations of men with God are not arbitrary, but dependent on the wisdom and the will of God Himself. Do we not see three distinct societies existing in the world?—the domestic society, or the family; the civil society, or the state; the religious society, or the Church? Now, God is the Author of the authorities which direct these three several societies: *Non est enim potestas, nisi a Deo.*[1] And when we say of the civil authority itself that it is of Divine right, we say simply that it is the will of God, Who created man for society, that he should be subject to an authority. But although God is the Author of all authority, He is not in the same sense its Author in every order of society. The civil authority is directed by God only in its substance, and not in its form; for the end of the state is only temporal, and subject to the variable conditions of time. It is not, and cannot be, thus with the authority which directs the family or the Church: the family, which is founded upon the institution of marriage, being necessarily of direct Divine and natural institution, as the principle of the natural life of man; and the Church, which depends on Jesus Christ, Who renders it fruitful, being also of direct Divine and supernatural institution as the principle of the life of grace—that higher life, which exalts every thing in human existence—marriage, the family, and the state—to bring all into harmony with the last and positive end of man. The authority in the family and the authority in the Church are thus Divine both in their substance and in their form, and emanate directly from God, the first principle and last end of man.

The commands of authority in the family and the precepts and commandments of authority in the Church oblige, therefore, in conscience according to the ordinance of God Himself, and in a grave matter they impose a grave obligation. Nay, even civil laws carry with them a conscientious obligation, not only, says the

[1] Rom. xiii. 1.

Apostle, *propter iram, sed etiam propter conscientiam*.[1] "And he who resisteth the power, resisteth the ordinance of God" (*Qui resistit potestati, Dei ordinationi resistit*).[2] How, then, can we venture to slight the laws promulgated by the Church, to remind us, according to the different necessities of the time, of the observance of the Divine laws, and to give us an opportunity of fulfilling them by works of charity, piety, or penance? Can obedience be less obligatory in the religious than in the civil or domestic society? If in the family or the state authority command what God forbids, we must assuredly obey God rather than men.[3] But God has not abandoned us to our caprices, or to the interested decision of our passions, or to the weakness of our reason itself, to judge between Himself and the powers which abuse the authority derived from Him. He has given to our weak nature since its fall a teaching authority, not only to raise it to a knowledge of truths and blessings of a supernatural order, but also to prevent it from going astray even in the order of natural truth and equity; and thus it is that the authority of the Church is at once the positive basis of liberty of conscience, with regard to the powers of the world, the guarantee against the abuse of that liberty, and the means to preserve it against being treated as impracticable, as those cause it to be treated who conceive of it as without any rule but its own will, and thus transform it into an intolerable licentiousness, furnishing an excuse and an occasion for the establishment of every kind of despotism.

It will be said that disciplinary laws are not unchangeable; we see them modified by time and varied by difference of place. Unquestionably they are variable, and ought to be so, because their object is to promote various ways of fulfilling the laws of God and practising virtues according to the diversity of time, place, and circumstance. But that which changes not is the authority which imposes them, and our obligation to obey it.

[1] Rom. xiii. 5.   [2] Ibid.   [3] Acts v. 29.

Let us, then, remember those words of Jesus Christ to the teaching authority which He established for ever: "He who heareth you, heareth Me." Let us observe the laws divinely established by that authority, and amongst those laws let us cherish with especial affection that which reminds us of the day of our Mother's deepest sorrow. And if the Church, for reasons which she judges sufficient, dispenses us on that day from the obligation of abstinence, let our hearts at least offer some voluntary sacrifice to Jesus and Mary.

Prayer.

O my God, how often should I have omitted to fulfil Thy commands; how often should I have neglected prayer, the sanctification of the day which Thou hast reserved for Thyself, or rather which Thou hast reserved for the use of my soul; how often should I have omitted attendance at Holy Mass, the practice of penance and good works, the reception of the Sacraments, and, above all, of the adorable Eucharist,—if Thy Church had not recalled me to my duty by her Festivals and her laws! What, O Lord, are the commandments of the Church, which I so often repeated in my childhood, but that Mother's voice recalling me to Thee? I will love them, then, as a child loves its mother's will, and I will fear to despise them, remembering those words addressed to her by Thyself: "He who despises you, despises Me." I will have it especially at heart, O my God, to offer the Sacrifice on Saturday in remembrance of her who suffered so intensely on that day, only because of the intensity of her love and Thine for us. Yes, I will love You in my turn, Jesus, my Saviour, and Mary, Mother of my Saviour; and I desire to prove my love to You by more than words. Aid me, my God, by Thy omnipotent grace, that I may be faithful to my resolution; and do thou, my Mother, obtain for me the grace of fidelity from thy Divine Son.

CHAPTER XXVI.

THE MONTH OF MARY.

THE works of God are full of life. Nature is a life, grace is a life, glory is a life. Nature lives, and whatever is not living in her serves at least to life. Grace is a higher and altogether supernatural life, because it is even here a participation in the uncreated life of God, although under the veil of time. Glory is the unveiled communion with that Divine life. God, Who is the Principle of all life, has quickened His creation by the intelligent or personal life and by the social life, having made man after His own image, and society also after the image of the eternal society of the Three Divine Persons in their indivisible unity. But there are various degrees of perfection in the social life. The life of the family, which is the divine root of the public life, is extended by the civil life and exalted by the religious life into the great family of the children of God, the universal Church, in which God diffuses the life of grace, and prepares the life of glory.

The living sap which circulates through the Church is not of earth: its roots absorb it from the " land of the living," which is not of this world, although it produces its fruits in this world. Her faith, her hope, her love, are unchangeable as their principle and their end; her faith is living, her hope is living, her love is living; and it is because of this abundant life that her fertility is inexhaustible and ever increasing. We know nothing more senseless than the astonishment of Protestantism and Jansenism at the sight of the new works of charity and piety which continually blossom on the Church's living stem at every season of the year, at every period of the life of humanity. The faith is always old, but its works are always new. The love of Christians for their Lord never changes, but it is proved by sacrifices as varied as the leaves of the forest or the flowers of the field. And a childlike love towards the Mother of our Lord began with the Church, and, like her, will never end, even in the kingdom of glory; but its acts are numberless and infinitely varied, as the expression of a child's love for a most dearly beloved mother.

Thus we see the Church multiply throughout the course of the year Festivals which set before our eyes the whole life of the Mother of God, and the examples of which that life is full. She consecrates to her that day in every week which especially calls to mind the heroism of her faith and of her sorrow, and offers to her thrice daily, at the sound of the Angelus, the Angelic Salutation which speaks to us of the Incarnation of the Word. Is it matter of astonishment, then, that, having consecrated to Mary three moments of every day and a day in every week, the Church should also have especially consecrated to her a month in every year?

Is it matter of astonishment, above all, that she should choose for honouring her who restored life to the world the month which seems to restore life to nature? All hearts here sympathise with the Church: they feel that the month of May is the most fitting for rendering homage to her whom God has fitted with grace; and while they adorn their Mother's altars with flowers, the filial hope arises within them that she will obtain for them from God the heavenly ornaments of sanctity.

Again, there is another thought of maternal charity in the choice made of this month by the Church. In this world evil closely follows good; and by the side of the gifts of God, we almost always find man's abuse of them. When Providence rejoices our hearts by the revival of nature, the passions also revive to disturb and embitter the purity of that enjoyment. It is truly, then, with a mother's thought that the Church in her turn would revive in the heart of her children the efficacious remembrance of that sweet Virgin, that loving Mother, whose very name is a reproach to souls that go astray, a pang of remorse to hearts which suffer themselves to be polluted, a hope to those who would return, a powerful aid to those who have fallen, a support to those who would persevere.

What, then, is our chief motive for honouring the month of Mary?

The love of Jesus, the love of His Divine Mother, the love of our own souls. Would not Jesus have us to love what He loves? Would He not have us to love intensely what He loves intensely? What has He ever loved more intensely than Mary? Let us, then, honour the month of Mary for the love of her, and we shall honour it for the love of Him. Let us also honour it for the love of our own souls; for a month of prayer cannot fail to be a month of grace.

What shall we do, then, that it may be a month of grace to us?

We must consecrate it by gratitude, by confidence, by fidelity.

S. Bernard says that, by mingling with our prayers thanksgiving for graces received, we move the Heart of God more effectually to grant us fresh favours than if we addressed Him simply by the prayer of supplication. We shall also move the heart of Mary, that living image of the Heart of God, to pray most fervently for us if we bear faithfully in mind what we already owe to her intercession. Our prayers will thus also be most closely conformable with those of the Church, who almost always begins her supplications by those grateful remembrances which open the heart to confidence and hope: *Salve* RADIX, *salve porta* EX QUA MUNDO LUX EST ORTA! *Salve Regina, Mater misericordiæ, vita, dulcedo et spes nostra, salve! Alma redemptoris Mater, quæ pervia cæli porta manes, et stella maris, succurre cadenti surgere cui curat populo!* In these, and in many other of her prayers, the Church reminds us of what Mary has been and still is to us, before she tells us what she will be if we have recourse to her.

And how can this sentiment of gratitude fail to
spring up within us when we think of her? Have we
not seen that Jesus willed the coöperation of her Mother's
heart in the gift of Himself to us? Do we not know
how much this coöperation cost her from the Incarnation even to Calvary? Did she not mingle her tears
with all the anguish of her Son's Passion? Did she
not descend even to the lowest depth of that abyss of
sorrow?—*Veni in altitudinem maris et tempestas demersit
me.* Was there one single pang of all the incomprehensible exterior and interior sufferings of the Divine
Victim which pierced not through her heart? How,
then, can we remember the Lamb of God, Who took
upon Him the burden of our sins, without remembering
His Mother and ours?

But it is not only this general remembrance of her
love which ought to move us, but the particular remembrance also of the numberless graces which her maternal
prayer has continually obtained for us. It will be no
less easy to us to feel gratitude for that series of graces
than for the immense benefit from which they all have
flowed; for every soul which marks attentively the leadings of Divine Providence will clearly recognise the hand
of Mary in that merciful guidance, and behold the great
graces which form epochs in the interior life stamped
with the invocation of the universal Mediatrix of intercession.

Gratitude will thus open our heart to confidence,
and the measure of our confidence will be the measure
of God's gifts to us; for confidence in Mary's prayer is
nothing else but confidence in God. If we deserve
nothing, if we merit nothing, Jesus has merited all
things for us; and in order to grant us His graces, He
needs only our prayer,—but it must be a confiding
prayer: *Credite quia accipietis, et evenient vobis.*[1] In
order to sustain our confidence, He has enjoined united
prayer: *Ubi enim sunt duo vel tres congregati in nomine*

[1] Mark xi. 24.

meo, ibi sum in medio eorum.[1] To rekindle this confidence, He bids us in His inspired Scriptures to pray for each other: *Orate pro invicem ut salvemini;*[2] and above all to have recourse to the "prayer of the just," because it avails much with God: *Multum enim valet deprecatio justi assidua.*[3] What, then, must be the efficacy of *her* prayer who is "full of grace," and who has not only drawn down the gifts of God from heaven, but God Himself into her bosom: *Fiat mihi?*[4] Therefore it is that the Spirit of Jesus Christ, the Spirit of grace and of prayer divinely promised by Him to His Church, has ever inspired her with those ineffable sighs which give such sweetness and such fervour to the prayers of the children of Eve to the Mother of mercy: *Ad te clamamus, exules filii Evæ! Eia ergo Advocata nostra, illos tuos misericordes oculos ad nos converte!* Yes, the month of Mary shall be to each of us a month of grace, because it shall be a month of confiding prayer.

But if gratitude leads us to confidence, confidence in its turn must lead us to fidelity and perseverance.

What shall we, then, offer faithfully to Mary on every day of this month?

First, a fervent prayer from the bottom of our hearts, and the attentive reading of some spiritual book, of which we shall find many at our choice: the present work may supply the needs of some. But let each choose what is best suited for his spiritual wants.

To this exercise let us join, if we can, an attendance at some church where the devotions of the month of Mary are publicly offered; for there are two things which God loves—to see His children come to Him in silence and in solitude—*Ora Patrem tuum in abscondito*[5] —and to see them gathered together before Him as a family.[6]

To these acts of piety, let us add daily at least one act of mortification, and at least one act of charity—of

[1] Matt. xviii. 20. [2] James v. 16. [3] Mark xi. 24.
[4] Luke i. 38. [5] Matt. vi. 6. [6] Matt. xviii. 20.

spiritual or corporal mercy—according to the ability which God gives us, and the opportunities with which His Providence will not fail to provide us.

Above all, let our intention be to obtain strength to overcome ourselves, and to destroy whatever is within us displeasing to the eyes of Jesus and His holy Mother.

Let us also perform our ordinary actions in union with the most Holy Virgin; let us do them *with her*. Let us meditate with her, and as she meditated: *Conservabat omnia verba hæc, conferens in corde suo*.[1] All meditation is comprised in these words: *Conservabat verba*—she remembered the Divine words which she had heard; *conferens*—she carefully reflected upon them; *in corde*—not only to think of them, but to conform all the sentiments of her heart to them, and to implore grace to fulfil them. Let us work with her, and as she worked: *Ecce ancilla Domini; fiat mihi secundum verbum tuum*.[2] Let this *fiat* animate all our works; we live but to fulfil the will of God. The desire of that fulfilment must therefore be the soul of all our actions and of all our sufferings, of our life and our death. Sin alone cannot be offered to God, except by repentance. All things beside may be and ought to be sanctified by conformity to the law of God and to the dispositions of His Providence, and become thus a chain of faith, hope, and love, by every link of which we are attached to God. Things most indifferent in themselves become the seeds of eternal life when connected with the fulfilment of duty. Whether we labour, then, whether we act, or whether we suffer, let us say always with our whole soul: *Ecce ancilla Domini; fiat mihi secundum verbum tuum;* let my soul, O Lord, do always that which pleases Thee. But let us make it our chief care to be present at the Holy Sacrifice of the Altar, and, in union with Mary, to offer the Divine Victim by the hands of the priest, as she offered Him on Calvary. This was the special devotion of S. Dominic, and it was

[1] Luke ii. 19. [2] Luke i. 38.

to him an inexhaustible source of confidence and grace. When we participate in the Sacrifice by Holy Communion, let us offer to Jesus Christ, then present in our heart, the heart of His Blessed Mother. Let us offer to Him the adoration of that heart, its love, its tears, its prevailing prayer. If we make only a spiritual communion, let us make use of Mary's intercession to enable us to make it well. If we say to her with all our hearts, " Hail, full of grace, our Lord is with thee," she will obtain for us that He may be also with us. Lastly, at night, before we lie down to sleep—that striking image of death preceding the morning of the resurrection—let us again offer to Mary the Angelical Salutation, in which the Church teaches us to invoke her for our last hour; and let us ask, through her, for grace to say with our whole heart that Divine prayer, which comprises all the acts of a good death as well as of a holy life. Happy they who shall offer every evening a *Pater* and *Ave* in this spirit! they shall be mightily assisted by Jesus and Mary at the hour of their death.

Prayer.

Mother of grace and love, I desire to honour thee during this whole month, which I consecrate to thee; and I offer it to thee, in order to obtain by thine Immaculate Heart the fidelity which I owe to thee. If I am faithful to thee, my Mother, I know that thou wilt make me faithful to God. *Virgo fidelis, ora pro me.* Yes, thou wilt obtain for me a lively, firm, and unchanging faith, an unshaken hope, a boundless confidence in the merits of Jesus, and a proportionate distrust of myself and my own weakness; a true love for the Spotless Lamb, the Majesty of God, become my Brother in the Incarnation and Redemption, and the very Spouse of my poor soul in the adorable Eucharist. Lastly, thou wilt obtain for me a deep sorrow for my sins, and a true and effectual change of life. O Mother of my soul, I beseech thee to watch over me all the days of my life;

but I look for thee above all at the moment of death. Thou wilt come to me then, tender Mother of the dying, to aid me in that last passage, in company with thine Angels and mine, and thou wilt receive my soul, to offer it to its Creator, its Saviour, and its Eternal Life. Amen.

CHAPTER XXVII.

CHARACTERISTICS OF TRUE DEVOTION TOWARDS THE BLESSED VIRGIN.

Veneration, love, confidence.

A DEVOTION which is merely external is not true devotion. This is a truth which every one knows; but it becomes an error in the mouth of those who reject exterior worship and exterior acts of piety, in the name of Him Who wills to be worshiped "in spirit and in truth." True piety comes from the heart; and if its source be not in the soul (*in spiritu*), if it be not interior, it is only a vain image, a shadow of piety, and sometimes a mere hypocrisy. It is no less true, that it cannot be in the heart without showing itself externally in some way or other, and without finding expression in acts. Man is made up of soul and body; and if humility of soul induces the body to kneel, the prostration of the body causes the soul to humble itself and bow down before God: to affect a piety exclusively interior is to attempt something contrary to nature, contrary to the established law of God; it is to desire to serve Him in *spirit*, and not in *truth*.

Do not believe, then, in the piety of those who say,— As for us, we do not care for all those external practices to which you attach so much importance; we serve God in spirit and in truth. No, do not believe that they serve God in spirit. When there is sap in a tree, it shows it by its leaves, its flowers, and fruit. If it bear neither leaves, flowers, nor fruit, it is a dead tree. Doubtless there may be hypocrisy in exterior practices; but if the wolf (says S. Augustine) sometimes assumes the skin of the sheep, must the sheep therefore assume the skin of the wolf? Because there are exterior practices without piety, is it necessary that there should be piety without exterior practices? Piety is essentially practical and active. A religion which pretends to be wholly interior is only an illusion; it is the dream of a proud spirit, which evaporates in its own fancies.

The true principle, therefore, is, that the exterior practices of piety should be animated by an interior spirit. But, to apply this general principle to the particular subject which occupies us, where shall we find this spirit, this soul, of the devotion towards the Blessed Virgin? Many will answer,—In the imitation of her virtues. Without this imitation, devotion to Mary is nothing.

At first sight this seems a solid answer; but though there be some truth in it, it is not entirely correct: were it so, poor sinners would be much to be pitied, for they would be incapable of real devotion to their tender Mother till after their perfect conversion. This answer, therefore, taken in its strict sense, is false, since it is an acknowledged, and happily an unquestionable fact, that devotion to Mary daily brings back many a sinner to God. A person may, therefore, be devout to the Blessed Virgin without having yet attained to the imitation of her virtues, provided he have a sincere desire to be converted, and to lead a really Christian life.

In order, then, to give an exact answer to the question proposed, several things must be considered,—the principle of the devotion to the Mother of God, the essential characteristics of this devotion, the fruit which it ought to produce, the different degrees of perfection of which it is capable.

The principle of this devotion consists in the *knowledge* of Mary. He who knows what Mary is in herself, or what God has given her, and also what God has willed she should be to us, will immediately feel a *filial piety* towards this divine Mother of souls spring up in his heart. This is why the first part of this book treats of the knowledge of Mary. Devotion to Mary is the expression of filial piety; and the essential characteristics of this filial piety are veneration, love, and confidence,—veneration for her incomparable dignity of Mother of God; love for the true Mother of souls ; confidence in the powerful intercession of the Mother of God, and in the tender heart of the Mother of men.

The imitation of the virtues of Mary, in the degree which God requires of us in the fulfilment of the duties of the state in which His Providence has placed us, and through the graces which He offers us, is rather the fruit of devotion to Mary than its essence. We should certainly destroy the essence of this devotion if we did not wish to partake of its fruit; but whoever has recourse to Mary with a filial, that is to say, a loving and humble confidence, that he may be protected and assisted by her, will infallibly feel the desire of leading a better life, and of accomplishing in all things the will of God, increase in his heart. We understand sufficiently by what has been said that there are different degrees of perfection in our devotion to Mary ; that the most miserable sinner may possess it in some degree; that if he be faithful to it, it will increase in his poor soul, and the light and grace of God will increase with it. It is, therefore, a very great error to say that there can be no sincere devotion except that perfect devotion which produces the excellent fruit of imitation. Imperfect devotion may be very sincere; it is at least a divine seed, which, if preserved and cherished in the heart, will in the end produce the fruits of penance, and effect a change of life.

Let us, then, never say, that without the imitation of the virtues of Mary, devotion to her is of no avail. Doubtless, it is not yet all that it ought to be; but it is a step, and a very blessed step. Is not this, moreover, happily confirmed by frequent experience ?

Those who are intrusted with the secret of consciences

will all bear witness to this fact; well-known examples of souls restored to virtue, grace, and peace, by devotion to the Blessed Virgin, occur continually every day; and there is nothing for which we may not hope from a heart which is faithful to this devotion, a heart which does not lose hold of that merciful chain by which God has bound the hearts of His prodigal children in all ages to Himself. No wonder, then, that theologians give devotion to Mary as one of the most certain signs of predestination. How should it be otherwise? Has not our Lord Jesus Christ said, "Unless you become as little children, you shall not enter into the kingdom of heaven"? Humility, candour, and real simplicity of soul, are therefore the conditions of salvation; and these conditions of salvation are also the characteristics of devotion to the Blessed Virgin, of that filial love of which we have been speaking. It is because heresy is the offspring of pride, that it cannot hear Mary spoken of without a feeling of impatience, and a sort of irritability; and if that vain "knowledge which puffs up" take the place in the heart of that which is true, and of the "charity which edifies," it will at once expel the devotion to Mary, and efface this true characteristic of the children of God.

Prayer.

O my God, I wish never to lose this characteristic of Thy children; but I desire, on the contrary, that this really filial love for the Mother whom Thou hast given me may increase in me daily more and more. And do thou, tender Mother of my soul, obtain for me an increase of the love I bear to thee, and of my confidence in thy powerful prayers. How great would be my blindness if, knowing what I do, I did not expect great graces from thee! Never, then, O Mary, suffer me to forget what I owe thee, that so the remembrance of the past may support me at the present moment, and teach me to expect with great confidence a happy eternity. I do not deserve it, but the merits of Jesus Christ have obtained it for me, together with grace to follow the road that will conduct me thither. He is pleased to bestow this grace on fervent, persevering prayer: *Credite quia accipietis, et evenient vobis* ("Believe that you shall receive, and it shall be done unto you"). My prayer, then, shall be full of confidence, because it will not remain desolate, cold, and unworthy of Him, but it will be conveyed to Him through the heart of a Mother to whom He can refuse nothing. He Himself has recommended the union of prayer; He Himself has said that He will hear those who are joined together to invoke Him. I will be one of these; I will be among the number of the children of God, united among themselves and to their Mother, in order to do violence to the Heart of our Lord after a manner well pleasing to Him. The sweet experience of graces which are infallibly received by this union will make me persevere in it on earth, till I shall go to bless thee in heaven for all that thou hast obtained for me; to love thee, and with thee to love the Sovereign Good for evermore. Amen.

CHAPTER XXVIII.

CHARACTERISTICS OF TRUE DEVOTION TOWARDS THE BLESSED VIRGIN (*continued*).

The love of Mary.

WE have seen that veneration, love, and confidence are the distinguishing characteristics of the filial devotion of the children of Mary. But we will not content ourselves with this speculative and somewhat dry analysis of a sentiment so full of life and heat. Shall we say nothing more of the veneration which is due to the Mother of Jesus Christ, true God and true Man, of the love which our own Mother feels for us, and of that which she expects from us, and also of the confidence with which her prayers, as the Mother of God and of men, ought to inspire us?

We will say no more of the veneration due to her greatness, because almost the whole of the first part of this book has been devoted to this subject, and has shown us Mary invested with the highest dignity which can be bestowed on a mere creature; peerless in her dignity, peerless in her grace, her merits, her virtues, her trials; peerless in her sufferings as in her glory.

We have spoken also of her title of Mother as regards ourselves, and shown her to be the true Mother of the superior supernatural life, which God has given us in Jesus Christ; we have seen her from the manger to the cross, bringing us all forth to this life of grace in sorrow and in tears.

But we have not yet said all that is to be said of the love of this Mother's heart; and how can we say it? Can human language express what the human understanding cannot fully comprehend? Where can words be found to speak what is unutterable? Let us at least understand why Mary's love for us is necessarily incomprehensible. It is because her love for our souls is *in proportion to her love of God*, and that the Divine flame which consumes her heart is more ardent than that of the love of all the Angels and Saints together; because her grace was of an order apart, and necessarily superior to that of all other graces;[1] her perfect correspondence to that grace increased it immensely;[2] and her glory— that is to say, her light and beatific love—were proportioned to her grace, and to the fidelity of her correspondence with that grace.[3] It is incomprehensible also, because she loves our souls *in proportion to what they have cost her*. And what have they cost her? The Passion of her Divine Son, His agony, His scourging at the pillar, His crowning with thorns, the insults and sufferings of Calvary, the dereliction on the cross, the death of Jesus Christ, the blood of the Man-God,—*i. e.* an infinite price. It is incomprehensible, because she

---

[1] See above, chap. v.   [2] Chap. x.
[3] Chap. xi.

loves our souls as she was bidden to love them by those words which fell from the dying lips of the Lamb of God concerning all mankind: "Woman, behold thy son!" She loves us, then, *in proportion to her desire to fulfil the last recommendation, the last wishes, of Jesus Christ with regard to us.*

But when we would speak of the love of Mary, we must yield the pen to S. Alphonsus. We said at the commencement of this work that one of our reasons for publishing it was the hope of leading our readers to appreciate the *Glories of Mary*. Since, then, we are now at the end of our work, it is time to open the *Glories of Mary*, and to listen to S. Alphonsus:

"Since all men have been redeemed by Jesus Christ, Mary loves and cherishes them all. S. John saw her clothed with the sun: *Et signum magnum apparuit in cælo, mulier amicta sole*[1] ('And a great sign appeared in heaven: a woman clothed with the sun'). She is said 'to be clothed with the sun,' to signify, that as no one on earth can escape from the heat of the sun—*Nec est qui se abscondat a calore ejus*[2] ('There is nothing hid from the heat thereof')—so, in like manner, there is no one here below who does not feel the effects of Mary's love, according to the expression of the learned Idiota: *A calore ejus; id est, a dilectione Mariæ*[3] ('From the heat thereof; that is, from the love of Mary'). 'Ah!' exclaims S. Antoninus, 'who can understand the care of this tender Mother for us all?' (*Oh! quanta est cura Virgini Matri de nobis?*) 'She offers and bestows upon all, without exception, the tenderness of her mercies' (*Omnibus aperit sinum misericordiæ suæ*).[4] As, therefore, she has desired the salvation of all, and has coöperated in the work of their salvation, it is certain, says S. Bernard, that 'she was full of anxiety for all the human race' (*Constat pro universo genere humano fuisse solli-*

---

[1] Apoc. xii. 1.
[2] Ps. xviii. 7.
[3] *Contempl. de V.M.*, in Præ.
[4] P. 4, l. 15, c. ii.

citam).¹ Those servants of Mary have adopted a very useful practice, who, as Cornelius A'Lapide relates, are accustomed ' to pray to our Lord to grant them all the graces which the Blessed Virgin asks for them' (*Domine, da mihi quod pro me postulat sanctissima Virgo Maria*). The reason of this is, acccording to the same author, that ' our august Mother desires for us far higher graces than those we can desire for ourselves' (*Ipsa enim majora optat, quam nos optare possumus*). And the pious Bernardine de Bustis assures us, ' that Mary desires more ardently to do us good, and to pour forth graces upon us, than we desire to receive them' (*Plus desiderat ipsa facere tibi bonum et largiri gratiam, quam tu accipere concupiscas*).² So also Blessed Albert the Great applies to her these words of the Book of Wisdom: *Præoccupat qui se concupiscunt, ut illis se prior ostendat* (' She preventeth them that covet her, so that she first showeth herself unto them').³ Mary prevents those who have recourse to her, and desires, so to say, that they find her before they seek for her. The love of this good Mother for us is so great, adds Richard of S. Victor, that as soon as she sees us in any need she immediately comes to our assistance, even before we invoke it: *Velocius occurrit ejus pietas quam invocatur*.⁴

"Now, if Mary is so good to every body, even to the ungrateful and careless, who hardly trouble themselves to love her and invoke her, how much more will she take pity on those who love her and frequently pray to her! *Facile videtur ab his qui diligunt eam, et invenitur ab his qui quærunt illam* (' And is easily seen by them that love her, and is found by them that seek her').⁵ ' Oh,' exclaims Blessed Albert the Great, ' how easy is it to find Mary when we love her, and to find her full of tenderness and love !' She declares that she cannot help loving those who love her: *Ego diligentes me diligo* (' I

[1] *In Ass. B.V.*, s. 4.
[2] *Mariol*, p. 2, s. 5.
[3] Sap. vi. 14.
[4] *In Cant.*, c. xxiii.
[5] Sap. vi. 13.

love them that love me').¹ And although this most loving Queen loves all men as her children, yet, says S. Bernard, *agnoscit et diligit*.² She recognises those who love her most, and feels most affection for them. Idiota assures us, that those who have the happiness of loving and serving Mary are not only beloved by her, but are also helped by her, and receive all manner of good at her hands: *Inventa Virgine Maria, invenitur omne bonum, ipsa numque diligit diligentes se, imo sibi servientibus servit.*

"We read in the Chronicles of the Order of S. Dominic, that Brother Leo of Montpellier commended himself to this Mother of Mercy two hundred times in the day. When he was at the point of death, he suddenly saw a Queen of surpassing beauty standing by him, who said to him: 'Leo, will you die, and come to my Son and me?' He answered: 'But who are you?' And the Blessed Virgin replied: 'I am the Mother of Mercy, whom you have so often invoked; I am come to take you; let us go together to paradise.' Leo died that same day, and we feel confident that she took him to the abode of the elect. 'O sweet Mary, happy is he who loves thee!'

"The Blessed Brother John Berchmans, of the Society of Jesus, used to say: 'If I love Mary, my perseverance is assured, and I shall obtain from God all that I desire.' This pious young man, therefore, was never weary of renewing his resolution of loving her; and he often repeated to himself: 'I will love Mary! I will love Mary!'

"Oh, how much does the love of this good Mother surpass that of all her children! 'Let them love her as much as they can, she will always love them more,' says S. Ignatius Martyr (*Cum devotis devotior, id est cum amantibus amantior*).³

"Let them love her as much as S. Stanislaus Kostka,

[1] Prov. viii. 17.   [2] *In Salve Reg.*, s. 1.
[3] Auriemma, *Aff. Scamb.*, p. 1, c. i.

who so tenderly loved this Mother of his heart, that it was sufficient to hear him speak of her to be inspired with the same desire of loving her. He had devised new expressions and new titles by which to honour her. He never began any action without first turning towards an image of Mary to ask her blessing. When he recited the Office, or the Rosary, or any other prayers in her honour, he seemed by his manner, and the expression of his countenance, to be speaking face to face with Mary. When he heard the *Salve Regina* sung, his heart was all on fire, and even his face was in a glow. A Father of the Society going with him one day to visit an image of the Blessed Virgin, asked him how much he loved her, and he answered: ' What can I say more, Father ?—she is my Mother !' This Father used to say, that the holy young man pronounced these words in accents so sweet, and with such loving and heartfelt emotion, that you could have thought you heard an Angel speaking of the love of Mary.

"Let them love her as much as Blessed Herman Joseph, who called her his loving Spouse, Mary having deigned to honour him with the title of Spouse,—as much as S. Philip Neri, to whom the mere thought of Mary brought consolation, and who called her his Delight,—as much as S. Bonaventure, who addressed her not only as his Lady and his Mother, but, in order to show his tender affection for her, called her also his Heart and his Soul: *Ave, Domina mea, Mater mea ! imo, Cor meum et Anima mea !* (' Hail, my Lady, my Mother ! my Heart and my Soul !')[1]

"Let them love her as much as that great servant of Mary, S. Bernard, who so loved this tender Mother as to call her the Ravisher of Hearts (*Raptrix cordium*); adding, in order to express his ardent love for her, that she had ravished his heart (*Nonne rapuisti cor meum ?*).[2]

"Let them call her their Beloved One, with S. Ber-

---

[1] *Stim. Div. Am.*, p. 3, c. xvi.   [2] *Med. in Salve Reg.*

nardine of Sienna, who went daily to visit a pious image of Mary; addressing this beloved Queen of his heart in affectionate colloquies; and who, when he was asked whither he went every day, replied that he went to seek his Beloved One.

"Let them love her as much as S. Aloysius, who was so consumed with the love of Mary, that as soon as he heard the sweet name of his beloved Mother, his heart was all on fire, and the colour visibly mounted to his face.

"Let them love her as much as S. Francis Solano, who, as if transported to a holy madness by his love of Mary, used to sing before one of her images; saying that, after the fashion of lovers in the world, he wished to serenade his well-beloved Queen.

"Let them love her as much as the multitude of her servants, who have not known how to express the intensity of their love. F. John Trexo, of the Society of Jesus, took great pleasure in calling himself the Slave of Mary; and, in token of his servitude, he often went to visit her in one of her churches, where he was so overcome by the tender emotion of his love for Mary, that he watered the church with his tears, which he wiped with his kisses, kissing the pavement over and over again; so greatly was he affected at finding himself in the house of his dear Lady. F. James Martinez, of the same Society, had, from his great devotion to Mary, obtained the privilege of being ravished to ecstasy to heaven, among the choirs of Angels, on the days of her Festivals, that he might see with what honour these are celebrated there; and he used to say: 'I wish I had the hearts of all the Angels and Saints, to love Mary as they love her; I wish I had the lives of all men, to consecrate them all to the love of Mary.'

"Let them strive to attain to the love of Charles, the son of S. Bridget, who used to say, that he knew of nothing in the world which gave him so much consolation as to know how much Mary is beloved by God. He added, that he would willingly have accepted any suffering rather than Mary should lose—if it were possible she could lose—the least portion of her greatness; and that if the greatness of Mary had belonged to him, he would have renounced it in her favour, in consideration of her incomparable merits.

"Let them desire, like Alphonsus Rodriguez, even to give their life in proof of their love of Mary; or to engrave the sweet name of Mary with a sharp instrument on their breast, as did the monk Francis Binaus, and S. Radegund, the wife of King Clotaire; or even to mark it with a hot iron, so that the impression may be stronger and more durable, as was done in their transports of love by her devout servants, John Baptist Archinto and Augustine of Espinosa, both of the Society of Jesus.

"Let them, in short, do, or desire to do, all that it is possible for a lover to do to show his affection for the object of his love; yet never will they succeed in loving Mary as much as she loves them, according to the words of S. Peter Damian: *Scio, Domina, quia benignissima es, et amas nos amore invincibili*[1] ('O my Queen,' he said, 'I know thou art more loving than all those who love thee; thou lovest us with a love which will not suffer itself to be overcome by any other love').

"The venerable Alphonsus Rodriguez, of the Society of Jesus, was one day at the foot of an image of Mary; and there feeling his heart burn with love for the Blessed Virgin, he uttered these words: 'My loving Mother! I know that thou lovest me; but thou dost not love me as much as I love thee!' Then Mary, as though she felt her affection hurt, answered by the image: 'What are you saying, Alphonsus? what are you saying? Oh, how much greater is the affection I feel for you than that which you feel for me! I can tell you that the distance is less between heaven and earth than between my love and yours.'

[1] *In Nat. B.V.*, s. 1.

"S. Bonaventure was right, then, when he exclaimed: 'Blessed are those who love this tender Mother, and serve her faithfully' (*Beati quorum corda te diligunt Maria! Beati qui ei famulantur*).[1] 'Yes,' adds another author, 'for this generous Queen never allows herself to be outdone in love by her devout servants; and, in imitation of Jesus Christ, the loving Redeemer, Mary repays twofold by her graces and favours the love which is shown her' (*Nunquam in hoc certamine a nobis ipsa vincetur, amorem redhibet, et præterita beneficia novis semper adanget*).[2]

"I will exclaim, therefore, with the burning love of S. Anselm: *Vestro continuo amore langueat cor meum, liquefiant omnia ossa mea!* May my heart always burn, and my soul be consumed, with the love of Thee, O my beloved Saviour Jesus; and with the love of thee too, Mary, my dear Mother! *Date itaque supplicanti animæ meæ, non propter meritum meum, sed propter meritum vestrum; date illi, quanto digni estis, amorem vestrum* ('And since, without your grace, I cannot love you, O Jesus and Mary; grant, I beseech you, by your merits, and not by mine, that I may love you as much as you deserve to be loved'). *O Amator hominum! tu potuisti reos tuos et usque ad mortem amare, et poteris te roganti amorem tui et Matris tuæ negare?*[3] ('O God, Who art full of love for men! Thou hast died for Thy enemies, and canst Thou refuse to him who asks it the grace to love Thee and Thy holy Mother?')

"*Prayer.*

"*O Domina, quæ rapis corda!* O my beloved Queen! may I say to thee, with S. Bonaventure, Thou who dost ravish the hearts of thy servants by the proofs of thy favour and thy love, touch my poor heart also,

---

[1] *Psalt. B.V.*, pp. 31-118.
[2] Paccucch. in Ps. lxxxvi. exc. 2.
[3] *Orat.* 51.

which desires to love thee much. What! my august Mother! has thy beauty touched the heart of God, and drawn Him down from heaven to dwell in thy bosom, and shall I live without loving you? No, surely! and I will say with another of thy children, a son who loved thee much, the Blessed John Berchmans, of the Society of Jesus: *Nunquam quiescam, donec habuero tenerum amorem erga Matrem meam Mariam* ('I am resolved to take no rest till I feel sure that I have learned to love thee fervently and tenderly, my Mother'); for thou hast loved me tenderly, even when I was so ungrateful to you! O Mary, what would have become of me, if thou hadst not loved me, and obtained so many mercies for me? Since, then, thou didst look so kindly on me when I did not love, what may I not expect from thy goodness now that I love thee? Yes, I love thee, my Mother; and I wish I had a heart which could love thee for all those poor creatures who love thee not. I wish I had a tongue which could praise thee as with a thousand tongues, to proclaim to all the world thy greatness, thy holiness, thy sanctity, thy mercy, and the love with which thou lovest those who love thee. If I had riches, I would employ them all in honouring thee; if I had subjects, I should wish them all to be filled with love for thee; nay, if needful, I would sacrifice my life itself for thy glory and love. I love thee, then, my Mother; but, alas! I fear that I do not love thee; for I hear it said, that love makes those who love like the one beloved: *Amor similes invenit aut facit.*

"I have reason, then, to feel that I love thee but little, when I see how far I am from resembling thee. Thou art so pure, and I so stained with sin; thou so humble, and I so proud; thou so holy, and I so guilty. But it is for thee to effect this marvellous change. O Mary! since thou lovest me, make me like thyself. Thou hast the power which is necessary to change the heart; take my heart, then, and change it; let the world see what thou canst do for those thou lovest. Make me holy, make me worthy to be thy child. This is my hope; so be it!"[1]

CHAPTER XXIX.

CHARACTERISTICS OF TRUE DEVOTION TOWARDS THE BLESSED VIRGIN (*continued*).

Confidence in her intercession.

PROTESTANTS reproach us with dishonouring God when we have recourse to the intercession of the Saints, the Angels, and the holy Mother of Jesus Christ; as if, by so doing, we showed a want of confidence in the Divine goodness. But do I dishonour God when I ask you, my brother, to pray for me? Far from doing so, He is pleased when I ask your prayers, because I show thereby, not that I mistrust His goodness, but that I mistrust my own unworthiness. I please Him when I ask your prayers, because I pray then with greater humility myself, and my prayer is, consequently, more pleasing to His eyes; for Jesus never treated any but the proud with severity.

But let us leave those who argue thus miserably against the confidence of Christians in the intercession of Mary, and continue to prove, by happy experience, the truth which has been so well expressed by him who called the Mother of God "Suppliant Omnipotence." This is indeed the name which she really deserves. Wherefore? Because she is the Mother of God. *Oratio Deiparæ*, says S. Antonine, *habet rationem imperii, unde impossibile est eam non exaudiri.*[2] Mary is always heard, because when she prays her prayer exercises the *empire* of love over her Divine Son. *Filius, quasi exsolvens debitum, petitiones tuas implet.*[3] "Thy Son," said

[1] *Glories of Mary*, ch. i. s. 3.
[2] P. 4, l. 25, c. xvii. s. 4.
[3] S. Greg. Nicom., *Or. de Ingr. B. V.*

S. Gregory of Nicodemia to Mary, "always hears thee, as if to acquit Himself in this way of the obligation which He willed to contract towards thee by taking His Human Nature from thee." The Son, omnipotent in Himself by nature, has made His Mother omnipotent by grace, *i.e.* by her prayers, according to the well-known verse: *Quod Deus imperio, tu prece, Virgo potes!*[1]

Mary, then, can obtain every thing; but will she do so? We have previously answered this question, when speaking of her love. She loves souls in proportion to their love of God; and she will therefore assist us with a love equal to the power of her "suppliant omnipotence." "Neither the power nor the will can be wanting to her," says S. Bernard (*Nec facultas ei deese poterit, nec voluntas*).[2] She can certainly assist us, because she is the Mother of God; and she will always be ready to aid us, because she is our Mother. Who ever found himself forsaken after having had recourse to Mary? "Ah!" exclaims the same Saint; *Sileat misericordiam tuam, si quis te invocatam meminerit defuisse*[3] ("If any one can recollect that he ever invoked thee in vain, O Mother of God! let him cease to praise thy mercy"). According to S. Bonaventure, Mary so ardently desires that we should pray to her, in order that she may bestow her favours on us more abundantly, that she feels herself injured, not only by those who revile her, but also by those who do not ask her for graces: *In te, Domina, peccant, non solum qui tibi injuriam irrogant, sed etiam qui te non rogant.* It is not necessary to make long prayers to this Mother of Mercy, in order to obtain her help; it suffices to ask her with confidence. *Velocius occurrit ejus pietas, quam invocetur* ("So great is her goodness, that she comes to our aid even before we have invoked her"). Richard of S. Victor speaks in the same manner, and he gives us the reason, namely, that Mary cannot behold our misery without being moved

---

[1] Works of S. Alph., t. i. *Prep. for Death*, p. 343.
[2] *In Assumpt.*, s. 1.   [3] Ibid., s. 4.

to assist us (*Non potest miserias scire, et non subvenire*).¹

But does Mary feel this Mother's love for poor sinners? How can we doubt it? Was it not for them that Jesus died? To whom should mercy be shown, if it be not to the miserable? and what greater misery is there than sin? If only the sinner have no attachment to his sin, and heartily desire to be free from it, Mary is ready to stretch out her arms, and lead him back to her Son, and obtain for him those graces of which he stands in need, and which Jesus Christ has purchased for him. "Mary does not examine into the merits of those who have recourse to her goodness," says S. Bernard, "but she stretches out a helping hand to those who pray to her" (*Maria non discutit merita, sed omnibus sese exorabilem præbet*).² S. Alphonsus says: "She receives every sinner who comes to her with tenderness, if only he have a good will; and she does not disdain to dress and heal his wounds."

Prayer.

O Mary, I will therefore say to thee, with S. Alphonsus: August Mother of my God! since to thee is committed the cause of the greatest criminals and of the greatest sinners, who have recourse to thee, behold me at thy feet, calling upon thee and saying, as did S. Thomas of Villanova, *Eia ergo, Advocata nostra, officium tuum imple*³ ("Therefore, O our Advocate, fulfil thine office"), thine office of Mother and Advocate of sinners—take my cause in hand. It is true that I have made myself very guilty towards my God by offending Him, after having received so many graces and benefits from Him,—but the evil is done; and now it rests with thee to succour me. This thou canst do. It is sufficient for

---

¹ *In Cant.*, c. xxiii.; S. Alph., Novena to the B.V.M. from her Litany.
² *In Sign. Magn.*   ³ *In Nat. B. V.*, con. 3.

thee to say to our Lord that thou wilt undertake my defence; He will pardon me, and I shall be saved.[1]

I confess that I feel but little sorrow for my sins, and that my love of God is very cold; but if my contrition be imperfect, and my love cold, it is because my soul is still sick, sullied, paralysed, blind, deaf to eternal truths, blind in the midst of the light which rejoices other eyes! Behold, then, O my Mother, thy child overwhelmed by all the miseries which the omnipotence of thy Son alone can cure. Perhaps I am yet buried in sin, and lying in the corruption of a spiritual death; but the voice which called Lazarus forth from the grave still listens to thee. Tell it to speak, and it will speak, and I shall hear it from the recesses of my tomb; and I shall come forth, and I shall live, and I shall love the Son Who has restored me to life, and the Mother who has obtained this restoration for me; I shall love them both in time and in eternity! *Fiat mihi, Maria, secundum verbum tuum, ut fiat in me secundum verbum Dei! Amen* ("Be it done unto me, Mary, according to thy word, that it may be done unto me according to the word of God! Amen").

CHAPTER XXX.

OF VARIOUS PIOUS PRACTICES IN HONOUR OF THE BLESSED VIRGIN FOR EVERY DAY, WEEK, MONTH, OR YEAR.

The Hail Mary—The Rosary—The daily visit—The consecration of the Saturday—The Feasts—The Month of Mary—The frequent invocation of the name of Mary.

AMONG the numerous pious practices by which the Church puts it into the heart of her children to honour and invoke the Mother of God, the first is undoubtedly the Hail Mary. She places it immediately after the Lord's Prayer, at the beginning of all her offices; and she

---

[1] *Visits to the Saints and B.V.*, 21st Visit.

calls upon us to offer it to the Blessed Virgin three times a day, at the sound of the Angelus, in memory of the benefits bestowed on us by the Incarnation of the Word.

The Hail Mary is an admirable prayer. Where could we find words with which to honour Mary to be compared with these?—" Hail, full of grace, the Lord is with thee; blessed art thou among women ;"—angelic words, which Heaven teaches to earth, and which we ought to ask grace fully to understand and devoutly to recite, through the intercession of S. Gabriel, the Angel of the Incarnation, by whom they were addressed from God to the second Eve. We ought also to ask, through the intercession of the holy mother, of the Precursor of Jesus Christ, of her who received the Holy Spirit at the sound of Mary's voice, grace to understand and realise those other inspired words: " Blessed is the Fruit of thy womb !"—words of unspeakable meaning, which announce to fallen humanity the restoration of its lost blessing. The same Holy Spirit, promised to the Church, and always abiding in her, will also teach us to say from our hearts, with the whole Church militant : "Holy Mary, Mother of God, pray for us sinners, now and at the hour of our death. Amen."[1]

[1] " So be it" (*Amen, Fiat*) have the same meaning, or rather, are the same word. This word, which concludes all our prayers, sums them up in one fervent supplication : *Amen, Fiat* (" Let it be so"). It is the great word both of God and man. It is the word of creation: *Fiat lux, dixit, et facta sunt; mandavit, et creata sunt* (" Let light be made, He said, and it was done; He commanded, and it was created"). It is the word of the Incarnation: FIAT *mihi secundum verbum tuum* ("Be it done unto me according to Thy word"). Human nature, in the person of the second Eve, accedes to the will of God : *Fiat mihi*—" And the Word is made flesh." It is the word of redemption : *Si non potest hic calix transire nisi bibam illum*, FIAT *voluntas tua* (" If this chalice may not pass away unless I drink it, Thy will be done"). Human nature, in the person of the Man-God, agrees to the atonement to be made for all, and mankind are saved. *Amen, Fiat*,—this is the main point on which the salvation of each of us depends,—submission to the will of God. It is supereminently an effective prayer, and supereminently a prayer of petition. It is love, which wills what God wills ; and it is con-

The title alone of Mother of God, of which we are reminded when praying to Mary, will awaken our confidence in her all-powerful intercession; and our condition as sinners will not deprive us of this confidence either now or at the hour of our death, because Mary will obtain for us repentance through the merits of the Lamb of God, Who takes away the sins of the world.

The Hail Mary is a sublime combination of prayers, in which are united the voices of Angels and men, of heaven and earth. It is the melody of the Church triumphant and militant, of joy and sorrow, blended in one common affection. The true children of the universal Church, therefore, like her, join together in their prayers the Lord's Prayer and the Angelical Salutation, "because," according to the remark of the venerable Cardinal Bellarmine, "we have no advocate who can plead our cause so effectually with Jesus Christ as His Mother. As soon, therefore, as we have recited the *Pater*, which He Himself has taught us, we beseech His Mother to obtain for us what we have asked, just as, when we have presented a petition to a prince, we recommend the matter to the most powerful advocate we can secure at court."[1]

Cardinal Bellarmine here manifestly expresses the mind of the Church.

This same mind of the Church, and consequently of the Spirit Who animates her, led S. Dominic to diffuse the devotion of the Holy Rosary, in which the Lord's Prayer, that Divine prayer which reveals to us the Heart of Jesus, and comprises the whole Gospel, is offered to God in a chain of the mysteries of redemption, and followed by another chain of Hail Marys, like an ardent and prolonged desire, which can find but one word to express

fidence, which obtains the grace to will it. Let us, then, often say, *Amen, amen! Fiat, fiat!* with humble confidence, and we shall finish by saying it with deep affection: *Sive vivimus, sive morimur, et Domini erimus in æternum* ("Whether we live or whether we die, we shall be the Lord's for ever").

[1] *Expla. of Christ. Doct.*, ch. v.

it (*eundem sermonem dicens*).[1] *Da amantem et sentit quod dico*, says S. Augustine ("Give me one who loves, and he will understand me"). Yes, those who truly love prayer, those who have received the spirit of prayer, will understand what treasures of faith, hope, and love are contained in the practice of the holy Rosary. Those only will not understand it who think to please God by a multitude of fine words (*putant quod in multiloquio suo exaudiantur*).[2]

The Rosary is full of the Spirit of grace and of prayer (*gratiæ et precum*).[3] It has guided many chosen souls to the most sublime degree of prayer; it has converted a multitude of sinners; it has been to countless numbers of the faithful the chain of prayer, to which has been linked the chain of graces, which secured their perseverance.

The Hail Mary and the holy Rosary, or at least a part of the Rosary, shall be our daily offering to the Blessed Virgin.

But we will not content ourselves with the Hail Mary of our morning and evening prayers, with those which we offer daily at the sound of the Angelus, or those which form the blessed links of the Rosary. No; like most faithful children of Mary, we will offer that sweet prayer to her before and after all our principal actions; and, to use the expression of a Saint, "We will place all our works between two Hail Marys, that so they may be truly full of grace."

We will imitate also those who love to recite three Hail Marys daily in honour of the Immaculate Conception, to return thanksgiving to the Most Holy Trinity for having preserved our Mother from all stain, and to obtain by the intercession of that Immaculate Mother an exceeding purity of heart and body. Lastly, during the holy Sacrifice of the Mass, we will recite the Angelical Salutation at the priest's Communion, to obtain grace to make a good spiritual Communion, saying with our whole

[1] Matt. xxvi. 24.   [2] Matt. vi. 7.   [3] Zach. xii. 10.

heart to Mary: "Our Lord is with thee; obtain from Him that He may be also with me."

Another pious practice, which will obtain great graces for us daily, will be to combine a visit to Mary with our visit to the Blessed Sacrament, according to the recommendation of S. Alphonsus, in the most widely diffused of all the books of prayer which have ever been offered to the piety of Christians. Amongst all the prayers of this book, those which seem to us most fervent, most inspired, if we may use that expression, are the seven which he distributes among the seven days of the week, in which this Apostle of the Blessed Virgin teaches us to ask of God, by the intercession of His Mother, the pardon of our sins, perseverance, and the spirit of prayer, a good death, deliverance from the eternal punishment we have deserved, heaven, the love of Jesus, and the maternal protection of Mary.

The Hail Mary, the Rosary, or part of the Rosary, and the visit to Mary, will thus consecrate each day of our lives to the Mother of God, and will keep us united to God in her sweet company. Our weeks, our months, and our years will be thus consecrated to Jesus and to Mary; but we will join something special to the acts of each day, still further to consecrate every week, every month, and every year to the Mother of life. In every week the Saturday shall be specially consecrated to her by some work of charity or mortification, and by some pious lecture, to remind us of our Mother's greatness, love, and power of intercession. In every month we will celebrate some one of her Feasts,—in January, her Virginal Marriage with the purest, the humblest, the greatest of Patriarchs; in February, her Purification; in March, her Annunciation; in April, her Compassion and her Sorrows; in May, we will give her the whole month of the awakening of nature, thereby to consecrate the whole year to her; in June and July, we will prepare for the Feast of the Visitation, which will obtain for us the sanctifying Visitation of Mary, on the day on which her voice sanctified S. John the Baptist and his Mother; in August, we will celebrate her Assumption; in September, her Nativity; in October, the Festival of her holy Rosary; in November, her Presentation; and lastly, in December, her Immaculate Conception. On each of these Festivals, which remind us of the principal acts of the life of our Mother, and of the dispensations of Divine Providence towards her, we will seek, as we have said before,[1] light to illuminate our own life by the maternal example given us by Mary of faith, hope, the love of God and our neighbour, holy suffering, humility, purity, the obedience, the courage, and the patience which God requires of us all.

We have spoken of all the practices of piety used by the Church for the honour and invocation of Mary every day, every week, every month, and every year of our lives; but we have said nothing yet of the act which touches most closely the heart of our Mother, and proves to her most effectually that we are truly her children. How does a child prove his confidence in his mother, when he is in need, trouble, or danger? Is it not by calling her to his aid? Does not the name of his mother then rise at once to his lips? Even so the invocation of Mary,—the prompt invocation of Mary's name, above all, in trouble, trial, or temptation,—is the principal sign of the confidence we owe her. He prays not enough who prays only when he is on his knees. The spirit of prayer is chiefly manifested by ejaculations, by those habitual aspirations which go straight from the heart of man to the Heart of God, together with the prayers of Angels and Saints, and of the Queen of Angels and Saints. The frequent, habitual invocation of Mary shall be, therefore, our chosen practice of piety, our most cherished devotion, the devotion that shall sanctify, not only every day, but every hour, nay, the best moments of all the days of our lives. S. Peter of Alcantara used frequently to repeat: " O Mary, Mary, Mary!" This is the true proof of the love of children for the Mother of souls. The mere name of their Mother speaks to them

[1] See chap. xxiv.

more powerfully than all books, all sermons, or all the sublime thoughts which come rather from the head than from the heart.

Prayer.

Yes, blessed name of my most loving Mother Mary, thou art to me, next to the Name of Jesus, the sweetest word that I can hear, the sweetest that I can speak. Thou shalt be inseparably united to that thrice-holy Name both in my heart and on my lips; thou shalt be there in all my troubles; thou shalt be there in all my wants; thou shalt be there in all my struggles; above all, in all my temptations, from their first beginning till they shall be overcome. Thou shalt be there in my falls, to raise me; in my victories, to receive my thanks; in my whole life, that, by thy intercession, it may be pure and faithful; and lastly, in my death, that it may lead me whither thou art, in the bosom of my Father and my God, to love Him with thee, with all my strength, for all eternity.

These graces, O my Mother, are too great for me, and I acknowledge myself to be wholly unworthy of them; but if they are too great to be granted to my prayer, they are not too great to be granted to thine. I hail thee, then, "full of grace," and I hope that thou wilt obtain for thy poor child something of the plenitude of his Mother's abundance. "The Lord is with thee;" but is He also with me? I remember His presence in the days of my childhood, His Divine and often-repeated visits to my soul; I remember His illumination, His unction, His light, which raised me far above the world and myself. But thou knowest, holy Mother, better than I do, that I went away into a strange land, far from God and from Thee; and that there I fell into great misery,—suffering cold and hunger in that, alas! too-willing servitude. But thou didst come and say to me: Remember thy better days, and return by me to thy God. And I have returned, but exhausted by my long and faithless flight, and hardly able to recover my strength. *Redde mihi lætitiam salutaris* tui! Restore to me, O my Mother, the first joy of Jesus my Saviour: *stolam primam* ("the first robe of my soul"). Restore to me innocence, by repentance. Restore to me *charitatem primam* ("my first love"). Thou canst do it, and thou wilt do it. Thou wilt do still more; thou wilt not be content to see me recover lost love, lost light, lost unction, lost strength, lost life; but thou wilt obtain for me that love, light, unction, strength, and life shall increase within me now and all the days of my life; and that the hour of my death shall be that in which I shall have most loved my God in time, that so I may go to love Him with all His Saints throughout eternity. Amen.

CHAPTER XXXI.

THE ROSARY.

WE have already spoken of the holy Rosary,[1] but we will again revert to this practice of devotion, in order the more fully to develop its beauty, its sweetness, and, above all, its utility.

I. In the first place, it is sweet and beautiful in its origin and its history, for it breathes the perfume of Christian antiquity and the memories of God's merciful providence over His Church.

The Christians of the early ages were accustomed to lay garlands of flowers at the foot of their altars and holy images, and in doing so they gave expression to a touching truth, namely, the obligation we are under of referring the gifts of God to their source, of honouring God in His works, and especially in His work of predilection, the victory of His Saints. In accordance with this pious custom, S. Gregory Nazianzen composed garlands of spiritual flowers, so that the offering of the faithful might ascend to heaven with the incense of prayer. S. Bridget—a humble virgin, living in Ireland

---

[1] Chap. xxx., *supra.*

in the sixth century[1]—being desirous to facilitate this practice, and to make it more general, composed crowns of the two principal prayers used by Christians,—the *Pater* and the *Ave Maria*. And in this she only followed the example of the anchorites of the first ages of the Church, who, when they were prevented from reciting the Great Psalter, or the hundred and fifty Psalms, supplied the omission by offering the Lord's Prayer to God a certain number of times; and made use of a chain of small stones, or something else of the same sort, similar to the beads of the chaplet, by which to reckon the number of their prayers.

This number was not to them an object of superstition, but a help to perseverance in prayer, and a remedy against spiritual sloth. There are some who think that they prove their spirituality by turning numbered and measured prayers into derision. But we would know if these fastidious critics themselves pray without measure. The custom of reciting the Angelical Salutation in the same manner as the *Pater* established itself afterwards, as it were, spontaneously. S. Albert and Peter the Hermit—who lived long before S. Dominic—propagated the popular practice of reciting the *Pater* and *Ave*, as a means of enabling the faithful to unite themselves with the Canonical Hours. But S. Dominic was the true author of the Psalter of Mary,—*i. e.* of the practice of reciting one hundred and fifty Hail Marys, divided into decades, in honour of the principal mysteries of the faith. This pious practice at first bore the name of *Chaplet*, from a Latin word which signifies "a little crown;" as the word *Rosary* signifies "a crown of roses," or odoriferous prayers. S. Dominic was moved to establish the devotion of the holy Rosary by an im-

---

[1] She must not be confounded with the S. Bridget who is so celebrated for her revelations, who lived in the fourteenth century, and founded the Order of the Bridgettines, for men and women; the priests of this Order were the first who received powers to indulgence Chaplets.

pulse of grace, which has been proved to be a true inspiration by its marvellous effects. Mighty as was that great Saint in deed and in word, he had laboured and suffered almost in vain to bring back to the truth the new sect of Manichees, called "Albigenses;" a proud and fierce set of men, addicted to impure doctrines, who, to mention but one of their infamous errors, condemned the institution of marriage. The virgin Apostle, being one day in prayer, besought the Virgin of virgins on behalf of these miserable men; and it was revealed to him, by an interior voice, that he was to triumph over this hitherto obstinate error less by argument than by the humility of prayer, combined with the simplest possible exposition of the faith. He saw by that interior light what kind of prayer, and what exposition of Christian doctrine, Mary would offer to these souls by his hands. That exposition consists in the chain of the Mysteries of the holy Rosary; and that prayer in the *Pater* and *Ave* poured forth at the feet of Jesus and Mary, with the simplicity of filial piety, which hopes for all things from Jesus by the prayer of Mary, invoked with confiding importunity: *usque ad importunitatem*. The Apostle of Mary followed this inspiration, and the father of lies was vanquished. Souls returned in multitudes to truth and to chastity,[1] and the holy Rosary has thus

---

[1] "For more than forty years," according to the words of Bergier, "missions, instructions, and every means which Christian charity could suggest, had been employed to reclaim the Albigenses; nor were measures of severity resorted to until they were rendered indispensable by the violence of the sectaries. When S. Bernard went to them, in the year 1147, he was armed, like S. Dominic at a later period, with the word of God and his virtues alone. It was not till the year 1179 that the General Council of Lateran pronounced an anathema against them; adding: 'As to those who respect neither churches nor monasteries, and who spare neither orphans, nor age, nor sex, we command the faithful courageously to resist their ravages, and to defend Christian people against these wicked men' (Can. 27).

"We have no intention," adds Bergier, "to justify the ex-

borne from its very origin the sign of victory. Mary
has taken care to preserve for it this character, of which
the Festival of the holy Rosary alone is a twofold proof.
The great Pope Pius V. first established it, under the
name of "Our Lady of Victory," in thanksgiving for
the triumph of Christendom at Lepanto. The Popes—
and this is not one of their least glorious characteristics
—have ever been the first to perceive that the repression
of the invading and barbarous power of Islamism is a
question of life and death, not for Christianity, which
cannot perish, but for Christendom, *i.e.* for the society
of Christian nations, which may be destroyed, and for
souls which may be lost. In the days of S. Pius V.
the Moslems were masters of the Mediterranean, of
Hungary, and Greece, and threatened to fall upon Italy,
after subduing Malta and Cyprus. S. Pius V. had to
overcome inconceivable difficulties, in appeasing the
jealousies among princes and nations, before he could
unite them under the standard of the Cross. By dint of
exhortations, prayers, and patience, he at last succeeded,
and appointed Don John of Austria commander-in-chief
of the combined fleet. The Pope, another Moses to the
people of Christ, another Aaron to the Church of God,
lifted his hands to heaven, while the defenders of Christendom were carrying out his great designs; and Rome
knelt with her Pontiff before the Blessed Sacrament,
during the prayers of the Perpetual Adoration, which
were offered most fervently of all by S. Pius himself.
Now, on the very day on which the confraternities of
the holy Rosary had offered a solemn supplication at

cesses which may have been committed on both sides by armed
men during a long war; we know well enough that as soon as
the sword is drawn, men account all things to be allowable, and
that one instance of cruelty committed by one of the parties
becomes a motive and pretext for bloody reprisals. We have
seen this in our civil wars of the sixteenth century, and surely
there was not greater moderation in the thirteenth" (See *Le
Dict. Th.*, art. "Albigeois").

the desire of the Pope, Monsignore Bussotti, one of the ministers of his Holiness, came to speak to him at the Vatican. He was laying an important matter before him in the presence of several prelates, when Pius V. suddenly imposed silence by a movement of his hand, rose hastily, and went to the window, which he opened, and stood by it for some minutes lost in contemplation. His countenance and his attitude evinced profound emotion; then he returned and exclaimed: " Let us not speak further of business, this is not the time for it! Hasten to give thanks to God in the church; our army has gained the victory!" He had scarcely finished these words when he dismissed his astonished attendants; and before they had fairly left the room, the holy Father threw himself, in tears, upon his knees in his oratory.

Bussotti, and the prelates who had witnessed this miracle, went to impart it in confidence to the Cardinals of greatest consideration in Rome and to other eminent persons. *They all together noted the day and the hour* of the holy Father's vision—the 7th of October, at five o'clock in the afternoon—and this was precisely the day and the hour when the Cross triumphed in the Gulf of Lepanto![1]

This occurrence was so publicly known both in Rome and out of Rome—*in urbe et in orbe*—that the Protestant historian Ranke says plainly: " On the day of the battle Pius V. had an ecstasy, in which he beheld the victory of the Christian armies."[2]

In thanksgiving for this victory—which took place on the first Sunday in October 1571—S. Pius V. instituted an annual Festival of Our Lady, under the title of " S. Mary of Victory."

Two years afterwards, Gregory XIII., wishing still further to perpetuate the remembrance of what had taken place at Rome and at Lepanto, on the 7th of

[1] See the Life of S. Pius V., by M. de Falloux.
[2] *History of the Popes*, t. ii. p. 174.

October 1571, changed this title for that of "the Rosary." "Clement X. extended the Feast to all churches under the dominion of Spain. Finally, the army of the Emperor Charles VI., having defeated the Turks near Temeswar, on the Feast of 'Our Lady's Church of the Snow' (*Sancta Maria ad Nives*), in the year 1716, and these infidels having raised the siege of Corfu on the Octave of the Assumption, in the same year, Clement XII. ordered the Office of the Feast of the Rosary to be used by the whole Church."[1]

It is true, therefore, that the Rosary, both in its origin and its history, is full of the most touching associations. But if it ought to be dear to us on account of its historical interest, still more ought it to be so from its intrinsic value.

II. This results from the union of the two great means of salvation which the Rosary presents to us, by making us both *meditate* and *pray*.

It makes us meditate on "the truth, the way, and the life,"—the truth as regards our end, the way which leads us to it, of the life which is prepared for us hereafter,—by fixing our attention on our Lord Jesus Christ, who is at once *Via, Veritas, et Vita* ("the Way, the Truth, and the Life"). The Rosary makes us meditate on this without effort and yet effectually. The meditation on eternal truths, a certain degree of meditation, at least, is undoubtedly necessary for all men; since, if we cannot succeed in any thing without thinking about it, no more can we succeed in saving our souls if we do not think of our salvation, of the fulfilment of the Divine law which is its condition, and of the means of fulfilling it. But many think they meditate when they do nothing but speculate and endeavour to excite fine thoughts, and discourse beautifully to themselves. These persons lose their time, which they would employ much better in

---

[1] Butler, 1st October.

saying their Rosary attentively; for by simply letting their thoughts dwell on the adorable mysteries of the life, the passion, the death, and the glory of their Divine Master, they would see more clearly what they ought to know and to suffer than they can learn in their ambitious meditations. Meditation is only salutary because it leads to mental prayer; that is to say, because it leads us to pray in spirit, and offer to God with all our heart, and not only with our lips, acts of faith, hope, love, contrition, holy resolutions, and, above all, prayers to obtain the grace to carry these resolutions into effect. Now, there is no way more easy, and, at the same time, more efficacious, of exciting us to these acts and these prayers, than the simple contemplation of Jesus and Mary in the Divine mysteries of redemption. God forbid that in speaking of mental prayer we should overlook the utility, the great utility, of the books and methods which assist us to make it well; especially when these books are used less to excite reflections than to teach us to apply those which they contain, and which apply to ourselves. But it is not the less true—as all the Saints have taught us, and as S. Ignatius has shown us so clearly in his *Exercises*—that Jesus Christ is the Book of books,—the one that can supply the place of all others, which are of no avail without it; the one in which a multitude of ignorant persons have learnt that which many learned men have yet to learn. Thus there is no doubt but that poor peasants, as they follow the Way of the Cross, or quietly recite their Rosary, make mental prayer much better than do many learned men, who think themselves far superior to the rest of mankind; whose supercilious prayers, however, only leave them full of themselves and devoid of God.

The simple elevation of the soul to Jesus,—suffering in silence, bearing the Cross which our sins had deserved, scourged for our souls, which had become the vile slaves of the flesh, crowned with thorns for our pride, crucified for the vile affections of our hearts—those hearts made by God and for God—forsaken in His sufferings that we might not be forsaken in our sins, dying to give us life; rising again to show us the life which He has prepared for us, ascending to heaven to draw us up thither also,—this simple contemplation of Jesus and also of His Blessed Mother—not only in the mysteries of the Passion, but likewise in the mysteries of the glory of her Son, as in those of the Incarnation, the Visitation, the Nativity, the Presentation, and of the Finding of that Divine Son in the Temple—this simple gaze of the poor and lowly Christian, who does not pretend to reason, but to see and learn, will teach him more divine truths than the books of the learned. We designedly repeat the expression "simple gaze," that it may not be supposed we wish to turn the holy Rosary into a laborious meditation.

No; let the Rosary continue to be a sweet and simple prayer, which will not prevent it from being a real prayer of the heart; a prayer in spirit and in truth; true mental prayer, if we only repeat the *Pater* and *Ave* with our thoughts fixed on Jesus and Mary.

The *Pater* is a Divine prayer, and the soul of all other prayers, since by it we ask for all that man ought to desire and ask for. What ought we to desire? Our end. For what end has God created us? For His glory and our happiness. "Our Father who art in heaven, hallowed be Thy Name;" this is the end of God. "Thy kingdom come;" this is the end of man. But how shall we come to reign in heaven with God? By letting Him reign in us on earth. "Thy will be done on earth as it is in heaven." The glory of God and heaven; this, then, is our end, and the accomplishment of the will of God is the way which leads to it. But strength is necessary for us, in order to walk day by day in this path. "Give us this day our daily bread;" both for soul and body,—the word and the bread of life. We have the end, and the means of attaining it, but we must also overcome the obstacles which we encounter by the way. The first of these obstacles is sin, which makes us unworthy of God: "Forgive us our trespasses, as we forgive them that trespass against us." Jesus Christ teaches us to be merciful, in order to obtain mercy. Temptations are the second obstacle; the wars waged against our soul by the world, our passions, and that irreconcilable enemy of our salvation, the fallen angel and his companions: "And lead us not into temptation, but deliver us from evil;" from the moral evil of sin, and from the evil of the punishment which is due to it. Amen (" So be it").

Thus we see every thing is comprehended in this prayer; but that which shows us still more clearly its Divine origin is the inexhaustible fertility of its meaning. We have indeed just considered its true signification, but this true signification contains many others, according to the state and wants of our souls; especially when we offer the prayer to Jesus, and contemplate His life and passion, His death and His glory. For His life is the rule of our life, His sufferings the explanation of our sufferings, His death the consolation of our death, His glory gives us hope in our trials. Every thing, indeed, in Jesus Christ is full of light and instruction, which He freely bestows on all who seek them. It is then that great desires are kindled in us, and the *Aves* of the holy Rosary scarcely suffice to allay the blessed thirst for the graces which we seek in Jesus through Mary: *Gratiam quærentes, et per Mariam quærentes* (" Seeking graces, and seeking them through Mary"); the graces of faith, humility, purity, charity, obedience, patience, resignation, increase of the love of God, and of that divine confidence which shall never be confounded.

Prayer.

Yes, I will seek these graces, and I will seek them in Jesus Christ by thy prayer, O Mary! holy and true Mother of my soul! I should be very ungrateful if I were not faithful to the recitation of thy sweet Rosary, if I did not love this Chaplet, which has withdrawn me from the world and drawn me to God, and which continues daily to draw down upon me so many graces. The remembrance of the past, the experience of the present, the certain expectation of mercies yet to come, —all bind me to the Chaplet, which I lovingly kiss, as one of the most sure means of perseverance.

O Mary, hearken to me! I have worn it about me for a long time past, and thou knowest that I have never found it a burden. Wilt thou suffer me to die without it? No, thou wilt never permit this to happen. And as its links have bound me to thee on earth, so by them thou wilt also raise me up to thee in heaven; where thou wilt unite me to thy Father and my Father, to thy Saviour and my Saviour, to the Spouse of thy soul and of mine, in the bosom of the Father, and of the Son, and of the Holy Ghost. Amen.

CHAPTER XXXII.

THE SCAPULAR.

LOVE is essentially active. It is a flame tending continually to its centre. The loving soul seeks always to please the object of its love, to manifest and prove its love, and thus to attract the love of the object beloved. If this be true of unlawful affections, which sully and delude the heart, and which always perish self-punished, how will it be with the true love, the love of souls, the love which comes from God and leads to God, and, above all, with the love of God Himself? It will be more active than any other, more anxious to manifest itself, to prove its strength and reality, and thus to attract in an increasing measure the love of God, Who is at once the Father, Brother, Friend, Lover, and Spouse of souls.

The soul which loves Jesus Christ naturally feels drawn to love all that He loves, and will not require to be urged to love the one amongst all creatures whom Jesus loves the best,—His most sweet and Blessed Mother. The love of Jesus, then, leads to the love of Mary, and the love of Mary, being the fruit of the love of Jesus, will be like that from which it springs,—active, anxious to make itself known and felt, and thus to attract the love of the Mother of God and of men.

For this reason the affection of the children of Mary is not satisfied with the pious acts of devotion which we have already mentioned, and by which they seek daily, weekly, monthly, and yearly to please her. What they want is an act of love, which shall be in some sort permanent, as that of the foolish lovers of the world, who carry about with them every where a remembrance of the object of their love, thus expressing the invariable and constant attachment of their heart and thoughts to the vain idol which has seduced them. The affection of the children of Mary is not less than that of these blind votaries; wherever they may be, they always wear some remembrance of their Mother, some medal or image of her Immaculate Conception, of her Heart, of her Love, and of her Sorrows, and still more constantly that blessed sign of her protection, the holy Scapular, which is at the same time the noble badge of an innumerable family, and the sure pledge of a union of prayers, which necessarily brings many graces.[1]

There are persons who fancy themselves clear-sighted, but who are only purblind, who will tell us that these remembrances are the amulets of Christians. In reply, we say of amulets and other superstitious badges of false religions, what we say of the religions which inspire them, that they are an adulteration and a profanation of the truth. Magical signs themselves are

---

[1] Union of prayers is one of the advantages of pious associations. See what S. Alphonsus has written in the *Glories of Mary* of the utility of these associations.

only chimeras in the eyes of the half-educated. In reality they are a badge of sacrilegious servitude or bondage, a means of procuring the fatal assistance of fallen and wicked spirits, who only aid men temporally in order to ruin them eternally, when the justice of God lets them take their own course, and permits them to give this fatal assistance to ungrateful and obstinately faithless men, and thus to lead them into sin, "because they receive not the love of the truth, that they might be saved;"[1] "giving heed to the doctrines of the spirits of error,"[2] "by which they perish."[3] An intelligent being never gives, receives, or wears such tokens in vain, because they are the expression of a thought, an affection, or a desire.

Are not the Sacraments tokens from God? Undoubtedly they are the visible sign of His love, and the channel of His invisible gifts; but Divine Omnipotence alone can give to the expression of His will that marvellous efficacy which no creature can attach to any sign whatsoever.

But though these tokens of our affections do not, like the Sacraments, possess efficacy in themselves, they still have power to influence those whom they concern on earth or in heaven. We do not yet see God, nor the elect, nor the Angels, nor the Queen of Heaven, because we do not yet enjoy the light which they enjoy; but if our eye perceives from this spot in the universe, which we call earth, the physical light of the stars at an immeasurable distance, how clearly must our souls be perceived by beings illuminated by the light of God Himself, in whose eyes they are greater than a thousand worlds!

You would yourself be touched by hearing that a person, out of affection for you, always wore something belonging to you. Be not uneasy, then; the inhabitants

---

[1] 2 Thess. ii. 10.   [2] 1 Tim. iv. 1.
[3] 2 Thess., *loc. cit.*

of heaven know what we do for them,[1] because they see Him face to face Who sees every thing, and enjoy His light Who is present every where, to Whom distance is as nothing, and to Whom are finally directed all the acts of devotion which we offer them, all the prayers which we address to Mary, to the Angels and Saints, to the celestial hierarchy of intercession which comes from God, returns to God, and leads us thither with it.

An ancient writer said: *Si vis amari, ama* ("If you will be loved, love; love attracts love"). It is love, then, which makes us wear a remembrance of Mary; and, consequently, this is a means of gaining the love of her Heart.

We need not, therefore, be surprised at the promises made by the Mother of God to those who wear her Scapular faithfully till death, according to the celebrated revelation related in the Office for the Feast of Mount Carmel; a revelation which, though not an article of faith, is not the less a belief founded in reason, as the learned and severe criticism of Benedict XIV. has shown. What, after all, does this consoling revelation teach us? That constant, filial piety to the Mother of God will certainly obtain repentance for poor sinners and the perseverance of the just; and that Mary will hasten to deliver her most faithful children from the expiatory sufferings of purgatory. Is it not just that a great love of the Mother of God should obtain great mercies?

We shall say nothing here of the origin and history of the different Scapulars, nor of the graces, indulgences, and spiritual privileges which are attached to them, because books treating of these subjects are in the hands of every body; but we wish to repeat to the faithful that the devotion of the Scapular is a devotion of the *heart*, childlike, simple, affectionate, and easy; carrying with it an especial pledge of constancy; a devotion which will infallibly draw down on them the love of the

---

[1] *Vide* ch. xiv., *sup.*

Blessed Virgin, and, through the prayers of this holy Mother, the grace of repentance and perseverance.

Assume the Scapular, then, you who read these lines, since it only obliges you to love, and persuade others to assume it, if you would know by experience how Mary can reward, even in this life, those who induce others to love her. Here is one example amongst a thousand:

A young girl, gifted with high intelligence and excellent dispositions, having the gift of faith, though in a soul still in some measure given to the world, and whose piety was rather instinctive than enlightened, felt to the Blessed Virgin that of which a soul regenerated by baptism is never entirely destitute,—the childlike affection which is a fruit of grace, and which leads it to say, "My Mother!" to Mary, as it leads it to say to God, "Abba, Father!"[1] This incipient devotion to Mary had not, however, been developed in this young girl either by her education, or by the examples around her, or by the home in which she lived. One day, when she was approaching the Sacraments, which she did only at distant intervals, the priest who heard her confession asked her what she offered to our Blessed Lady every day. After a few moments' silence she replied: "Nothing but the Hail Mary which I say in my prayers." "Will you do something more than that?" rejoined the priest. "Yes, provided it be not too difficult." "Well, then, wear the Scapular." "But what is that?" "It is the badge of the children of Mary, the remembrance which they wear of their Mother, and which they never lay aside; the pledge of their affection for her, which they bear on their heart, where Mary sees it, though it is hidden from the world. By wearing the Scapular, we perform an act of piety which is lasting; and yet there is

---

[1] God has made Mary truly the Mother of men in the order of grace, or of the supernatural life. He, therefore, teaches us these filial sentiments of which we have spoken, as He does nothing imperfectly.

nothing easier, for it is not difficult to love one's Mother." "Give me the Scapular," was the immediate answer of the simple and generous-hearted child; "I will wear it with all my heart." Some weeks afterwards she returned to express her most grateful thanks to him who had induced her to offer to the Blessed Virgin an act of devotion which was to her the beginning of a chain of graces, the first of which had already changed her life.

Some years afterwards, this priest was leaving his house one morning about nine o'clock, with a book under his arm, wishing to escape from the town and enjoy the silence of the fields. As soon as he was outside the gates of the city, he resumed the perusal of his book on philosophy, at the place where he had left off; but it was in vain that he endeavoured to pursue his favourite study. In spite of all the efforts he made, he could not succeed in shaking off, not distracting thoughts, but simply an interior attraction, for which he could not account to himself. At length, overcome by this attraction, he shut his favourite book, almost in spite of himself, and bent his steps back to the church where he exercised his sacred ministry. As the attraction increased, he knelt, or rather he felt himself pressed down upon his knees by a powerful hand, at the foot of the tabernacle. There, instead of visiting Jesus Christ, he was rather visited by Him. A light, till then unknown in his soul, showed him Divine truths under quite a new aspect; but, above all, it was the sword of the Spirit of God which pierced his heart. Was it joy or sorrow? was it love or grief? It was one and all at the same time; but he would not have exchanged the least of the tears which ran in streams from his eyes for all the delights of the world. This Divine visitation lasted a long time, and left on him one of those impressions which can come from God alone, which remain in the soul as the germ of a higher life, and which we have only to call to mind to be awakened in spirit and in truth, according to these words of S. Paul: *Admoneo te, ut resuscites gratiam Dei, quæ est in te* ("I admonish thee, that thou stir up the grace of God which is in thee").[1]

When our poor priest came to himself, he exclaimed continually: "My God, what hast Thou done? I did not seek Thee, and Thou art come to me. Why has a grace like this been shown to me?" He repeated this during the day and night.

On the following day he received a letter, which began thus: "Yesterday, at nine o'clock, M—— made her vows. She is still too much absorbed in her retreat to write to you herself to-day, but she has begged me to do so instead, and to tell you that, immediately after her oblation, she recited an *Ave* with her hand on her Scapular; saying to Mary, with all her heart: 'Ask Jesus Christ to requite him for all the good which he has done to me.'"

The mystery of the preceding day was revealed, and it was also shown how ready Jesus is to hearken to the petitions of fervent souls in behalf of those who teach them to love His Mother. M——'s fidelity to the Spouse of Virgins continued to increase, and she died young, in sentiments of great fervour, after having offered her life to God to save that of another.

Prayer.

It is true, therefore, O Lord, that prayers are arrows, which ascend to pierce Thy Heart, and descend again from heaven to pierce ours. But I perceive that, in order to make those arrows effective, I must ask them of Thy Mother, and love that holy Mother much. I will love her, then, Lord; I will speak of her, that Thou mayst speak to me Thyself; I will love her, that Thou mayst love me; I will pray to her, that Thou mayst hear me; I will wear the symbol of her love, the remem-

[1] 2 Tim. i. 6.

brance of her affection, the Scapular of her chosen children; I will wear it always, living and dying, in the firm conviction that this token of the affection which I cherish for her will induce her to obtain for me, from Thee, the grace of repentance and of fortitude which will make me confess, detest, and do penance for my sins, and, above all, the spirit of prayer, which obtains the gift of perseverance.

And do thou, Mary, my incomparable Mother, behold the high estimate which I have formed of thy power and goodness! Yet art thou far more powerful and more loving than I can imagine or express. I shall not, then, be deceived in my expectations; thou hast but to say one word to Jesus, and it will obtain every thing from Him.

Velis tu, et omnia fient! Amen, Amen.

CHAPTER XXXIII.

THE IMITATION OF MARY.

A VERY useful book might be written upon the moral and theological virtues, considered first in themselves and then in Jesus Christ; Who is both the source and the model, the beginning, the means, and the end: *Veritas, Via, et Vita* ("the Truth, the Way, and the Life"); —then in Mary, the most perfect imitatrix of the Divine Master, the true mirror of the Sun of Justice, the true Queen of all the Saints. It is evident that we could not enter upon such a subject in a work like this, where we must confine ourselves to showing — in the principal mysteries of the life of Mary, according to the Gospels —the true light of our own lives, in the heroic examples of humility, faith, hope, love, wisdom, purity, obedience, poverty, detachment, gentleness, courage, and patience which our Mother has left us. Moreover, though we have not been able to add to this sketch of the life of the Blessed Virgin a speculative treatise on the nature, the material and formal object, the necessity, the excellence, and the fruits of virtue, we will console ourselves with the thought that God, by this ray from above, which is at once light, heat, and life, is able perfectly to communicate the perception, love, and practice of the virtues to a number of souls who are incapable of defining them, and who do not even know the names of *moral* virtues and *infused* virtues, and of their *material* and *formal* object, though they possess both, and are attached to their respective objects by the holiest and wisest motives.

Now, God is pleased to give this light from above to the words of Holy Writ, on behalf of those who read it, without presumption, to be enlightened as to their duties, and not to satisfy their curiosity, or give themselves the airs of doctors and judges of the faith.

Let us, then, lend an attentive ear to the words of the Gospel concerning Mary, or to the words of Mary in the Gospel, and we shall obtain from her Divine Son that ray of light, of heat, and of life which will give us a perception and a love of the virtues which those words will reveal to us in our Mother.

An Angel, radiant in light, descends from heaven, and salutes her as full of grace. Will Mary's first emotions be those of joy and delight? No; her first impulse will be to retire into herself, and to take counsel of God, for she knows well that the spirit of lies can transform himself into an Angel of light. "She thought within herself what manner of salutation this should be."[1] What prudence, what caution, what wisdom!

The Angel of God declares to her that she is destined to become the Mother of the Messias, the Desire of Nations, the Son of David, the Son of God. And Mary asks how these great things shall be accomplished in her, since, God having accepted her vow to remain a

[1] Luke i. 29.

Virgin, she faithfully chooses thus to remain rather than become the Mother of God: " How shall this be done, because I know not man ?"[1] What admirable purity !

The messenger of God reassures her, and announces to her the designs of Almighty Power and Wisdom, which has ordained that she shall be the Mother of the Saviour of the world, precisely because she resolves to remain a virgin. We expect now, at least, to see Mary burst forth in transports at the choice which is made of her, " the Woman blessed among women."[2] But Mary is overwhelmed by the thought of her own unworthiness, and experiences nothing but sentiments of humility: " Behold the handmaid of the Lord !"[3] And when Elizabeth, the mother of the Precursor, wonders that the Mother of her Lord should deign to come to her, sentiments of humility and gratitude alone arise in her heart: " My soul doth magnify the Lord, because He hath regarded the humility of His handmaid."[4]

Every part of Mary's character corresponds with this humility, the foundation of all other virtues.[5]

Her heroic faith, in the first place, which believes, on the word of God, what is impossible to nature, but not to the Author of nature: *Beata quæ credidisti* (" Blessed art thou that hast believed").[6]

Her confiding and generous obedience, which feels itself to be powerful in union with God: " Be it done to me according to Thy word."[7]

The unspeakable sublimity of her detachment and poverty: " She took the Child, and wrapped Him in swaddling-clothes, and laid Him in a manger, because there was no room for them in the inn."[8]

Her tender charity for others: she is troubled at the perplexity of the bridegroom at Cana, and says to her

---

[1] Luke i. 34. [2] Luke i. 28.
[3] Luke i. 38. [4] Luke i. 48.
[5] See upon the Humility of Mary, ch. xviii., *supra*.
[6] Luke i. 45. [7] Luke i. 38. [8] Luke ii. 7.

adorable Son, "They have no wine;"[1] for she is not afraid of asking for a miracle to satisfy her maternal heart.

Her maternal sweetness in her most bitter trial, when she lost Jesus, the light of her eyes, the life of her life: "Son, why hast Thou done so to us? Behold, Thy father and I have sought Thee sorrowing."[2]

Her courage and unexampled patience in her terrible martyrdom: "Now, there stood by the cross of Jesus, Mary His Mother."[3]

Finally, her love as Mother of the human race, which she brings forth to the life of grace in sorrow of heart, which resembled more nearly than any other suffering that of Jesus in His agony: *Et tuam ipsius animam pertransibit gladius*[4] ("And thy own soul a sword shall pierce."

Prayer.

And for myself, my Mother, I would have no sufferings; I would have neither poverty, nor humiliation, nor sorrow. I scarcely, therefore, realise the price of the cross; I scarcely believe in that Almighty Power Who has promised victory to those who submit and obey. I study only the interests of my self-love; since so cold is my compassion for the unfortunate, I do not really know how to love the poor souls of those who offend me, nor to do good to those who have done me evil; above all, my heart is so cold towards Jesus, that I have no courage to embrace the sufferings which He sends me, that so I may take my share in carrying His heavy cross, and thus give Him some proof of my love.

O Mary, so humble, so gentle, so obedient, so patient, so compassionate, so loving! wilt thou leave me in my pride and hardness of heart? Wilt thou leave me in my blindness, so that while I confine myself to the false vir-

[1] John ii. 3.   [2] Luke ii. 48.
[3] John xix. 25.   [4] Luke ii. 35.

tues which suit my inclination, I hold myself dispensed from that true charity without which " I am nothing"?[1] No; for after all I am, and I feel myself to be, thy child; I trust in thy pity and in thy prayers, and it shall not be said that I have thus trusted in vain. I will change my life; pray for me, and never weary of praying till thou seest that I have resolutely entered upon the path of Christian virtue; since it is not those who say, Lord! Lord! who shall enter into the kingdom of heaven, but those that do the will of God.

May this holy will be accomplished in me, both in my life and in my death, so that I may come to the place where thou art; that, being inseparably united with my Mother, I may dwell for ever with God!

CHAPTER XXXIV.

THE ARK OF THE COVENANT, MARY, AND THE CHURCH.

DURING the journey of the children of Israel through the desert, Moses placed in the tabernacle of the old covenant the holy ark, in which were the tables of the testament, the golden pot full of manna, and the rod of Aaron which had blossomed: *In qua urna aurea habens manna, et virga Aaron, quæ fronduerat, et tabulæ testamenti.*[2]

The rod of Aaron signified the sacerdotal or spiritual power, as is shown by the following passage from the Book of Numbers: "And Moses spoke to the children of Israel: and all the *princes* gave him rods one for every tribe: and there were twelve rods beside the rod of Aaron. And when Moses had laid them up before the Lord in the tabernacle of the testimony: he returned on the following day, and found that the rod of Aaron for the *house of*

---

[1] 2 Cor. xiii. 2.   [1] Heb. ix. 4.

Levi" (consecrated to the service of the tabernacle) "had budded."¹ It was from the ark of the covenant that *God manifested Himself* on behalf of His people: " And when Moses entered into the tabernacle of the covenant, to consult the oracle, he heard the voice of one speaking to him from the propitiatory, that was over the ark between the two cherubims, and from this place He spoke to him."²

The ark of the covenant was, therefore, a figure of Jesus Christ, of the Word of God manifest in the flesh: *Quod manifestatum est in carne*,³ of God appearing to the world in a visible manner in His sacred Humanity; confirming anew the law which He did not come to destroy but to fulfil,—the more perfect law of the New Testament; Who gave Himself as a victim Whose death was to give us life; coming down from heaven as the true Bread—*panem de cœlo verum*⁴—of which the manna was only the type; and finally establishing that new priesthood and spiritual power prefigured by Aaron's priesthood and the Levitical authority.

But if the ark of the covenant was the type of Jesus Christ, it was also the type of Mary, as we have already shown;⁵ since the Mother of God made man truly enclosed within her womb Him Who was at once the Word, or the uncreated Word of God manifest in the flesh, the eternal law made visible, the living Bread which gives life to the world, the Power which is the source of all other powers. Was it not in the womb of Mary that the Word took upon Himself His sacred Humanity, by which He has manifested His power, His wisdom, and His love? Was it not in the womb of Mary that He willed to take that Humanity, henceforth to be inseparable from His Divinity, by which we have received truth and life?

The holy Mother of God, prefigured by the ark of the covenant, is, then, in her turn, the living and beauti-

---

¹ Numb. xvii. 6-8. ² Numb. vii. 89. ³ 1 Tim. iii. 16.
⁴ John vi. 32. ⁵ Chap. iii., *supra*.

ful type of the Church of God, while at the same time she is its Queen.

It is, indeed, by the Church that Jesus Christ *manifests* Himself continually to the world, by making her the *unexceptionable witness* of His Divinity;[1] it is the Church which is the guardian of His word, either living, traditional, or written;[2] it is by her that He gives Himself to us as nourishment and Victim;[3] it is in her, and by her, that He leaves on earth that spiritual power, that authority in matters of doctrine or instruction, which is the sole, ever-faithful guardian of the truth, the sole indefectible organ of justice, the sole moral force against which all conflicting elements are, sooner or later, dashed to pieces;[4] the sole supernatural power, which gives us strength to overcome ourselves, to subdue our passions, and to lead a new life;[5] lastly, it is in the Church that He dwells with us, according to His promise: *Vobiscum suæ* ("I am with you"); and there He shows forth His power, His truth, and His life: *Imperium, magisterium, ministerium.*

Offering from the Author to our Lord Jesus Christ.

Thou knowest, O my God, the desire with which Thou hast inspired me to increase the love of Mary, Thy Mother and ours, and that of the Church, also our Mother and Thy Spouse.

Thou knowest, O Lord, how long I have suffered at hearing the unbeliever—deaf, blind, and headstrong—speak of Thy great work, of the true religion which never dies, as of a question purely of ancient history confined to the learned; and I have said to the poor

---

[1] See *La Quest. Religieuse*, c. iv.; *Le Libre Examen*, &c., 1st Entretien; *Les Lettres Theolog.*, 1st, 6th, 14th Lettres.
[2] *Quest. Relig.*, c. viii.; *Lettres Theolog.*, 13th Lettre.
[3] *Quest. Relig.*, c. x. xi.
[4] See *Quest. Relig.*, chap. i. s. 17.
[5] *Ibid.*, chap. ix. s. 16.

infidel, with all my power: "Listen, then, and see (*Audi et vide*). Listen to the Church, which anticipates your researches, which comes to meet you, saying, she is the messenger of God. Listen to what she tells you, look at what she shows you, and see what she gives you. Listen to what she tells you, and her words will reveal to you the mystery of our being, the mystery that is in yourself; look at what she shows you, and you will recognise by her characteristics, and her noble and lasting acts, the proofs of her origin and her mission; see what she gives you, and you will receive from her hands the remedy of the evil you carry about with you, the strength to overcome all that humbles you, the peace which you pursue without attaining it, the life to which you aspire but which you do not possess."

But I desired also, O my Divine Master, to say to poor souls: "'If you knew the gift of God,' the gift which He has bestowed upon you by giving you His Mother, what diligent use you would make of this gift, which will obtain for you every other!"

And now at length I have given utterance to these words so dear to my heart, and I offer them to Thee, all unworthy though they be both of Thee and of her; but Thou wilt nevertheless bless them as the offering of the poor.

Bless them, then, Lord, to the salvation of souls, to the salvation of my own. I expect this blessing through the merits of Thy blood, and through the tender heart of Thy Mother; and I hope, in full confidence, that at the moment when I shall go to appear before Thee, Thy Blessed Mother and the holy Church will both say to Thee: "Lord, this poor soul has loved us, he belongs to us; let him belong also to Thee!" *Agnosce, Domine, creaturam tuam, lætifica animam ejus; licet enim peccaverit, tamen Patrem, et Filium, et Spiritum Sanctum non negavit, sed credidit, et zelum Dei in se habuit, et Deum, qui fecit omnia fideliter adoravit* ("Acknowledge, O Lord, Thy creature; rejoice his soul; for although he hath sinned, he hath not denied the Father, and the Son, and the Holy Ghost; but hath believed, and hath had a zeal for God, and hath faithfully adored the Creator of all things").[1]

This is my hope, Lord, and it shall not be taken from me; because Mary, whose prayers Thou dost always hear, will obtain it for me during life, and, above all, at the hour of my death. Amen.

[1] *Ord. Comm. Animæ.*

THE END.

HYMNS AND SACRED VERSES.
From the Italian of St. ALPHONSUS. Neat pocket size, cloth, 2s.

The Universal 2s. Prayer-Book.
THE PATH TO HEAVEN:
OR, PEOPLE'S MANUAL OF CATHOLIC DEVOTION.

Being the most complete Prayer, Meditation, and Instruction Book ever offered to the English Public. Printed in a very clear type and convenient and portable form. Price Two SHILLINGS.

The Clergy and others desirous of circulating a work of this kind, especially among those who require but one book, will oblige by sending for a Specimen Copy, which will be sent free for 24 stamps.

THE COMPLETE CHOIR MANUAL.

A Collection of Easy and Attractive Catholic Music for the Morning and Evening Services during the course of the Ecclesiastical Year.

This work will carry on and complete the plan of "Webbe's Motetts," and other works of that kind, which are now found inadequate to modern requirements.

HYMNS FOR THE YEAR (288 HYMNS), 3d.,

Containing also Benediction and other Latin Pieces in general use. This *is the cheapest and most complete Hymn-Book ever issued.* It contains not only the favourite Hymns from the Oratory and other Catholic Hymnals, but also many new and beautiful Hymns by St. ALPHONSUS, &c. Price 3d.; covers, lettered, 4d.; strong cloth, 5d.

HYMNS FOR THE YEAR, with PUBLIC DEVOTIONS for every Evening. 6d.

HYMNS FOR THE YEAR bound with the POPULAR VESPER-BOOK. 1s. A very complete and cheap book for general use.

HYMNS AND MELODIES (1s.),

New edition, with an Introductory Part of "EASY MELODIES" (price 1s.), contains the Tunes for the above Hymn-Book, also for the *Oratory Hymns* (upwards of 100), *Holy-Family Hymns*, &c. &c. It supplies easy Hymns and Music for the Month of May, for Processions, Rosary, Quarant' Ore, &c. &c. Also, Music for Hymns at Vespers and Benediction. *Fourth Thousand.* Price 1s.; cloth, 1s. 6d.; or, with the Hymns, 2s.

THE BOOK OF VOCAL PARTS AND ACCOMPANIMENTS.
Bound in one volume, 10s. 6d.

FOR THE MONTH OF MAY.

Hymns and Carols for the Month of May; one for each day, with easy Music. Cloth, 2s.

Hymns and Carols, Words alone. 3d.; cloth, 5d.

Lyra Sanctorum. Hymns and Carols for the Feasts of our Lady, &c., with Vocal Parts and Accompaniments, complete. Blue cloth, elegant, 4s.

The Graces of Mary, for every Day in the Month. 1s. 6d.; or in cloth, 2s.

The Children of Mary: Narratives for the Young. 2s.

Segneri's Devout Client of Mary. Cloth, 2s.

The Month of May, for Interior Souls. 2s.; or in cloth, 2s. 6d.

Rosary, with Hymns and Music, for Children. 2d.

"The Joyous Birds are Singing." A new Part-Song for May, for Single Voices or Chorus (an easy and attractive Piece for Convents and Schools). 4d.; or 3s. 6d. per dozen.

The Month of May, for Children. 1d.

Ave Maria (Romberg or Klein), 1s.; (Haydn), 1s. 6d.

Sub tuum præsidium (Richardson). 1s. 6d.

Surge Amica Mea (Crookall). 1s.

Regina Cœli (O'Leary). 3d.

Lyra Liturgica, containing Poems for the Season. By the Very Rev. Canon OAKELEY. Cloth, 3s. 6d.; calf, 7s. 6d.; morocco, 10s.

The May Pageant. By the Rev. E. CASWALL. 2s.

Flowers of Mary. 3s.

Muzzarelli's Month of May. 1s.

With a large variety of French " Mois de Marie."

www.ingramcontent.com/pod-product-compliance
Lightning Source LLC
Chambersburg PA
CBHW032222230426

43666CB00033B/603